STUDIES IN ROMANCE LANGUAGES: 38

John E. Keller, Editor

ROBERT LIMA

Dark Prisms

Occultism
in
Hispanic
Drama

THE UNIVERSITY PRESS OF KENTUCKY

PQ
6102
.L56
1995

Publication of this book was made possible by a grant
from the Program for Cultural Cooperation
between Spain's Ministry of Culture
and United States Universities.

Copyright © 1995 by The University Press of Kentucky

Scholarly publisher for the Commonwealth,
serving Bellarmine College, Berea College, Centre
College of Kentucky, Eastern Kentucky University,
The Filson Club, Georgetown College, Kentucky
Historical Society, Kentucky State University,
Morehead State University, Murray State University,
Northern Kentucky University, Transylvania University,
University of Kentucky, University of Louisville,
and Western Kentucky University.
Editorial and Sales Offices: Lexington, Kentucky 40508-4008

Library of Congress Cataloging-in-Publication Data

Lima, Robert.
    Dark prisms : occultism in Hispanic drama / Robert Lima.
        p.   cm. — (Studies in Romance languages ; 38)
    Includes bibliographical references (p.   ) and index.
    ISBN 0-8131-1909-X (alk. paper) :
        1. Spanish drama—History and criticism.   2. Latin American drama
—History and criticism.   3. Occultism in drama.   I. Title.
II. Series: Studies in Romance languages (Lexington, Ky.) ; 38.
PQ6102.L56   1995
862.009'37—dc20   94-48397

This book is printed on acid-free recycled paper meeting
the requirements of the American National Standard
for Permanence of Paper for Printed Library Materials. .

To Sally

Contents

Human kind
cannot bear too much reality.

T.S. Eliot, "Four Quartets. Burnt Norton (I)"

It is one thing merely to believe in a reality beyond the senses and another to have experience of it also.

Rudolf Otto, *The Idea of the Holy*

That which is magical unequivocally takes on that nature when it surges from an unexpected alteration of reality (the miracle), from a privileged revelation of reality, from an unusual or singularly favorable illumination of the unsuspected richness of reality, from an amplification of the range and categories of reality, perceived with a particular intensity by virtue of an exaltation of the spirit.

Alejo Carpentier, "Prólogo," *El reino de este mundo*

Preface

Prisms are transparent bodies, usually with a triangular base, used for dispersing light into its components (the spectrum of insensible tangencies in the procession from the color of the longest wavelength, red, to that of the shortest, violet), or for reflecting light beams. The title *Dark Prisms* is metaphorical, not oxymoronic; it is meant to convey the passage of occult cultural icons from Hispanic life through the prism of drama, the images inexorably flowing from the bright side to the dark side of the spectrum. The resultant is a metaphysical state.

Metaphysics is not used here in the manner of the Aristotelian construct of exegesis on such as existence, causality, truth, among other first principles, nor does it refer to the seventeenth-century school of English poets whose principal exponent was John Donne and whose chief concern was expressing intellectual and philosophical matters through exotic conceits and ingenious wit. Rather, metaphysics is employed here in the sense conveyed by the protagonist in Christopher Marlowe's *The Tragical History of the Life and Death of Doctor Faustus* (1588) when, filled with excitement at the prospect of acquiring esoteric knowledge from the tomes placed into his hands by the thaumaturges Valdes and Cornelius, he exclaims:

> These metaphysics of magicians
> And necromantic books are heavenly;
> Lines, circles, signs, letters and characters—
> Ay, these are those that Faustus most desires. [Scene 1, 52–55]

It is the variety implicit in Faust's statement that concerns us in this study, for the sigils, symbols, seals, signets, and other semiotic elements in the grimoires consulted by Faust in his search for the meaning of the cosmos are but the external manifestations of a complex, universal, and interrelated system of arcane traditions whose origins may be lost in antiquity but whose impact is still felt. The quest of Faust is a universal one.

And perhaps because these modes of thought and being were first expressed through formal gesture, elevated speech, rhythmic movement, and ritual action—all basic elements of the ancient worship that gave rise to drama—they have continuing vitality in the written dialoguework and its counterpart, theater, the play on stage.

The chapters in this book present a comparatist's view of mythological, folkloric, and religious beliefs of the Western cultural heritage that have prompted a long and ongoing history of esoteric themes in theater and drama, from the Middle Ages to the present, in Spain and the Americas, either intact or syncretically. The terms *occultism* and *occult* are used here principally to describe the many ways that human beings have sought to fathom a secret knowledge intuited to exist but held to be inaccessible through normal means; turning to other possibilities, humans have sought the aid of supernatural agencies through alchemy, angelology, asceticism, astrology, demonolatry, divination, ecstasy, magic, necromancy, possession, santería, seances, voudoun, witchcraft, and so on. Because the list is extensive, the terms are meant to be more inclusive than exclusive.

The peoples of Europe were loath to give up the deities of millenia when Christianity confronted the pagan religions and overwhelmed them with its dogma and status after the fall of Rome. But despite the Church's drive and commitment to eradicating ancient beliefs it considered inimical to its message and mission, the peoples of Europe retained the old gods, nurturing them in the very cradle of the new faith, often vesting them with new identities and elevating them to sainthood without the formalities of canonization. Their festivals were integrated into the Church calendar in each vicinity, and their rites were practiced openly as if condoned by the religious authorities, as indeed was the case in the face of popular insistence. The result was that a pagan substratum thrived beneath what was in effect the veneer of Christianity.

That pagan tradition is still extant, not only in Europe but also in other geographical areas as well, including the Americas and Africa (indeed, wherever European colonizers took Christianity as part of their cultural baggage and imposed its tenets on the indigenous peoples they encountered, ever interpreting their religions as myths and damning their practice as sinful). Despite ongoing attempts at eradication, pre-Christian beliefs have persisted, continuing to inform and shape much modern thought. Hispanic drama is no exception.

Divided into three parts, *Dark Prisms* distinguishes the general from the specific in its assessment of theater and drama in Spain and Latin

America. The chapters in Part One present overviews of the topics they cover, while those in Part Two deal at length with the pertinent works of playwrights in which the occult canon is at the core. I have selected specific *plays* to discuss because of their focus on the occult. Some playwrights address this theme with greater frequency and import than others, thus their inclusion in Part Two. Part Three, the bibliography, is a compilation of plays in which occultism is central to the theme or is an important element therein.

In the chapters that follow, I first of all address, in addition to the metaphysical aspects of particular works, the human desire to know and connect with a supernatural order, whether through the formal worship of an established religion or through the attempt to effect personal control of the cosmos by the varied machinations of what is termed "magic." Be it the materialization of Hell on the medieval stage or the efficacious presentation of demonic pacts, astrology, alchemical operations, Cabbalism, witchcraft, Satanism, and so-called voodoo, the mechanism in human nature that prompts belief in these matters is the same: an intuitive sense of the existence of *something* beyond human cognition and attainment. The unknown prompts both fear and curiosity, the latter resulting in attempts to grasp its meaning, possess its hidden powers, engage in communion with hermetic forces and beings, or dabble in arcane doctrines toward illumination. It is all the result of ignorance about what lies beyond the human ken, along with the desire to have unlimited knowledge thereof and power over its operations, in short, to be godlike.

Second, the following chapters have many subtle interrelationships founded on shared topoi. For example, the belief in telluric forces and demons, which grew out of polytheistic animism, giving vent to the devils and pacts of medieval Christianity, the witches and magicians from the Renaissance through Salem, as well as the deities and their shamans taken out of Africa and brought to the Americas, where they mixed with Christian beliefs in Saints and miracles. It is all part of the pagan substratum, which is still extant in many parts of the world.

The topics herein also share the same roots in mythology and folklore—largely, but not exclusively, Greek and Roman. For one, the doctrines of the Cabbala are replete with Platonic ideas and Pythagorean principles that have attached themselves to that esoteric, mystical oral tradition of the Jews. Indeed, there are many European superstitions within the Jewish mystical system and, in turn, medieval occultism was greatly influenced by that oral tradition upon its transcription in numerous heterodox texts. The impact of the Cabbala is evident in the Faust legend and the theme of magic in early European drama, as well as in later plays.

Even where the gods are seemingly foreign to the European tradition, as in Africa, they parallel the deities in the pantheons encountered in the Western cultural heritage, often with surprising affinities, such as similar genealogies, myths, symbols, and ritual practices—among the latter, the use of snakes, states of possession, and the role of divination. Furthermore, the syncretism that took place in the Americas relates African and European beliefs meaningfully. Yet the superimposition of Western ideas does not obliterate the deeply embedded culture of Africa; at work there, as well as in Europe, is the pagan substratum.

Lastly, there are the shared factors of the human psyche, the interlacings and similarities of beliefs, rituals, and archetypal images that Jung saw as the result of "the collective unconscious" at work since prehistoric times. These universal elements have given rise to similar Creation and Flood myths, to name but two, in the Middle East and in the Americas, as elsewhere in the world. The Stith Thompson Motif Index attests to the human penchant for originating similar concepts in vastly different settings of time, place, and culture.

Dark Prisms explores a great many of these aspects of esoteric knowledge and practices as manifested in the drama of the Hispanic world—with an expansion into the Lusophone world of selected Afro-Brazilian plays because of their thematic proximity to the Cuban works studied—in order to show how the universality of human beliefs in the supernatural has given rise to a long tradition of staging and writing plays on that broad theme on both sides of the Atlantic Ocean.

Two of the chapters in this book first appeared in earlier versions in the following journals: Chapter 5 in *Journal of Dramatic Theory and Criticism* 4, no. 2; and Chapter 6 (in Spanish) in *Romance Notes* 24, no. 1. Chapter 8 contains passages from two articles that appeared respectively in *Latin American Theatre Review* 23, no. 2, and *Afro-Hispanic Review* 11, no. 1–3. Some entries in the bibliography were published in "The Occult Arts in the Golden Age," a special issue of *Critica Hispánica* 15, no. 1.

PART ONE

Evolution

I

Supernaturalism
in Medieval Spanish Drama

The term "supernatural" . . . denotes a fundamental category of religion,
namely the assertion or belief that there is *an other reality*, and one of
ultimate significance for man, which transcends the reality within which
our everyday experience unfolds.

Peter L. Berger, A Rumor of Angels

After the fall of Rome and during the rise of Christianity, the sophistication of the classical past was eroded. At best, only externals of the
greatness that had been Rome remained: roads, aqueducts, buildings,
and the like. Indeed, much of the Empire's great architecture fell into
decay through disuse or abuse. Classical Latin had long before given
way to the vulgar tongue, and now it was often unrecognizable in the
emerging languages of a disjointed Europe. A largely uneducated and
backward populace, concerned with problems of daily life, had no use
for the literature of the classical civilizations, and thus much of it was
lost as a consequence of ignorance, indifference, or hostility. Rightly or
wrongly, the period has come to be known as the Dark Ages.

Ironically, it was through the conquest of the Iberian Peninsula by the
followers of Mohammed that the knowledge of the West was returned to
it. The great literary, scientific, and philosophical texts of the past might
have perished had not the majority of them been preserved in Arabic by
Islamic scholars in such centers of learning as Baghdad and Cairo. These
texts, in turn, were brought to Al-Andalus where, in the caliphates of
Córdoba and Seville, they attracted scholars from all of Europe. These
Moorish courts were, in fact, the first European universities.

Much of ancient knowledge passed into Christian Europe through
such enlightened Christian courts as that of the thirteenth-century
monarch Alfonso X of Castile, who had many of the texts translated
from the Arabic and who compiled considerable knowledge and lore of
the era in encyclopedic works, earning the sobriquet "the Wise."

The conscientious toil of monks in monasteries illuminating manu-
scripts helped disperse such writings throughout Christendom. These

treasures of art as well as wisdom were securely placed in reading rooms within monasteries and in other libraries of the Church, later to be rediscovered in the great period known as the Renaissance.

In Spain the rebirth of interest in Humanism was to occur in the Siglo de Oro, or Golden Age, ranging from the consolidation of the Iberian Peninsula in 1492 under their Most Catholic Monarchs Fernando and Isabel, to the latter part of the seventeenth century when the death of Pedro Calderón de la Barca marked the end of literary greatness. It was a renaissance come full circle out of its origins in Muslim Al-Andalus.

In the centuries before the Renaissance, however, Europe led a curious life founded in large part on the struggle for survival of religious ideologies. A mixture of classical and barbaric mythologies gave medieval life a strong pagan substratum that Christian dogma could not eradicate; even the establishment of the Holy Office of the Inquisition relatively late in this period did no more than point out how deeply rooted were many of the pre-Christian traditions. Regardless of the outward acceptance of the Church by medieval Europeans through Baptism and other sacraments, there continued to exist an extrasocial underground of practices rooted in ancient beliefs (Eleusinian Mysteries, Druidism, Gnosticism, Mithraism, Christian heresies), many of whose origins have been lost in prehistory. The struggle of the Church with these incompatible forces, which were first termed superstitious and later condemned, is amply noted in the writings from the earliest apologists to Augustine and Aquinas.

While the Church sought to regulate and then eliminate these pagan traditions through excommunication (the assurance of eternal damnation), the state (frequently allied to the Church during this period) bolstered the spiritual attack through temporal tactics founded on laws that promised strong punishment for unorthodox practices. A case in point was the Spain of King Alfonso X.

The frequency of divination, necromancy, and other "black arts" in his thirteenth-century kingdom prompted Alfonso X to define occult activities and to attach suitable warnings against and punishments for their practitioners. These regulations were contained in his voluminous compendium of Gothic laws known as *Las Siete Partidas*. In Title 23, Law 1 of the last *Partida*, we read:

> Divination means the same thing as assuming the power of God in order to find out things which are to come. There are two kinds of divination; the first is that which is accomplished by the aid of astronomy, which is one of the seven liberal arts; and this, according to the law, is not forbid-

den to be practiced by those who are masters and understand it thoroughly; for the reason that the conclusions and estimates derived from this art are ascertained by the natural course of the planets and other stars, and are taken from the books of Ptolemy and other learned men, who diligently cultivated the science. Others, however, who do not understand it, should not work by means of it, but they should endeavor to study and master the works of learned men. The second kind of divination is that practiced by fortune-tellers, soothsayers and magicians who investigate omens caused by the flights of birds, by sneezing and by words called proverbs; or by those who cast lots, or gaze in water, or in crystal, or in a mirror, or in the blade of a sword, or in any other bright object; or who make images of metal, or any other substance whatsoever; or practice divination on the head of a dead man, or that of an animal, or in the palm of a child, or that of a virgin. We forbid impostors of this kind and all others like them to live in our dominions, or to practice any of these things here, because they are wicked and deceitful persons, and great evils result to the country from their acts; and we also forbid anyone to dare to entertain them in their houses or conceal them.[1]

The second law of the same Title contains the definition of necromancy and related subjects:

What is called *necromantia*, in Latin, is the strange art of calling up evil spirits, and for the reason that great injury happens to the country from the acts of men who engage in it, and especially because those who believe in them and ask for information on this subject suffer many accidents through fear caused by their going about at night looking for things of this kind in strange places, so that some of them die or become insane, or lose their minds; we therefore forbid that anyone shall dare to practice or make use of such wickedness as this, because it is something by which God is grieved and great harm results from it to men. Moreover, we forbid anyone to dare to make images of wax or metal, or any other figures to cause men to fall in love with women, or to put an end to the affection which persons entertain towards one another. We also forbid anyone to be so bold as to administer herbs or beverages to any man or woman to render them enamoured, because it sometimes happens that such beverages cause the death of those who take them and they contract very serious diseases with which they are afflicted for life.

The reach of the definitions indicates the widespread practice of these black arts and speaks for the necessity of strong regulatory laws. Alfonso completed the treatise by setting strict punishments for these crimes, which offended God and man; if convicted by the testimony of witnesses or by their own confessions, the accused were to die, and any who had aided them were to be banished from the kingdom for life. Practices with beneficial ends, however, were omitted from the third law's prosecution: "Such, however, as practice enchantments or anything else with good intentions, as, for instance, to cast out devils from the bodies of men; or to dissolve the spell cast over husband and wife so that they are unable to perform their marital duties; or to turn aside a cloud from which hail or a fog is descending that it may not injure the crops; or to kill locusts or insects which destroy grain or vines; or for any other beneficial purpose similar to these, cannot be punished, but we decree that they shall be rewarded for it." While the state sought to curb the malevolent practices of magician and witch through the promulgation of *Las Siete Partidas,* the Church promoted the damnation of the guilty as a deterrent. That neither was successful to any large extent is evident in the continuation of these nefarious activities over the centuries that followed and in the struggle of the civil and religious establishments to eradicate what they considered the Devil's plague, the work of anti-Christ.

Medieval Spanish literature also points to the prevalence of occultism, be it mystical or profane, in the daily life of court and populace. The earliest devil pact extant in Spanish literature dates from the middle of the thirteenth century; it is the *Miraglo de Teófilo* (Miracle of Theophilus), possibly derived from Rutebeuf's chronicle, which recounts the tale of a bishop's secular deputy who, being unjustly deprived of his post and then driven by resulting bitterness, sells his soul to Satan. Later, torn by his continuing resentment on the one hand and his deep Christian faith on the other, Theophilus finally selects the right-hand path and is saved by the Virgin Mary's intercession. This theme of the devil pact, with or without salvation, would become the core of many plays of the Golden Age; it would have particular delineation in Antonio Mira de Amescua's *El esclavo del demonio* (The Devil's Slave) and Pedro Calderón de la Barca's *El mágico prodigioso* (The Prodigious Magician).[2]

The story of Theophilus appears in two medieval Spanish works that stress the religious conception of the topic. In *Los milagros de Nuestra Señora* (The Miracles of Our Lady) Gonzalo de Berceo recounts the tale in miracle number twenty-four, and in *Las cantigas de Santa María* (The Canticles of Holy Mary) Alfonso X, "the Wise," gives his version in the third canticle. Both works contain many other references to the occult, such as miracles, wonders, superstitions, enchantments, possession and satanic pacts. Considered by some as pietistic collections, Berceo's *Milagros* and Alfonso's *Cantigas* continue to be studied as examples of dramatic staging, for there is some conjecture that the miracles in both texts may have been presented in the round. Indeed, certain miniatures in the *Códice Rico* of the *Cantigas* point to the use of current staging techniques in the artists' creation of the miniatures.[3]

Such novels of chivalry as *El caballero Cifar* (The Knight Cifar) and *Amadís de Gaula* (Amadis of Gaul), together with those Arthurian and Carolingian legends translated into Iberian romance, gorged themselves on the fantastic and the occult. The novel of chivalry became a milieu of esoteric operations presided over by Merlin and his kith and kin; the supra- and supernatural were unleashed to fly and leap, appear and disappear at the flick of a wand or the dropping of a demonic name. It was this exorbitance that impelled Cervantes to deal the genre, already moribund, its fatal wound in *Don Quijote*.

A similar interest in occult matters can be noted in the drama. The oldest extant play from the early Middle Ages in the Iberian Peninsula is a twelfth-century fragment of 147 verses, which has come to be known as the *Auto de los Reyes Magos* (The Play of the Magi); it is the real beginning of occultism as a subject for drama in Spain. The remnant of five brief scenes from the one surviving act of a longer work has been given its title solely on the basis of the motif on which it centers, a gloss from the Gospel of Matthew. The emphasis is on three personages who enter one by one—not the Three Kings of later tradition but the Magi of the Zoroastrian religion (or simply astrologers of Oriental heritage)—on their journey after a mysterious star, which each has followed from his realm.

> GASPAR (*Alone*): I do not know what star that is!
> This is the first that I have seen it,
> since its birth is very recent. . . .
> BALTHASAR (*Alone*): This star confounds me; I know not
> whence it comes, who brings or holds it.
> Why does this sign exist? . . .
> MELCHIOR (*Alone*): That star does not belong up there
> or I am not a good astrologer.
> GASPAR (*To Balthasar*):
> Have you ever seen such a wonder?
> A star has been born.[4]

Having joined in the quest to follow the star, they visit the court of King Herod, the puppet set up by Rome to rule over the Jews, hoping to learn the exact whereabouts of a newborn king whose sign in the sky has led them to the city. Upon their departure, Herod summons his astrologers, learned men, and seers to verify that what the foreign wise men told him was true.

The fragment is, of course, a segment of the familiar story of the Nativity and as such qualifies as a Mystery Play, dealing as a whole with an aspect of Christ's life. Yet, it is curious that the only verses of the longer play that have been preserved are the ones dealing with the supernatural aspects of the birth of Christ, itself an event of outstanding proportions, for it is the manifestation of God as man in the Christian belief system. Separated from the rest of the work as it is (historical irony or deliberate act?), this fragment acquires an aura of mystery and real poignancy: three astrologers from distant lands, a strange new star in the heavens, a superstitious King, court astrologers and seers. The only supernatural aspect of the original story missing from the Spanish fragment is that of the vision or dream of the Magi in which an angel advises them to leave Herod's court. The *Auto de los Reyes Magos* becomes another important indication of the occult tendencies of the medieval mind—a mind wherein religion and superstition cohabitated and were often synonymous.

Spain must have had an *early* medieval theater in Castilian akin to that of England, France, and Germany, among other European nations, but its existence has yet to be proven. Nonetheless, logic mandates recognition of its shadow existence in light of the presence of the thirteenth-century *Auto de los Reyes Magos*, whose first endeavors no doubt made possible the advances in style and dramatic technique that came about in the fifteenth century with Gómez Manrique (1412–90?), the first dramatist known by name, and Juan del Encina (1469–1529), considered the founding father of Spanish drama.

Although limited in number, there were other examples of medieval Peninsular drama, if in other than the Castilian tongue. As Peter Meredith and John Tailby record it, in the Valencia Corpus Christi processions of the early fifteenth century, salaries were paid in 1404 "to hire the men who walked in the dragons (*los drachs*)," in 1407 "[f]or repairing the wild beasts (*les figures de les besties feres*) of the blessed St. George" and "to the man who walked inside St. George's dragon (*la cucha de sent Jordi*)," as was done also in 1408, while in an indoor performance at the Aranzo estate in Jaén, Spain, in 1461, there was a fire-breathing dragon "[i]n front of the place where the Countess was seated[;] there then appeared the head of this huge dragon (*serpiente*). It was made of painted wood, and a device inside it (*su artificio*) propelled the boys out through its mouth one by one, and it breathed huge flames at the same time" (*Staging of Religious Drama*, 121–22).

Likewise, the *Misteri d'Elx* (The Mystery Play of Elche), which is held every year in two parts on the fourteenth and fifteenth of August, the Feast of the Assumption of Mary, has its origin in religious rites celebrated in the Basilica Menor de Santa María as early as the fourteenth century, the language being the Valencian variant of Catalan. Legend has it that around 1265 an ark was taken from the waters near Elche. According to José Antón, who held eighteenth-century Elche's equivalent of the post of attorney general, the vessel contained both an "*imagen*" (image? statue?) of the virgin of the Assumption and a book, *Consueta* (from the Latin *Consuetudine,* for a book of Church rituals), in which the text and music of what has come to be called "El Misteri d'Elx" were written. The year of this event seems to have been fostered because it coincided with the capture of Elche from the Moors by King Jaume I. But another, more reliable fourteenth-century date was promulgated by Pere Ibarra, who found a mention of Elche's celebration of the Feast of the Assumption of Mary in a letter written by Queen Mary of Aragon on June 7, 1370.

Whatever the date of its inception, the rite in the text honors the first woman in the Christian canon. She is the Virgin Mary, venerated as Nuestra Señora de la Asunción in Elche, of which she is the patroness. The *Misteri d'Elx*, divided into two parts, re-creates in song and spectacle the death and assumption into Heaven of the body of the mother of Christ. The first part, or "Vespra," takes place on August 14, while the second, "La Festa," occurs on the following day. Additionally, in even-numbered years the *Misteri* is performed again on November 1, All Saints Day, to accommodate the faithful and the many visitors who could not see it otherwise. On either occasion, it is a stirring drama.

What makes the play something other than a traditional medieval pageant, albeit a solemn one, are the machinations that take place during the performance. These are literally machine-produced effects that enhance the thaumaturgic nature of Mary's assumption into Heaven by creating through physical means that which is held to have been miraculously wrought. The special effects never fail to bring wonder to the eyes of onlookers, even to those who have repeatedly witnessed the spectacle over a lifetime, or to one who was privileged to have been admitted to Heaven, to have seen the "backstage" preparations, to have talked to angels, Christ, God the Father, and the Holy Spirit ("Ghost" in the old days), and to have witnessed apprehensively the actual machinations during the performance of the *Misteri d'Elx*.

In the first part, Mary, or La María, enters the basilica in the company of six acolytes, her attending angels, and Saints María Salomé and

María Jacobe. As she processes on the *andador*, the ramp that leads to the elevated platform under the dome, Mary laments over the separation from her Son. She stops four times in commemoration of her Son's Way of the Cross. She longs to join him in Heaven and prepares for death when she reaches the *cadafal*, her bier.

High above the platform, the dome is hidden by a canvas painted with clouds over a background of celestial blue. Its surface is broken only by a framed square opening—*les portes del cel*. When La María kneels on her bier, the first miraculous event occurs. A thunderous blast from the organ, accompanied by ringing church bells and the sound of fireworks, signals the opening of Heaven's door, through which emerges a huge, resplendent pomegranate that, on clearing the celestial opening, unfolds its eight "petals" upward to disclose an angel bearing a golden palm. Suspended by rope covered in celestial blue cloth, the deus ex machina descends slowly as the angel sings a greeting to La María. Upon landing the angel alights and tells Mary that her prayers will soon be answered, promising to honor her request that the Apostles attend her deathbed. Leaving her with the golden palm sent by Christ to his mother, the angel returns to Heaven in the same open pomegranate, singing anew. Afterward, the Apostles begin to arrive, singly or in groups, singing the praises of and offering greetings to Mary. Saint John is the first to enter and receives from her the golden palm. He is followed by Saint Peter, and six others enter thereafter. The remaining three Apostles meet on the *andador* in the scene known as the "Ternari," in which, led by Saint James (the patron saint of Spain, known there as Santiago), they sing in three-part harmony a piece that is the musical highlight of the *Misteri d'Elx*.

Upon the death of La María, the Apostles witness the descent from Heaven of what the *Ilicitanos*, the people of Elche, call the Araceli, an open-frame platform bearing five angels who accompany their slow progress toward the bier with voices, harp, and guitars. They take the soul of Mary, in the form of a small sculptured image of her, and ascend to Heaven with further celestial song. This great moment in Catholic belief—that the soul of the worthy will join God in Heaven upon the death of the body—forms the dramatic closing of the long first act of the *Misteri d'Elx*.

The events in the second and final act follow immediately on those of the first, although the time of presentation is delayed to the actual day of her feast. As the Apostles prepare her body for burial, a horde of Jews threatens to disrupt the proceedings in order to prevent the Christians from claiming for Mary the same resurrection of the body that they did for Jesus. But as the Jews appear to be winning the battle, Mary performs her first miracle after death and converts them. The burial ritual is interrupted anew as the opening of Heaven is announced by the organ and sundry other joyful noises, and the Araceli returns to earth, this time to take the body of Mary into Heaven. In the middle of its ascent, Thomas, the only Apostle missing, returns from India and makes his obeisance to the body of Mary. Shortly, another blast from the organ announces the arrival of a second conveyance out of Heaven. It is the Holy Trinity, descending to the Araceli in their own framework, the Trinitat, to crown Mary as Queen of Heaven. As the powerful bells of the basilica toll joyously, the Araceli and the Trinitat ascend to Heaven in a cloud of *oropel*, pieces of gold foil, falling from God's domain.

The greater mystery that the end of the play heralds is the miraculous favor accorded Mary upon entering Heaven with her uncorrupted body, underscoring her uniqueness as a human born without Original Sin, and thus Immaculate, fit to be a suitable vessel for the birth of her Divine Son. That mystery is now seconded by her Assumption, Mary's apotheosis.

Once again, medieval Spain has demonstrated an affinity for the mysterious and the miraculous, as attests the lore surrounding Santiago (Saint James) and his role in the reconquest of the Iberian Peninsula from the Moors. The ongoing veneration of the Virgin Mary under the title of Nuestra Señora de la Asunción, shows that in Elche, as elsewhere in Spain, the devotion to mysterious deities out of medieval tradition still survives.

It was not the type of Christian supernaturalism evinced in the *Auto de los Reyes Magos* and the *Misteri d'Elx* that concerned Alfonso X, however. The laws in *Las Siete Partidas* condemn such pervasive *secular* practices as divination and necromancy, perceived to be inimical to Christian teaching. If many of the extant works of the Middle Ages abound with sacred themes of a supernatural nature, many others deal with devil pacts, astrology, alchemy, fabled beasts, and perverse enchantments. These subjects are at the core of what is called occultism.

In Webster's definition, occultism is the "belief in hidden or mysterious powers and the possibility of subjecting them to human control."[5] In the broad context of this statement, it can be said that the medieval works discussed are occult in their orientation since they show the involvement of human beings with forces beyond human attainment through normal means. The involvement consisted in either attempting to control such powers (as through satanic aid) or using them to achieve a praiseworthy end (as the location of Christ's birthplace in the *Auto de los Reyes Magos*).

The nonreligious, that is, secular, work which is, perhaps, most representative of this use or attempted manipulation of occult forces is the *Tragicomedia de Calixto y Melibea*, attributed through an acrostic to Fernando de Rojas. The *Celestina*, as it is generally known because of its central character, was published in 1499 (although it was probably composed in 1492) and is a novelesque drama in twenty-one acts in its final version (sixteen in the first). Anticipating Cervantes and Shakespeare in the portrayal of character, Rojas presents a series of richly drawn figures within the tragic framework of Calixto's sensual love for Melibea. The best-drawn and most memorable character is the one who gave her name as the "new title" of the work.

In Celestina, Rojas created the definitive version of the old crone. More than a mere go-between and love broker, she is a practitioner of the black arts. A very human witch with many side talents, Celestina seems unbounded in the practice of her vocation: she takes in sewing, runs a house of ill repute, repairs the often lost virtue of supposed virgins, acts as a midwife, and concocts all sorts of medicines, cosmetics, and potions for sale to a large and eager clientele from all social classes. That she serves the needs of society is obvious in the lack of secrecy about her affairs and in the lucrative manner in which she is paid.

More often than not these services are aided by her conjurations of demonic forces. Pointedly in the third act, for example, Celestina prepares the ingredients that she requires to summon Pluto, classical lord of the Underworld; she instructs Elicia, one of her prostitutes to

> Run up to the garret over the sun porch and bring me that vial of snake oil, the one that's hanging from the rope I found in the fields that dark and rainy night. Then open the sewing cabinet; on the right you'll find a piece of paper written in bat's blood, under the wing of that dragon whose claws we removed yesterday. . . . If not there, go to the room where I keep the ointments and you'll find it in the hide of the black cat, where I told you to put the wolf eyes. Bring down the goat's blood too, and a few of his whiskers. . . .[6] [III.2]

These instructions leave no doubt that her pharmacopeia is replete with ingredients for traditional witchery. Using these unsavory (but effective) ingredients, Celestina proceeds with the lengthy and twisted conjuration of the pagan god:

I conjure you, dark Pluto, lord and master of the hellish depths, . . . I, Celestina, the best of your clients, conjure you through the potent force of these scarlet letters; through the weight of the names and signs written on this paper; through the venom in this snake oil now anointing this yarn. Come at once to obey my command and wrap yourself within this yarn; stay wrapped in it so that Melibea buys it, as she will, and upon gazing at it more and more her heart will soften to my request. Wound her heart and lance it with base passion and love for Calixto so that forgetting her virginity, she will reveal her passion to me and offer just rewards for all my work. Once this has been done, ask and demand what you will of me.

Her offering, made to a pagan rather than a Christian deity, does not necessarily imply the pledging of her soul to eternal damnation. Celestina's statement, in keeping with tradition, may contain the offer of her body for possession by Pluto, a not unsatisfying experience in the eyes of a witch. But her immediate concern is with the swift completion of the appointed task, and to assure its satisfactory end, Celestina adds a threat to her conjuring: "But should you fail to act with all due speed, I will become your greatest foe. I will pierce your dark and moody dungeons with shafts of light, denounce with venom all your lies, curse with harshest words your hideous name. I conjure you this once and once again. And trusting in my great power, I set out to my task with this yearn, knowing that I have you wrapped within."

Celestina's first visit to Melibea takes place in the fifth act; the witch is encouraged by the virgin's receptiveness and leaves her walled garden retreat muttering, "Oh, demon whom I conjured! How well you granted all I asked! I am in your debt. You tamed the shrewish fury of the girl and let me speak to her alone when you got rid of her mother. . . . Bless you, snake-oil; bless you, yarn! You've made everything work to my advantage!" (V.2). The tone of her speech shows that even the experienced witch can be surprised at the efficacy of her conjuration. The total fulfillment of it with the illicit union of Calixto and Melibea further attests to her powers—both occult and psychological. She has served society well once more.

Her success is marred, however, by the avarice of Calixto's servants, who expect to share in the reward their master has given the witch. Celestina reneges on her promise. But Sempronio cannot restrain his ire and attacks her with his sword. As he wounds her fatally, the servant shouts out her sentence of infernal damnation. Celestina screams pitifully for confession, but death has her in its grip and she dies in her sin.

She may have conjured the pagan Pluto, but in the eyes of Sempronio her soul will dwell with the damned in Satan's Hell.

The publication of the *Tragicomedia de Calixto y Melibea* marked the end of an era and the beginning of another, the work forming a bulwark between the Spanish Middle Ages and the Renaissance, known as the Siglo de Oro (Golden Age). Yet that bulwark does not imply that what is in the past will remain a relic; rather, the bulwark becomes a bridge that allows the continuation of traditional beliefs in supernaturalism in the new intellectual atmosphere, enriching it thereby.

II
Esoterica in the Golden Age Drama of Spain

Many pagan customs survived among the lower classes: enchantment, magical knots, the use of disguise as mythical animals, nightly assemblies of sorcerers, the use of talismans, herbs, stones and poisons, incantations, spells, demon worship, and many other practices of witchcraft. . . . Everybody believed in the power of magic, the scholars as well as the worldly rulers and the clergy.
                    Kurt Seligmann, *Magic, Supernaturalism and Religion*

The influence of the novelesque drama known as *La Celestina* has been great. In the two centuries that followed its publication, many plays make direct connection to the *Celestina* in their titles, while others offer characters whose ancestry in that work cannot be doubted. One of the first dramatists to follow this important current was Pedro Manuel Jiménez de Urrea, an Aragonese, who in 1513 wrote *Egloga de la tragicomedia de Calixto y Melibea*, a versification of selected episodes from the original. In 1534 Feliciano de Silva composed the *Segunda comedia de Celestina*, a play that capitalized on the original's ambiguity by resuscitating its principal character and explaining away the impossibility of such an event by stating that Celestina's death had been nothing more than a magical deceit she performed to avert her real death. Gaspar Gómez de Toledo wrote another sequel, *Tercera parte de la tragicomedia de Celestina*. This, in turn, was followed by Sancho de Muñón's *Tragicomedia de Lisandro y Roselia llamada Elicia y por otro nombre cuarta obra y tercera Celestina*, written in 1542, in which the young Elicia of the *Celestina* has matured and taken over the work of her mentor. Also in direct lineage are three plays of the seventeenth century: the anonymous *Baile de Celestina*, Salas Barbadillo's *Celestina* (1620), and the *Entremés famoso de la Celestina* by Juan Navarro de Espinosa. Menéndez y Pelayo, the great Spanish critic, noted that even Calderón penned a play titled *Celestina*, but this is among those texts presumed lost.

Other plays of the sixteenth and seventeenth centuries may not disclose an association with the *Celestina* through the title, but may include either a character with the same name or one with similar characteristics. Three anonymous plays of the period, for example, contain go-betweens of the Celestina type: *Tragicomedia alegórica del parayso y del infierno* (1539), which is an adaptation of Gil Vicente's *Auto da barca do infierno, Farça a manera de tragedia* (1517); and *Comedia Clariana* (1522). A character named Celestina appears in Francisco de Castro's *Entremés de los gigantones,* as well as in Antonio Diez's *Auto de Clarindo* (1535). In *El encanto de la hermosura y el hechizo sin hechizo* (late 1600s) by Agustín de Salazar y Torres, another Celestina—a daughter of the original—also performs as a witch. Her influence is visible in Quevedo's *Entremés de la ropavejera,* in several of Juan del Encina's églogas, in Juan de la Cueva's *Comedia del infamador* (1581), and in a host of other plays too numerous and minor to list.

Lope de Vega, an innovative genius considered the father of modern European drama, made use of the character Celestina in his play *El caballero de Olmedo* (The Knight of Olmedo). The work unravels the tragic story of Don Alonso, who falls victim to the jealousy and hatred that fate instills in his adversary for the hand of Doña Inés. The tragic action occurs despite the warnings given the knight by Fabia. The old crone of *El caballero* possesses the same qualities and vices that defined Celestina; like her, Fabia is a witch whose powers are available to all for a fee. Like her, too, she is hired to facilitate the seduction of a virgin. In the fifth scene of the first act, Fabia tricks Doña Inés into answering Don Alonso's letter, saying in an aside:

> . . . Come quickly,
> fierce dweller of the depths,
> and bring a scorching flame
> to sear the breast of this fair maid.[1] [I.5]

Fabia's words are as much an invocation to her familiar spirit or demon as were Celestina's to Pluto. Further, while Celestina only discussed how she obtained the ingredients for her spells and incantations, Fabia is seen in the actual process of gathering the same. In the eighth scene of the first act, Fabia bullies Tello, Don Alonso's comic servant, into accompanying her that night while she removes the molar of a recently hanged man—an operation that will assure the success of her spell. Tello, full of superstitious fear, objects strenuously because he is not an initiate in the black arts: "Fabia, you've been taught well/how to speak to the Devil. . . ./Are you a woman or a demon?" (I.8). Later, in the first scene of the second act, Tello discloses to his master the disconcerting work of that horrible evening:

I'm very frightened
that this love begins
with so much witchery,
for circles and conjurations
provide no proper cure
if honestly you strive.
I went along with her (would I had not)
to raid a hanged man's mouth
of a single molar; like Harlequin
I took a ladder to the gallows.
While Fabia climbed, I stayed below
and heard the highwayman speak out:
"Climb up, Tello, without fear
or I will have to come to you." [II.1]

Tello's fear—that of the superstitious and untutored rustic—contrasts
with Don Alonso's sophisticated assurance that such practices are vain
and false. The irony here, of course, lies in that the knight cannot hope
to achieve his amorous conquest of Doña Inés without the witchery of
Fabia, the effectiveness of whose spell she had indicated in an aside in
the last scene of the first act: "Oh, what strong effect have had/the
conjurations and the spells!/I know that victory's at hand." (I.17).

But while Fabia's magic works to win an illicit end, it cannot overcome the dictates of fate. An aura of doom hangs over Don Alonso,
but he fails to heed Fabia's prognostication of a tragic event. Through
her divining ability, Fabia perceived upon first meeting her employer
that he was born under unfavorable conditions; the knight himself had
experienced a daydream in which the eyes of his beloved warned him
not to return to Olmedo. Afterward, as he entered a chapel in pursuit
of Doña Inés, he felt a strange presentiment of death. Other warnings
of an unnatural type appear. In a highly dramatic moment, Don Alonso
meets his shadow and is unnerved by the ominous meaning he reads in
the encounter; he tries to dismiss the omen as a trick concocted by
Fabia, but as he walks through the foreboding night another startling
event occurs. He hears a peasant's voice in the dense forest, singing the
ballad of Don Alonso's death:

"How late at night
they killed the knight,
Medina's pride,
Olmedo's flower.
Shadows had warned
not to depart,

shadows had warned
the knight to remain,
not to depart. . . ." [III.18]

When questioned by Alonso, the peasant tells him that Fabia taught him
the song. The witch had sent the peasant (her familiar spirit in human
form?) as a last warning to the doomed man. Shortly, Don Alonso is
treacherously attacked by his rival. As he lies dying, the inevitable irony
of unheeded warnings comes to his mind. The sophistication that earlier
had ridiculed Tello's superstitious fears is now replaced with the recognition of the occult forces that had worked through intuition and
Fabia's magic. Here, as in the *Celestina*, the beneficial role of witchcraft
in society is made obvious, but Lope de Vega in *El caballero de Olmedo*
does more than indicate this fact or make a moral judgment; despite
Tello's comic antics and fears, the presentation of witchcraft in the play
is serious, showing that the occult cannot be dismissed with a shrug and
a leer.

Besides Celestina and her descendants, Golden Age drama contains
many witches and magicians of fact and fantasy. Zoroaster appears in
Juan de la Cueva's *Comedia de la constancia de Arcelina*; Circe is a
central figure in Mira de Amescua et al.'s *Polifemo y Circe*; Merlin is the
lead character in Rey de Artieda's *Los encantos de Merlín*, and appears,
too, in *La casa de los celos y selvas de Ardenia* by Cervantes. Ruiz de Alarcón's *Quien mal anda en mal acaba* (Evil to Him Who Evil Does) deals
with Román Ramírez, a Moor who was arrested and punished by the
Inquisition on charges of being a magician; it is a typical *comedia* of in-
tricate plot and superimposed identities maneuvered by Satan. Another
reputed magician, Pedro Vallalarde, is the subject of Salvo y Vela's
El mágico de Salerno (written between 1715 and 1720); another
eighteenth-century dramatist, Valladares de Sotomayor, wrote numerous plays in which magicians are protagonists.[2]

A particularly attractive subject for Golden Age drama of the occult
was Marthe Brossier, a Frenchwoman born in 1547. Accompanied by
her ambitious and unscrupulous father, Marthe toured the country,
feigning demoniacal possession, and for many years made a handsome
income from public exhibitions, many of which were arranged by street
preachers anxious to dramatize their sermons. When she was uncovered
as a fraud, the pope and king acquiesced in her return to her own town
in order to avoid the scandal that a trial would bring. Marthe slipped
into near anonymity and would remain as a curious historic personage
were it not for the many dramatists in Europe who saw her life as a

ready-made plot; in Spain important eighteenth-century plays were written about her by Cañizares, Ripoll, Concha, and Ramón de la Cruz.[3] One of the more fascinating historical characters who figures prominently in the works of the Golden Age is the Marqués Enrique de Villena, the Aragonese nobleman born about 1384, who published an influential treatise on the "evil eye" (*Libro de aojamiento*, [1425]),which caused him to be branded a sorcerer and inspired the Church to burn his library upon his death in 1434. The confrontation between the Church and a member of the nobility could not help but be dramatic, and its appeal to the major playwrights of this period is evident in their works: Ruiz de Alarcón's *La cueva de Salamanca*, Calderón's *Los encantos del Marqués de Villena*, Rojas Zorrilla's *Lo que quería ver el Marqués de Villena*, and Lope de Vega's *Porfiar hasta morir*.

Another magician who interested the Golden Age playwrights was Don Illán de Toledo, whose story can be traced back to Don Juan Manuel's *El libro de Patronio, e por otro nombre, el Conde Lucanor* (circa 1323–35), the medieval collection of examples in which Patronio instructs Count Lucanor. In Example XI, Patronio develops the tale of the renowned magician who, testing the veracity of a pupil's promises, weaves a spell that makes the ambitious subject think he has achieved all his desires; within the framework of this magical future, however, Don Illán learns that the promises made him will not be kept, and he then abruptly returns the deceiver to the present, having taught him not the magic he wished to learn but a real lesson in human fickleness. In *La prueba de las promesas* (1618 or 1634?), Ruiz de Alarcón adapted Patronio's tale in a three-act *comedia*. In it, Don Illán makes certain that his daughter's eyes will be opened to her preferred suitor's opportunism by creating a new time and place in which honor and fame come to Blanca's pretender. In the process, as in Patronio's tale, the shallowness and deceit of Don Juan are clearly seen, and Blanca, back in reality with her virginity intact (as her name implies) recognizes the worth of her other suitor. In the *comedia* an hour elapses between the time that Don Illán casts his spell and the moment when he breaks its effect; in the course of that period Don Juan has been made to experience a lifetime. The operation is purely magical.

The occult in the Golden Age extends into other areas, too. There are countless plays in which astrology and other forms of divination are basic motifs or frequent elements. Such is the case with many of Lope de Vega's dramas (e.g., *Roma abrasada*, *La niña de plata*, *El sufrimiento de honor*, *La Arcadia*, *La niñez del Padre Rojas*, *El mejor alcalde el Rey*, *El acero de Madrid*). Likewise, the plays of José de Cañizares exhibit a particular interest in astrology as an occult science, apart from their great attention to magical operations. The tracks of the astrologers can also be found in Guillén de Castro's *Las mocedades del Cid* (The Cid's Youth), Ruiz de Alarcón's *El anticristo* (Anti-Christ), Bances Candamo's *El esclavo en grillos de oro* (The Slave in Golden Fetters), and Nanclares's *La hechicera del cielo* (Heaven's Bewitcher). Calderón also incorporated astrology into various works, especially *La vida es sueño* (Life Is a Dream), *Apolo y Climene*, and *El laurel de Apolo* (Apollo's Laurel). Further, there are a number of dramas and *entreméses* in which the principal character is an astrologer, as exemplified by the anonymous *Entremés del astrólogo borracho* (The Drunken Astrologer), Bances Candamo's *El astrólogo tunante* (The Roguish Astrologer), Arroyo y Velasco's *Entremés del astrólogo burlado* (The Astrologer Tricked), and Calderón's *El astrólogo fingido* (The Fake Astrologer). The treatment of astrology in these and other plays of the Golden Age ranges from slapstick to serious, encompassing all the gradations in between. This variety of approaches indicates the mixture of social, religious, and political attitudes toward astrology. While in most instances astrology is acknowledged as an impressive phenomenon, it is at the same time treated mundanely in most of the works in which it plays a role, and therefore loses much of its occult character. Thus is the fate of the esoteric when it comes into vogue.

There is yet one major facet of occultism in the Golden Age that remains to be considered. It is the role of Satan, the Devil. Although the lord of Hell appeared frequently on the medieval stage, he did not possess the grandeur and the potency that the Golden Age dramatist was to give him. Even in the *Celestina* and *El caballero* de Olmedo the dark beings on whom the witches call have only a power implicit in the words of their conjurers; indeed, these deities never materialize, and the effectiveness of their power is ambiguous. But in important plays by Cervantes, Mira de Amescua, and Calderón, the Devil emerges as an impressive, and dangerous, being. To these dramatists Satan was not the ridiculous or rustic creature that he often was on the medieval stage. Rather, he was the great archangel whose pride and arrogance drove him and his followers to open rebellion against the majesty of God. To the classically oriented Golden Age, Lucifer was not unlike Prometheus, although the dichotomy in their relationships to man strained the comparison.

In the Middle Ages the Devil had emerged with mixed characteristics derived from sources far-flung in time and locale. The animism of primitive societies, for one, ascribed all phenomena to personal agencies—superhuman beings who were either good (i.e., gods) or evil (i.e., demons). The gods were generally separatists, not easily accessible to human call. But the demons were usually in close contact with man, perhaps because in man's mind he saw his own animal nature reflected in the essences he called demons. These evil beings were exotic and appealed to the human sense of drama and mystery.

The Egyptians personified the base side of their deities through various animal forms (the serpent Apap) and demiurgic identities (Set being the primary lord of evil); the Babylonians employed the dragon Tiamat along with a host of demons, among which are distinguished Beelzebub, Baal, Astaroth, and Asmodeus; the Hindus identified as their evil deities Ahi, Siva, and Kali; the Aztecs had their Mictlantecutli; the Greeks, their Titans, Furies, Harpies, and Circe.

Many of the demonic figures of ancient religions bore the horns of goats, stags, rams, or bulls. These adornments, symbolizing the fertility of the respective animals, along with their strength and abilities considered magical, are universal in their usage. Such dispersion of this custom over time and place has given rise to the proposition that humankind developed a fertility religion whose deities were horned gods and earth mothers. While the female figure eventually lost its high place in societies that were largely patriarchal, the figure of the horned god thrived even among the more civilized cultures. In Greece and Rome the representatives of this already ancient tradition were Pan (half man, half goat) the horned satyr and Priapus, his phallic counterpart.

When Christianity arrived in Europe these religious beliefs, and others, were well entrenched. The Christian priests brought with them their own concept of evil and their personal view of its instigator. The early Christian personification of evil in Satan was founded largely on scattered Old Testament references to a "satan" (by which is meant merely an opponent or antagonist), on the acceptance of the story of the angelic fall as recounted in the pseudepigraphal *Book of Enoch* (from 200 to 100 B.C.), and on the literal interpretation of the Gospels, particularly the one dealing with Christ's temptations while fasting in the desert by a "satan," undoubtedly meant to be taken in the Old Testament sense. These are the sources that Origen, Augustine, and Aquinas, among the more prominent, employ in the formulation of their detailed views of Christian demonology. In the fourth century Saint Jerome borrowed Isaiah's Lucifer (Hebrew for "shining star") and applied the term to the Devil, although the Old Testament prophet used it simply to disguise a reference to Nebuchadnezzar. In A.D. 547 the Council of Constantinople defined the Devil and established the existence of Hell. But it was Peter Lombard in the twelfth century who most forcefully fixed the identity of the Devil to that of Lucifer, the name now accepted for the rebellious archangel.

As Christianity converted pagan Europe, it found it necessary to deal with the myriad deities, many of the horned variety, that it encountered. In the process, the Church created in the minds of the populace the belief that their gods were false, and in some cases demons. In the movement of the centuries, the association led to the equating of pagan deities with Satan and his followers. It is not too difficult to see, then, how Satan got his horns or to understand how medieval Christians pictured him with cloven hoofs and goat skin.

In the Golden Age, the Devil was interpreted in more sophisticated terms. He lost his association with Pan and other satyr figures; in the course of change he also lost much of the physical grotesqueness that had made him terrifying in earlier days. Further, the influence of Mithraic and other dualistic religions added to the Christian concept of Satan the near equality of the evil being to the deity. Through these refinements of his outwardness, accompanied by purgations of his character and role, the Golden Age Devil became an epic figure not unlike Ahriman in the Zoroastrian pantheon. In his new grandeur Satan was evil incarnate. A tragic figure in that through his own action he had denied himself the divine vision for eternity, he sought to derail from God's path as many souls as inhumanly possible into the sharing of his wretchedness.

In *Auto sacramentales* and other religious dramatizations of this era, the Devil is introduced in the guise that Christianity eventually came to grant him. In Lope de Vega's *La Maya,* he is the Prince of Darkness who vies with the Prince of Light for the soul in a Christian approximation to the Mithraic *agon.* The parallels to Zoroastrian dualism or the Manichean heresy are incidental to Lope's treatment, which is largely canonical in its stance.

Quite different is the case of Cervantes's *El rufián dichoso* (The Fortunate Rogue), in which the Devil is the purveyor of temptations and the means to their satisfaction, the latter through an act of despair or a contract signed in blood. Lucifer's emissaries, grotesque still in this play, attempt to make Padre Cruz return to the amoral life he had led in Seville before his dedication to the service of God. His temptations come in all types, often in the form of succubi with their lascivious intent. But the priest is able to overcome their carnal enticements. The attempts of these lesser demons are to no avail and they have recourse to the great Lucifer. He appears with the regalia of his kind to oversee the final torments of the priest, but Padre Cruz dies in his holy state. Lucifer and his cohorts, furious at their defeat, rush to vent their anger on the corpse, but the rosary that adorns the bier prevents the devils from their vengeful act. The devils mocked and defeated is a Christian motif characteristic of the age. Characteristic of the play is the mixture of conceptions regarding the devils; in the case of Lucifer Cervantes presents the "new" view, while in the treatment of the minor devils he returns to the medieval depiction. The *comedia*'s principal interest as an example of occultism in Golden Age drama rests, therefore, on its bridging two attitudes toward the Devil.

In *El esclavo del demonio* (The Devil's Slave) by Mira de Amescua, the plot centers on a satanic pact made by a rogue who would later become Saint Gil de Santarem. In his treatment of this Portuguese legend, the playwright creates a Faustian figure that compares favorably with Marlowe's creation, although it lacks the element of damnation.

The plot evolves through many complications in typical *comedia* fashion. Marcelo has ordained that his daughters, Leonor and Lisarda, follow his guidance; the first is to become a nun and the second is to marry Don Sancho. While Leonor accedes to her father's wish, Lisarda rebels. She is in love with Don Diego, despite the irony that he was responsible for her brother's death in a duel. Lisarda plots with her lover as a willing abductee. Don Diego, accompanied by his servant Domingo, arrives that night and starts to climb Lisarda's balcony as prearranged, but he never reaches his dishonorable goal; a reputed holy man, Don Gil, enters and convinces him of his error. But, after Don Diego exits, his reprimander, giving in to the temptation of the flesh, himself ascends and in the dark and silent night enters Lisarda's room. The unknowing girl gives her virginity to Don Gil; only at dawn does she realize what has transpired. Don Gil creates the lie that Don Diego asked to be replaced in order to avenge himself fully on Lisarda's father. Willfully dishonored, lasciviously deceived, Lisarda does a totally unexpected thing: she runs off with Don Gil, swearing vengeance on Don Diego. She devotes herself to a criminal life of robbery and murder while waiting for the opportunity to hold her intended victim in her grasp. Don Gil, always by her side, adds other rapes to his growing list of offenses.

The plot takes another twist when the duo waylay Lisarda's father and sister. After a struggle between the hatred and love that rages inside her, Lisarda allows them to depart. But on seeing Leonor, Don Gil feels the cravings of lust stronger than ever before. Since there is

now no plausible way to achieve his desire, Don Gil pronounces some
damning words when he stands alone:

> Since relish and intent
> indeed condemn a man,
> I'd give my soul
> to ravish you, Leonor.[4] [II, ll. 371–74]

No sooner are the words spoken than the Devil, disguised as a rake,
materializes to accept the offer. Replying to Don Gil's desire, the Devil
identifies himself:

> I am your friend,
> although till yesterday
> I was your foe.
>
> .   .   .   .
>
> You're following my steps;
> I once enjoyed the grace of God
> and in an instant fell
> and lost forever hope of making
> a prodigal's return. . . . [II, ll. 1384–91]

Angelio, as this devil calls himself, offers to teach Don Gil the necro-
mantic arts that will vitalize all his desires:

> If learning necromancy
> is your wish, I'll teach you then
> for I have learned it all in old
> Toledo's caves, and here instruct
> within my own in magic
> arts to sate all vices
> and let all appetites
> run wild without remorse.
> If in the shadows of dark nights
> at sepulchers you conjure
> hell with bones
> you'll know of things to come.
> In all four Elements you'll
> see strange signs—
> in plants, in animals and
> in the movements of the stars.
> Your wishes will be infinite;
> with freedom and resolve

you'll give free rein
to all your appetites. [II, ll. 1399–1418]

Don Gil is astonished by Angelio's awareness of his lust for Leonor and captivated by the world of possibilities that has opened before him. He enters the devil's cave to sign the blood pact and to don the garb of the demonic slave. Lisarda enters unexpectedly and instinctively tries to kill Angelio, who only scoffs and forces her to witness Don Gil's ritualistic pledge and the reading of the pact.

At the start of the final act, Don Gil recounts his evil deeds but shows dissatisfaction with mere sinfulness. His real desire is to possess Leonor, and Angelio whets his lust by showing him the girl. Seeing his satisfaction at hand, Don Gil rushes into the cave to enjoy the prize for which he has repudiated God and salvation. As he approaches the seductive Leonor, Don Gil discovers that the Devil has tricked him: it is not Leonor who stands before him, but a skeleton wrapped in finery— a succubus. Full of remorse now that he has experienced the Devil's deception, Don Gil turns to God in a desperate prayer. Literally fuming, Angelio dissolves in a puff of smoke accompanied by a great noise. Having denied God and the Holy Virgin Mary, the Devil's slave turns to his guardian angel for help. Suddenly, a host of angels comes to his aid and in the fierce battle that rages above him, Don Gil sees the pact wrested from Angelio's hands. He has been saved. His redemption is complete, however, only when he confesses before the king of Portugal the crimes he has committed against Lisarda, Don Diego, and others. The play ends with this apotheosis. The triumph of Christian values over satanic wiles may have been the most moving moment of the play, but the most interesting in the context of occult lore is the interpretation of the demonic pact with its ritual pledge, its contractual assurances, and its bloodletting.

Calderón patterned one of his best plays, *El mágico prodigioso*, on Mira de Amescua's outstanding drama, but there are other examples of Calderón's use of the occult as subject matter for his plays. In *La dama duende* (The Lady Ghost) the dramatist would seem to be an enemy of popular superstitions regarding ghosts, familiars, witches, magicians, succubi and incubi, and the like. But in his attack through comic ridicule Calderón in fact reiterates the frequency and seriousness of these beliefs among Golden Age Spaniards. Regardless of his attitude in *La dama duende*, Calderón never laughs at the Devil. He portrays him in the accepted fashion of the period as a doomed figure of tragic proportions. It is in this way that the Devil appears in the plays in which he is an important character: *El José de las mujeres* (The Woman's Devil), *Las cadenas del demonio* (The Devil's Fetters), *La Margarita preciosa* (Precious Margarita), and the aforementioned *El mágico prodigioso*. All four works have leading characters born and raised in pagan cultures with polytheistic religions, and the basic conflict emerges as an attempt by the Church to gain these souls away from Satan. In these plays, then, the Devil is a composite of pagan and Christian traditions, personifying falsehood in opposition to truth, superstition in conflict with faith, the principle of evil in furious combat with the Supreme Deity.

In *El José de las mujeres*, the Devil has the task of preventing the pagan Eugenia from pursuing the Christian tenets she has discovered in the epistles of Saint Paul. His adversary is the Carmelite monk Eleno, miraculously transported to the scene by God's power. The arraignment seems uneven in the face of the monk's humility contrasted with the Devil's hubris. In the debate that ensues (monotheism versus polytheism), however, Eleno emerges victorious. The Devil also plays a leading part in the love theme of the *comedia,* inhabiting the corpse of one of the pretenders to Eugenia's favors and pursuing the girl in the hope that she will succumb, but the heroine has become a Christian convert and in her resolve gives the Devil his final defeat.

In *Las cadenas del demonio* there is yet another theological base in which argumentation decides the issue, but the play also contains other elements. The real power of God (and his church) over Satan is demonstrated by Saint Bartholemew when he chains his adversary with fire, preventing him from moving or speaking without leave. In another sequence, the apostle exorcises the princess, whom the Devil has possessed through an explicit pact. The magic of the Cross!

La Margarita preciosa, of which Calderón wrote only the last act, is based on the life and martyrdom of the Christian saint whose feast is celebrated on July 20.[5] In the play, Margarita's suitor and her father, under the instigation of the Devil (who adopts human form), attempt to force her to render homage to the pagan gods whom the girl has abandoned for the monotheism of Christianity. Perservering in her obstinacy, Margarita attains the martyrdom that assures her sainthood. The Devil has been cheated in yet another way, and in a curious context that naively places him (a Christian!) in a position of influence over pagans. Calderón and his coauthors evidently sought to exalt the Church, even through such miscasting.

The travails of Satan as outlined in these selections are typical of the treatment he received in the Golden Age at the hands of Christian dramatists. Indeed, all aspects of occultism during this period came to be considered in the context of the Christian faith. Despite this change of venue, magic, witchcraft, divination, and other esoteric arts continued to hold their own as fundamentally pagan expressions. Their survival was assured because they offered an alternative way of seeking out the answers to human existence, answers that Christianity had not been able to give. Faith alone was not enough and, as history reveals, a great many people looked elsewhere with the desire to make real what they intuited. The Church may have branded them heretics, but society always employed the talents of its "gifted ones."

The drama of Spain from its inception through the Golden Age portrays this reality. It shows that even in a highly Christianized nation of Europe, such as Spain, there is a pagan substratum that defies all attempts at eradication. Christian dogma may have been imposed upon the populace of Europe with apparent success but beneath the churches of the continent lie the remains of pagan temples; just outside towns with churches at their centers lie the wooded sites where witches congregated for sabbats and esbats; before them, Celtic rites were held in the same places. People continued to accept as true what they had long believed; not infrequently such matters were classified as heretical by the Church. Among these was "the belief in hidden or mysterious powers and the possibility of subjecting them to human control."[6]

III

The Demonic Pact and
the Quest for Esoteric Knowledge

> Here, Mephistopheles, receive this scroll,
> A deed of gift of body and of soul.
> —Marlowe, *The Tragedy of Doctor Faustus*

The demonic pact looms large in folklore and literature because it embodies the aspiration of humans since Adam and Eve to possess supernatural knowledge. Prohibited from such an attainment by each deity in the major contributory cultures of the West—by the Yahweh of the Garden of Eden and by the Zeus who punished Prometheus—human beings turned to devious, unorthodox means to ensure the fulfillment of ends become illicit.

A biblical story that typifies this quest is narrated in 1 Samuel, chapter 28 (1 Kings). King Saul, having promulgated an edict against divination and other occult practices, disguised himself in order to obtain the services of the Witch of Endor; abandoned by Jehovah, Saul sought to know the outcome of a crucial battle through the unnatural agency of the diviner. The Witch of Endor summoned the spirit of Samuel as the King had prompted her to do. The Hebrew judge and prophet informed Saul of his impending defeat at the hands of the Philistines, of his death, and of David's ascension to the throne of Israel.[1]

Apart from intrinsic elements, this is a curious tale in the history of necromancy because it does not contain either a threat of God's punishment or the implication of danger to the conjuror from those spirits brought from the realm beyond the natural. Despite periodic laws against the practice, trafficking with spirits did not have an explicitly negative aspect in the Old Testament.

In later tradition, however, the magus or conjuror who sought direct communion with other-worldly beings had to prepare constraints against the possibility that his body and soul would be endangered in the unnatural encounter. To that end, rituals that the magician believed to be both effective in procuring the visitation of spirits and protective of his human frailty were devised.[2] Through such ritual (or ceremonial) magic, the celebrant sought to gain knowledge and to affect the material world by its application; in effect, he wished to tamper with natural law through cosmic means yet remain immune to danger. His audacity was bolstered by elaborate preparations. He ensconced himself within a magic circle that, upon being closed, prevented the entry of the horrific creatures he would summon, yet permitted him to view, converse with, and order them as he desired.[3] This safety was achieved through the use of the deity's name, inscribed together with magical formulas and other Words of Power within the bounds of the circle's circumference.[4] Thus empowered, the magus could safely command demons and the spirits of the dead to appear before him and do his bidding. Later artistic interpretations of the provocative episode regarding the Witch of Endor include this protective motif, some with the witch and Saul inside the circle, others (less orthodox) with the spirit of Samuel in its confines to prevent it from harming those outside.

The ancient belief that secret knowledge, when used by an initiate, could force the denizens of the supernatural dimension to accede to human demands came to be supplanted by a new concept when Christianity emerged as the only unitive force in the wake of Rome's demise as an empire. In a theology that held that Lucifer, although fallen from God's grace, had the power to seduce human souls into damnation, it was impossible to believe that a human being, even if an adept, could command communion with the supernatural order without the assistance of the Devil himself.[5]

Thus, the Church came to look upon magical practices as demoniacal in nature and their seeming efficacy as a hoax perpetrated on humanity by the Devil. The magician, who traditionally was held to be aloof from any religious commitment to the powers he called forth, became suspect as a willing agent of Satan. Since the magus was the beneficiary of the conjuration, and since the personality of the Devil did not contain an iota of altruism, it was reasoned that a quid pro quo arrangement existed between them. This agreement came to be known as the demonic pact.

Just as the Old Testament provided a seemingly authoritative basis for subsequent (i.e., Christian) attitudes toward necromancy, so too was it the source for the idea of the demonic pact. Unlike the story of the Witch of Endor, however, which does concern the practice of divination through the dead, the reference from which Christianity drew its pactual concept was read erroneously and out of context.[6] The Book of Isaiah (28:15) states: "We have entered into a league with death, we have made a covenant with the nether world."[7] Taken in its proper setting, the language of the prophet is symbolic, not literal; he is not referring to a hellish pact but to the despicable alliances that the Jews had made with Egypt and Babylonia to prevent the destruction of Israel. Therefore, the Christian conception of human-demonic relations is postulated on a false premise, through either negligence or design.[8] In fact, the Church's schema on the unholy pact was developed primarily in the intellectual world of theology, using the Old Testament as the foundation for interpretations of gospels and legends.

Origen (A.D. 185–254), Saint Augustine (354–430), and Saint Thomas Aquinas (1227–74) were among the most influential theologians of the Church to address themselves to diabolical matters, including the pact. In *De doctrina christiana*, Augustine declared: "Therefore, all superstitions of this kind, either trivial or noxious, arising out of the damnable consortium of men and demons . . . are to be intrinsically repudiated as the covenants (*pacta*) of a false and treacherous friendship."[9] He was referring specifically to forms of divination, as was Aquinas in his *Summa theologica:* "Divination is a kind of curiosity with regard to the end in view, which is foreknowledge of the future; but it is a kind of superstition as regards the mode of operation. This kind of divination pertains to the worship of the demons, inasmuch as one enters into a compact, tacit or express, with the demons. . . . All divination by invoking demons is unlawful for two reasons. The first is gathered from the principle of divination, which is a compact made expressly with a demon by the very fact of invoking him. This is altogether unlawful" (Question 95, Articles, 2 and 4). It was taken for granted subsequently that the demonic pact was a requisite for human endeavors of the kind stipulated by the theologians. Augustine's dictum became the cornerstone of canonical law on the subject when in the twelfth century Gratian compiled the *Decretum*, the prime text on ecclesiastical matters in the Middle Ages.

Later works expounded upon the topic of demonic pacts with example and anathema. Cesarius of Heisterbach in the thirteenth century told in *Dialogus miraculorum* how two miracle workers appeared in Besançon, France, and amazed the populace with their sorcery. Suspected by Church authorities of being in league with the Devil, they were seized and examined for physical evidence of the alliance; the process revealed that they carried demonic pacts beneath the skin of their armpits. Once the documents were removed, the two were burned as heretics.

This and similar stories represent the socioreligious current that prompted the formulation of canonical laws through the writings of the Church fathers. Such narratives had their roots in non-Christian cultures. Legends of human liaisons with deities (either positive or negative in nature), occurred with frequency in classical, near-eastern and oriental mythologies. Some of these came into Europe via Spain upon the conquest of the Iberian Peninsula by the Moors in the eighth century; others were absorbed from Byzantine sources during the several Crusades.

In geographic areas where East met West, or wherever the pagan and Christian faiths confronted each other, it was not unusual to find embedded in the life of a saint one or more episodes in which the holy man or woman prevented Satan from collecting the soul of one who had made a demonic pact. The earliest known of these tales concerns Saint Basil, a fourth-century bishop of Caesarea in Asia Minor; he was called upon to rescue from eternal damnation a servant named Proterius, who had obtained the otherwise impossible love of his master's daughter by signing a pact with the Devil. Saint Basil extracted the damning document from the clutches of Satan, thus defeating his vicious design. Possession of the pact, from this first legend on, was considered necessary for the Devil to be able to drag his victim to Hell.

A European example of early vintage is found in the life of Saint Cado who, at the supplication of his parishioners, sought out the Devil to bargain over a bridge the Evil One regularly prevented the townspeople from completing. Saint Cado, knowing Satan's affinities, offered to grant him the first soul to cross the bridge, if he permitted the work to be completed. The verbal pact was honored by both parties—the Devil allowed the bridge to be finished, and Saint Cado saw to it that a cat was the first to cross the span. To this day the tricking of the Devil is remembered in numerous European communities by a Devil's Bridge, although some are so named because of the difficult locales they span and the intrepidity it took to construct them.

Both of these stories, each in its unique way, typify the popular optimism of early Christians; they saw God as a guardian of his human creation who acted through the actions of holy men and women to defeat the Devil. Not all ecclesiastics were cast in a positive role, however; many were viewed as sinners who had dealings with God's adversary. An anticlericalism that grew as Christianity became the establishment of the Middle Ages scourged those who served the Church badly or hypocritically for personal, political, or other reasons. Prominent churchmen were sometimes singled out because they abused their power or special status or simply because of their great learning. Three examples, among many, of individuals who were believed to have achieved success within the Church through a pact with the Devil were Theophilus, Gerbert, and Roger Bacon.

Theophilus of Adana was a sixth-century cleric affiliated with a church in Cilicia in Asia Minor. According to the Greek legend, he had refused the offer of a bishopric out of humility. The man who did accept the post vindictively deprived Theophilus of his, confiscating goods and money in the process. Unlike the biblical Job, the destitute Theophilus ranted against Heaven for permitting such an inequity. Receiving no satisfaction, he renounced God and sought the aid of the Devil to regain his position, wealth, and honor; in exchange, he offered his soul. Seven years after the Devil's compliance with his request, Theophilus sincerely repented his willful fall from grace and prayed fervently to Mary. The Virgin, of course, rescued his soul from eternal damnation.[10]

The second case also presents a last-minute conversion and salvation of a covenantor, but without the direct involvement of Mary or a saint. Gerbert of Aurillac was a brilliant churchman who became Pope Sylvester II in 999. Adversaries within and without the Church hierarchy promoted the gossip that Gerbert had been elevated to the throne of Peter with the Devil's help. It was said that the mediation of an Arabic sage at Toledo, where Gerbert had resided for some time, had brought the cleric into contact with Satan, to whom he bound himself in exchange for the papacy. It was also affirmed that Satan himself instructed Gerbert in the construction of an oracular head.[11] Among many other alleged prognostications made to Gerbert through that medium was that he would not die until he had celebrated the Mass in Jerusalem; rather astutely, Pope Sylvester II avoided acting upon any suggestion that he visit the Holy Land. One day, however, while officiating at a mass, the pope felt his life ebbing away inexplicably; fearing for his life, he inquiried as to his whereabouts and he learned that the church was dedicated to the Holy Cross of Jerusalem. The prediction of the oracular head in mind, Gerbert made a hasty but sincere confession.

While Gerbert's salvation is demonstrative of how God's grace can rescue a sinner even at the last moment of life, the third example shows how a wise man can fool the Devil by cleverness without risking his soul. It was said of Roger Bacon (1214?–94), the English scientist, philosopher, and friar, that he had promised his soul to Lucifer on the condition that he died neither in church nor out of it. The Devil, who seems to enjoy the self-assurance of humans because he has often used it to his advantage, accepted Bacon's offer and granted his desires. But the friar never intended to be damned. Knowing it was God's plan that the Devil suffer in every conceivable way, Bacon proceeded to prove that a human could trick the fallen angel. Pursuing his plan, he built a cell in the wall of the church—neither inside nor outside—and repaired there to die when he felt his earthly days were nearly over. Satan had kept his bargain, but he was deprived of his prey by an intellectual ruse.[12] Though dangerous, such abuses of the Devil were considered laudable by medieval Christians, who thought it only right to trick the great trickster.

Besides the documentation found in theological tracts and legends of the saints, the belief in the reality of demonic pacts is attested by the literature of medieval Europe. *Le miracle de Théophile*, composed around 1261 by the *trouvère* Rutebeuf, is the second oldest miracle play extant in France and the first to use the Virgin as a character.[13] The 663 verse lines of the drama tell the story of Théophile, the same cleric of Adana whose involvement with Satan had shocked earlier Christians. Rutebeuf does not rely on suspense—the legend was too well known by his audience—but achieves a cathartic end through the skillful use of the mimetic art.

Guided by the Jewish magician Salatin, Théophile approaches the Devil in "great fear."[14] The stage directions indicate that the dispossessed priest kneels "in feudal submission" before the Lord of Darkness, who takes his hands between his own, thus accepting Théophile into his service. Théophile then asks for his Master's assistance:

> Witness the homage I make to you.
> If I could just get back my loss,
> Great Master, for the rest of my life.

The Devil's reply secures the verbal part of the agreement:

> In return, I make this pact with you:
> I'll set you up in such great power—
> They'll not have seen a greater lord
> Than you.

But Rutebeuf was not satisfied with mere verbiage; reflecting popular beliefs of his time as well as Church doctrine, he introduced a new element into the tradition of the miracle play: the agreement between the Devil and Théophile was metamorphosed into a *written* document signed in human blood. The impetus for the blood pact comes from the Devil:

> And now, since we've agreed,
> You ought to know that for your part

I must have deeds of covenant,
Sealed and unequivocal.

The Devil offers as explanation for his demand the experience of past encounters with human users of his unique services: "Many folk have
cheated me/Because I did not take their deeds—/That's why I like
things cut and dried." The stage directions then indicate how Théophile
proceeds to comply with the Devil's demand: "Théophile makes his
deed, writing in his own blood and sealing the document with his ring."
There is no hesitation on his part. Neither does he have to be instructed
in the proper execution of the blood pact. Théophile performs with the
assurance of one who has prior knowledge of such contracts. The fallen
cleric then hands the document to the Devil.

Rutebeuf chose not to reveal the wording of the pact, preserving the
mystery inherent in such deeds of gift, for the sake of both his credulous audience and posterity. This secret pact written in blood captured
the imagination of the medieval Christian and became the literary
progenitor of scripted alliances with the Devil in later periods. Rutebeuf's pact may, in fact, have influenced the historical evolution of the
concept and its application to a larger, previously uninvolved segment
of the population—those who still practiced a pre-Christian religion
that came to be known in Europe as Witchcraft.[15]

In 1398 the theory that witchcraft involved a pact with the Devil was
confirmed at no less a center of learning than the University of Paris's
Sorbonne. This conclusion was reached upon the inability of the
Church to eradicate the Old Religion, which personified in the Horned
God (Pan, Cernunnos) and the Great Mother (Diana, Gaea, Cerridwen,
Ishtar), the fertility of nature. Long before the end of the fourteenth
century, the association of the Christian Devil with the Horned God of
the witches had been forced upon the populace to accentuate the
Church's view that fertility worship was sinful. The syncretic process
gave Satan the outward characteristics of Pan, the half-human, half-goat
deity who was most prominently worshipped in Mediterranean Europe.
In time it was common belief that witches worshipped the Devil. (After
all, did not their deity have the physical aspect of Satan?) The witch,
largely ignored during the rise of Christianity, was now denounced as a
heretic; she (or he) was brought before the inquisitorial boards of Protestant and Catholic churches, accused of having denied Christ, and,
finally, of having made a pact with Satan, signed in blood.[16] Under torture, the witch confessed to these heretical transgressions. And so the

demonic pact, traditionally associated with the magus and dissident clerics, now blighted the existence of the witch.

Theologians gave inquisitors two types of demonic pacts to work with, the distinction having been made by Albertus Magnus.[17] The first was termed *Professio tacita* , an implicit, tacit, or private pact in which allegiance was given to the Devil indirectly through another or by the performance of acts considered heretical or demoniacal in inspiration; magical practices fell under this category. The second type was the *Professio expressa*, a solemn pact made either during a sabbat through a prescribed ritual, such as the *Osculum infame*, or privately by signing the contract with one's own blood. It was this document that was often provided by the prosecutors at trials as the ultimate evidence against the witch or magus.

While the form of the pact varied according to locale and period, the general conditions that accompanied its execution were well defined. In his *Compendium maleficarum* (1608), Francesco Maria Guazzo detailed these in outline form. Most pacts were unilateral, stipulating above the signature of the human being his demands of the Devil and his payment upon their fulfillment or after a specified time. The Devil was not expected to make a document specifying his agreement or even to sign the mortal's pact; his word was thought to be sufficient, since he stood to gain a soul in the bargain. In some rare instances, however, a second pact—signed by a demon or demons—was introduced as evidence.[18]

The idea of a mutually binding pact (or pacts) was a reflection of changes in European life. A bourgeois class had developed over the centuries with the growth of mercantilism and other commercial endeavors; business relationships required the formalization of rights and duties through legally binding contracts. This commercial standard was reflected in the terminology of demonic pacts brought before inquisitors; the cautious wording and exact stipulations of real contractual arrangements was also reflected in literature.

The most representative and important literary example of such pacts is found in Christopher Marlowe's *The Tragical History of Doctor Faustus*, written and produced in the late sixteenth century.[19] The Faust theme was first formulated in Germany, apparently on the evidence of a historical model (whose biography is polemical).[20] The first compilation of data on Faust appeared in 1587 in the anonymous *Faustbuch* (also known as *Volksbuch*), published at Frankfurt am Main by Johann Spies. It was probably the English translation of this book—*The History of the*

Damnable Life and Deserved Death of Doctor John Faustus—that served as the foundation for Marlowe's tragic work because the incidents depicted therein parallel those of the Spies book, although there are many aspects that Marlowe eschewed.

In the crucial Scene 5, having verbalized his aspirations and offered his soul to Mephistopheles, Faust listens to the demon's stipulations: "But, Faustus, thou must bequeath it solemnly/And write a deed of gift with thine own blood, / For that security craves great Lucifer." [21] There is an implicit reluctance in the learned Dr. Faust's failure to comprehend the explicit instructions. He proceeds to cut his arm, intending the mere flow of blood in the manner of a primal bond as support for the words he had previously uttered, but such an action is not sufficient in the context of this period. Because Faust lives in a bourgeois society that insists on the formalization of agreements, and because not to require a written contract would lessen the impact of the obligation, Mephistopheles instructs him further to that end. Lucifer's agent mandates that Faust not only draw up a promissory note and sign it with his blood, as earlier tradition had it, but also draft the entire document with his "own blood." Complying, Faust writes the opening sentence ("Faustus gives to thee his soul"), but his blood immediately thereafter congeals; unable to continue, he asks in amazement, "What might the staying of my blood portend?/ Is it unwilling I should write this bill?" The question, of course, is rhetorical. Faust knows the phenomenon to be an explicit warning from God yet chooses to ignore it. When Mephistopheles offers hot coals, undoubtedly from Hell, Faust himself applies their heat to the wound to cause the blood to flow once more. The document is then signed. Before the deed is delivered to complete the infernal transaction, though, Faust receives yet another warning: a phrase in Latin warning him to flee God's wrath appears on his arm. Still, Faust has resolved to follow the left-hand path and so delivers the parchment to the demon:

> Here, Mephistophilis, receive this scroll,
> A deed of gift of body and of soul;
> But yet conditionally that thou perform
> All articles prescribed between us both.

For his part, Mephistopheles binds himself verbally, as was the convention from earliest times: "Faustus, I swear by Hell and Lucifer/ To affect all promises between us made." Marlowe then departed from the theatrical convention established by Rutebuef in *Le Miracle de Théophile,* wherein the wording of the pact is not revealed.[22] Ever the Elizabethan, Marlowe opted for dramatic impact over mystery; his character pronounces with relish the terms and conditions of his covenant with Lucifer:

> First, that Faustus may be a spirit in form and substance.
> Secondly, that Mephistophilis shall be his servant and at his command.
> Thirdly, that Mephistophilis shall do for him, and bring him whatsoever.
> Fourthly, that he shall be in his chamber or house invisible.
> Lastly, that he shall appear to the said John Faustus at all times, in what
>   form or shape soever he please.
> I, John Faustus of Wittenberg, Doctor, by these
> presents do give both body and soul to
> Lucifer, Prince of the East, and his minister
> Mephistophilis, and furthermore grant unto
> them, that twenty-four years being expired,
> the articles above written inviolate, full
> power to fetch or carry the said John Faustus
> body and soul, flesh, blood, or goods, into
> their habitation wheresoever.
>   By me John Faustus.

As if desirous of Faust's repentance and giving him the opportunity to rescind his deed of gift, Mephistopheles prompts further discussion on it:[23]

> MEPHISTO: Speak, Faustus, do you deliver this as your deed?
> FAUST: Ay, take it, and the Devil give thee good on't.
> MEPHISTO: Now, Faustus, ask what thou wilt.

The outcome of this daring venture had to be the damnation of Faust. He had willfully and without extenuating circumstances (unlike Theophilus), renounced the Christian God and compacted with his adversary, the Devil. Within the theology of Protestant Germany (based on Martin Luther's schismatic view of Lucifer's power on a near par with God's), the illegitimate and blasphemous quest for esoteric knowledge that Faust implemented through the demonic pact had to be punished by the God who burdened humanity with Original Sin for its first transgression against his authority. Also, Lutheranism did not tolerate the deus ex machina approach to salvation that characterized such legends as that of Theophilus. Depleted of miracles, the Reformation theology within which the legend of Faust was fashioned could not justify salvation for one who had willfully traded his soul to the Devil. Thus, in his recognition scene (scene 14), Faust acknowledges the gravity of his sin and concludes that he merits eternal punishment: "But Faustus' offense can ne'er be pardoned." The protagonist himself never asks forgiveness of God (and, of course, he is theologically impeded from having recourse to the Virgin or the saints). For it to have been otherwise in the context of Lutheran Germany and Elizabethan England would have been untenable.[24]

It was Marlowe's tragedy, not the *Faustbuch*, that gave rise to a rash of dramatic and other literary works on Faust and related themes in England.[25] On the continent, English actors performed *The Tragical History of Doctor Faustus* in Germany during the late sixteenth and early seventeenth centuries; these performances influenced German popular drama, including the puppet theater. They may have also similarly affected drama in other nations.

As in France and England, the demonic pact found acceptance as a dramatic theme in Spain, especially during the latter part of the Golden Age (1492–1680).[26] Among the earliest of major *comedias* to deal with the subject in this period was *El esclavo del demonio* (The Devil's Slave), written and published by Antonio Mira de Amescua in 1612.[27] The plot concerns the fall from grace of Don Gil Nuñez de Atoguía, a Portuguese priest who made a pact with the Devil in order to satisfy his lust for Leonor, a beautiful young woman destined by her father to be a bride of Christ.[28] Don Gil voices his lecherous ideas in a soliloquy:

> Since relish and intent
> indeed condemn a man,
> I'd give my soul
> to ravish you, Leonor.[29] [II, ll. 1371–74]

Immediately his solitude is shattered by the ironic presence of the Devil, who presents himself in the guise of a rake and gives his name as Angelio. The Devil has overheard Don Gil's offer and is eager to accept it. In exchange for his tutelage in the black arts, the Devil expects Don Gil to become his slave eternally; he tells the priest the stipulations of the formal ritual:

> The God Himself you will deny
> and pledge to me to be my slave
> by signing with your blood, a writ
> and to abort your chrism's grace. [II, ll. 1431–34]

Upon further verification of his intent to accede to Angelio's requisites, Don Gil is taken off by two other slaves to be bled in preparation for the writing of the pact. The document is composed in Angelio's cave and when Don Gil again appears on the stage, he is a changed man. His clothing and manner indicate his servility to the Devil. The apparent is verified as fact when Don Gil proclaims his pact at Angelio's command:

> If subtle Necromancy I should learn
> (which Catholics affirm is so barbaric)
> and, far exceeding all my normal powers,
> will soon possess fair Leonor,
> I state that I, Gil Nuñez de Atoguía,
> fearless in the face of hellish pain,
> will give up Heaven, my Baptism's right,
> renouncing faith in God and courtesies due Him
> His Name I'll blot out from my memory.
> Your slave forever I'll become,
> to live in pleasure through this transient life,
> and will renounce my path to Glory's Gate,
> which Mother Church has granted me outright
> through God's own breast, an open door.
> I deed it thus. [II, ll. 1499–1513]

Don Gil's contractual words notwithstanding, the total commitment of the priest must be impugned on the evidence of two other statements—the first preceding the compact (Angelio says, "porque a ser mi esclavo empieza" to which Don Gil retorts, "Yo a ser discípulo voy") and the second, directed at Don Gil's companion-in-crime, Lisarda, after the signing of the document ("que no soy demonio yo/que arrepentirme no puedo"). These statements indicate a reservation on Don Gil's part—he seems to be leaving himself a way out of his obligation to the Devil, in the first by not accepting the total commitment that "esclavo" makes explicit, and in the second by acknowledging God's mercy toward a repentant sinner. This idea of hedging his bet parallels (but does not duplicate) the trickery of Roger Bacon. That in effect Don Gil is leaving himself a loophole is verified toward the end of the play when he recognizes the Devil's wiles (instead of Leonor, Angelio has given him a succubus) and then addresses God: "And even when I left You, Lord, / I never gave up hope/despite denial of the Faith" (III. 2813–15). He knows, however, that having spurned God and Mary, he cannot have recourse to them in his moment of need; seeking supernatural assistance to liberate himself from Angelio (who holds the pact), Don Gil receives an inspiration: "Who is it that can shelter me?/Alone, my Guardian Angel have I/not denied. But would he intercede?" (III. 2838–40). Falling on his knees, he prays. Immediately, a battle between angels and demons ensues above his head; shortly, his guardian angel enters, triumphantly bearing the pact he wrested from Angelio's clutches. On receiving the paper, Don Gil stuffs the pieces in his mouth. The angel assures him of God's forgiveness.

El esclavo del demonio, like Rutebeuf's miracle play before it, is as Catholic in its positive resolution as Marlowe's tragedy is Protestant in the damnation of Faust. For Mira and other Golden Age dramatists the eternal punishment due one who died out of God's grace was an impressive deterrent to dying unrepentant; yet it mattered more to them to show how God's mercy was extended even to the greatest of sinners, such as Don Gil. The Catholic playwright of the period recognized human frailty as such and sought to have his character overcome it through the grace of a merciful God; this was impossible for the author of the *Faustbuch* (*Volksbuch*) and for Marlowe.

This application of Catholic theology to the denouement of Golden Age plays dealing with demonic pacts is equally characteristic of two works by Pedro Calderón de la Barca (1600–1681). Chronologically, the first of these is *Las cadenas del demonio* (1636; The Devil's Fetters), which is premised on the evangelization of Armenia by Saint Bartholomew. The plot focuses on Princess Irene who, like the great Calderonian protagonist Segismundo in *La vida es sueño*, has been isolated from society by her father. His cruelty stems from the revelation of his court astrologers that Irene will cause havoc in his kingdom. The long years of captivity in a distant castle have brought Irene to despair of ever being free, and so she calls upon the nether gods of her pagan religion to release her from the fetters that the gods of the upper region have unjustly imposed on her:

> . . . to you appealing,
> o infernal deities,
> I offer life and soul,
> exchanging these for liberty.[30] [I, p. 738]

Her offer is accepted immediately by a young gallant whom she recognizes as the embodiment of the statue of Astaroth worshiped in the temple.[31] It isn't the pagan deity, however, who offers her the freedom and the legacy she craves; it is the Devil, the personification of evil in Christianity, who has materialized in order to seduce her soul: "I will provide your liberty/if you but once again will vow/to be forever mine" (I, p. 739). Deceived by the supposed Astaroth, Irene complies willingly: I pledge myself as/yours, O Astaroth, in life/as well as death" (I, p. 739). The Devil accepts her word as bond. There is no requisite of a written pact signed in blood. Calderón may have wanted to avoid the incongruity of superimposing a Christian concept on a pagan culture, or he may simply have been looking for a departure from the tradition current in his day, or perhaps he wished to lay the rational groundwork for the next diabolical twist. This is prompted by the evangelical fervor of Saint Bartholomew. The possibility that Irene will convert to Christianity forces the Devil to seek a reinforcement of the pact; he does so not by securing a written document but by possessing her (she had promised to be his "in life"). It is to no avail because Saint Bartholomew is empowered to exorcise demons. Once he has ousted the spurious Astaroth, thus freeing Irene in the true sense, he secures her conversion to Christianity. Later, after Saint Bartholomew has been martyred, the Devil attempts to repossess Irene, but she confronts him boldly with the strength of her new faith:

> While it is true that once
> I promised you my life and soul
> if you would give me liberty,
> I find myself released from debt
> by the new faith I now profess. . . .
> I am freed from that pact. [III, p. 763]

The Devil's defeat is the climax of the play but not its termination. Bartholomew is seen on a heavenly throne while at his feet the bound Devil confesses his impotence before the might of God. As the new saint ascends to Heaven, the Devil is cast once more into the abyss of Hell.

Another Calderón play to fix upon the demonic pact is *El mágico prodigioso* (1663; The Prodigious Magician). Like the majority of its predecessors in this thematic area, the *comedia* is based on a medieval legend. The life of Saint Cyprian, with its historical mixture of pagan and Christian elements, provides both a variant on the scenario of *Las cadenas del demonio* and a return to the blood pact as depicted in the work by Mira de Amescua.

Disguised as a traveler, the Devil interrupts Cipriano's intellectual musings on the nature of divinity. Cipriano, an Athenian, has been reading Pliny's analysis of the problem, a view compatible with Christian theology. Fearing that Cipriano would succumb to the argument of a First Cause in creation and thus come to acknowledge the one God, the Devil, ever the fallen theologian, enters into an ingenious discussion with the student. Satan tries to confound Cipriano with the tenets of ancient beliefs in dualism, but the intellectual prowess of his intended victim confounds him at every turn. The Devil changes tactics when he sees the futility of argumentation; instead, he probes the emotions of Cipriano for a weakness. Through a series of machinations, the Devil makes Cipriano fall in love with the virtuous Justina, a Christian convert, but she rebukes his declaration of love. Tortured continuously, Cipriano abandons his studies. Proving that an idle mind is the Devil's workshop, Cipriano entertains conjectures of an illicit conquest of Justina:

> So much does passion
> drag my thoughts through dust,
> and to my woe this torment
> works upon my fantasy,
> that I would give . . .
> my soul to endless
> grief and suffering
> to have this woman for my lust. [II, p. 823]

The Devil accepts the offer but his offstage voice is not heard by Cipriano. Again dealing with a pagan (as in *Las cadenas del demonio*), the Devil knows the futility of involving Cipriano at this moment in a scheme of self-damnation under Christian terms. He feigns, as before, to be someone other than his diabolical self. This time, however, he presents himself as a magician, and Cipriano unwittingly enlists him in his quest for Justina. As Cipriano's guest, the Devil works subtly toward his host's damnation and Justina's downfall. Having earned Cipriano's confidence, the Devil openly accepts the offer of his soul (still without disclosing his identity). Cipriano is skeptical, however, about the powers of his guest. The Devil then gives him a demonstration of prodigious magicianship that stuns him—a vision of Justina. Imediately, Cipriano rushes to possess her, but the Devil has a demand to make of him first: "Hold back! Until you sign,/affirming words that you have said,/ she's not for you to touch." The Devil seeks the blood pact as "merely a safeguard:/a deed of gift bearing a signature/by your own hand and with your blood" (p. 832). Impassioned by the vision of Justina, Cipriano accedes to the conditions. He pierces his arm with his dagger and writes upon a piece of white linen; the words of the pact precede and follow parenthetical remarks that show the fevered state of Cipriano's mind as he promises that I will give my soul immortal

.   .   .   .

to whomsoever trains me in the arts

.   .   .   .

through which I might attract Justina
to my arms. . . . [p. 832]

The Devil takes his victim (together with Cipriano's servant, caught spying on the scene) to a secret cave to learn the magic lore—the signs, the rituals, and the words of power—that composes the lesser aspect of the pact.

A year later, Cipriano's apprenticeship completed, the Devil moves to the seduction of Justina, but his lures and enchantments fail to woo her away from Christian virtue, and she defeats the Devil through God's grace. All that remains for the Devil to do is to trick Cipriano into believing that the conjuration has been effective; and, indeed, after an initial failure, Cipriano holds in his arms the figure he takes to be Justina. Passionate, ready to possess physically the woman for whom he has bartered his soul's salvation, Cipriano disrobes her. To his horror, he discovers that the figure he has held is a skeleton.

In the confrontation that ensues with his master, Cipriano demands the return of the pact, declaring it null and void for nonfeasance, and re-signs from further association with him. The Devil is then forced to play his final card: he reveals his true identity, to Cipriano's amazement and consternation. But the victim becomes the victor in his struggle with the Devil when he invokes the Christian God who had made Justina steadfast. At the play's end, the Devil oversees the martyred remains of both his intended victims; forced by God, he proclaims Justina's virtue and the nullification of Cipriano's pact. Once again, the Christian God has triumphed, demonstrating himself to be the veritable "prodigious magician."

It is difficult to ascertain the impact, if any, of Spanish theological dramas on European dramaturgy, either contemporary or sequential. Mira de Amescua was the first playwright to counter Marlowe's damnation of the Christian renegade with repentance and salvation. Calderón and other Golden Age dramatists followed suit. Theirs was a Counter Reformation theology that rejected the heresy of predestination and ex-ulted the doctrine of free will and faith in God's mercy. Calderón went further than Mira (who still reflected the medieval notion of miraculous salvation) by positing that reason is a proper channel for salvation. His characters are frequently led from evil (or ignorance) to good (or knowledge) through a rational process. Thus, Cipriano has an intellectual concern with the nature of God and seeks through study to arrive at the truth; if he is sidetracked from his purpose by the Devil's arousal of his passion, he sees clearly once more when the veil of ignorance is removed, revealing the Devil's deception. In Calderón's system, reason is the key to epistemology, and thus to redemption.

Later periods confronted the moral implications of the demonic pact within the framework of religious and social codes then pertinent. The eighteenth century—which prided itself on its emphasis on reason— saw Faust as a human being with a laudable quest rather than as a perverse figure who verified the modern link to Adam's fallen nature. Faust's thirst for knowledge was considered not unlike that which typified the Age of Enlightenment, especially in the research endeavors of the Encyclopedists and "philosophes." Consequently, the matter of Faust's damnation came under revision. Perhaps the popularity of Mira de Amescua's *El esclavo del demonio* and the power of Calderón's *El mágico prodigioso* had helped effect a change beyond the Pyrennees.

Dramatists contemporary and subsequent to Goethe, in Germany and elsewhere, did not follow the idealization of Faust. Perhaps the philosophical and poetic heights of Goethe's masterpiece preempted attempts at imitation of the treatment; perhaps Marlowe's approach had greater appeal because it touched on esoteric aspects of the human personality, which thrills to the hermetic mystery of the demonic pact and the horror attendant upon its execution. The danger of eternal damnation is ever more horrifically interesting than the intellectualization of redemption; this is particularly true in the theater, where the suspension of the audience's disbelief is one of the goals of the playwright. Likewise important is the arousal to pity and the lamentation over perverted destiny, as in Greek tragedy; Goethe's model seeks none of these.

Beyond Goethe's *Faust* and the borders of Germany, other dramatic works dealt with Faust or parallel characters—fictional or historical— who made verbal or written pacts with the Devil. In Spain, Alejandro Casona (1903–65) wrote two plays on the topic, *Otra vez el Diablo* (1935; The Devil Once More) and *La barca sin pescador* (1945; The Boat without a Fisherman).[32] The Argentine playwright Conrado Nalé Roxlo in *El pacto de Cristina* (1945; Christina's Pact) returns to the disguised Devil who deceives the unwary into signing a pact. In this play Cristina herself is not to suffer the consequences; rather, the Devil plans that her firstborn son shall be his to employ against whomsoever comes into contact with the beautiful child and loves him—unwittingly, an anti-Christ.

Eclecticism has typified plays on the subject of the demonic pact, from Rutebeuf onward. Unlike many of his predecessors, the modern dramatist is not constrained to express any single idea or ideology, as was Marlowe in Elizabethan England or Calderón in baroque Spain. In the context of the twentieth century, it would be impossible to identify which religious, political, or social dogma is representative enough to warrant the assimilation of the Faustian theme into its corpus. Consequently, there is no possibility of distinguishing a "modern" approach. Eclecticism is the hallmark of our times, and of the timeless subject of the demonic pact, through which some were damned and others found an ironic means to redemption.

PART TWO

Devolution

IV
Ancient Ways: Occult Lore in the Plays of Ramón del Valle-Inclán

My work reflects the life of a people near extinction.
My mission is to annotate it before it disappears.
—Ramón del Valle-Inclán

Ancient ways still survive in the northwestern sector of the Iberian Peninsula, the region of Spain known as Galicia. It is a lush, hilly land of old, as attested to by numerous prehistoric remains, by Phoenician trade objects and the cult of the serpent, by Celtic settlements, traditions, and placenames dating to the Iron Age, by Roman culture and language, by feudal customs out of the Suevian and Visigothic early Middle Ages, and by the age-old myths of intrepid mariners from all over the Mediterranean world and barbaric invaders from elsewhere in Europe.[1] At one time after the fall of Rome a distinct kingdom that encompassed much of Lusitania, Galicia became a mere province after the inception of the Castilian hegemony and, as a consequence, its language, once the joy of lyric poets, lost its high status.[2] Nonetheless, for centuries pilgrims have flocked from all over Christendom on the many land and sea routes leading to the important shrine in Galicia believed to house the bones of the apostle James. Santiago de Compostela, the cathedral city named after him, became second only to Rome as a pilgrimage site in Europe after the saint miraculously led the Reconquest, the only successful Crusade against the followers of Islam.

The rich Galician lore that resulted from so many intertwinings permeates much of the writing of Ramón del Valle-Inclán (1866–1936), a native of the region, from his earliest short stories through his novels and poems, being particularly notable in his dramaturgy, throughout which folk superstitions and quasi-religious beliefs are sprinkled liberally.[3] A gnomic poem of unkown authorship is axiomatic of the proclivity of Galicia to the occult: "Teño medo d'unha cousa/que sinto e que non se vé."[4] Besides the principal occult elements to be discussed here, Valle-Inclán has many other esoteric motifs peppered throughout his plays, as a summation of some of these illustrate.[5] Small supernatural beings, similar to the little people or fairies in Celtic lore, appear in *La cabeza del dragón* where a *duende* (an impish creature) plays an important role; in *Romance de lobos*, *Voces de gesta*, and *Cara de Plata* there are passing references to *trasgos*, little demons who enter houses through chimneys seeking hearthfires, although none of the creatures materialize in the plays. Invisibility of another sort is alluded to by La Mozuela's character in *Ligazón* in her reference to a ring that grants its wearer invisibility, as in the one fabled to have been used by Gyges.

Omens, in a variety of guises, appear in *El embrujado* and *Tragedia de ensueño*, as elsewhere in his dramatic works along with fortune-telling by Tarot cards (in *Águila de blasón*, *El embrujado*, *Divinas palabras*, *Cara de Plata*), by palm-reading (in *Comedia de ensueño*, *Cara de Plata*), by hydromancy (in *Ligazón*), or by birds trained to pick out a piece of paper (in *Divinas palabras*). Astrology is evident in *Voces de gesta*, *Ligazón*, and *Los cuernos de don Friolera*. The interpretation of the future through dreams appears with some frequency in *El Marqués de Bradomín*, *Águila de blasón*, *Romance de lobos*, and *Divinas palabras*, while premonitions or intuitions figure widely, as do clairvoyance and telepathy, in *El yermo de las almas*, *Voces de gesta*, and *Ligazón*.

Other popular superstitions also appear in his plays. The belief that two people drinking from the same cup reveals the first one's secrets appears in *La cabeza del Bautista* and *Ligazón*. Although the practice of placing a horseshoe over a doorway has died out in Galicia, the time-honored practice of touching iron is still a sign of protection (as in *Los cuernos de don Friolera*, where a grating provides the means). The use of a horn or horns to protect a house or granaries, known as *hórreos*, from witches is still commonplace there and, in passing conversation, is treated as such in *Ligazón*, although the stone decoration is a stylized remnant of the phallus used in ancient fertility practices. The association of dogs and death is also common in Galicia, as marked by the howling canine in *Tragedia de ensueño* and the motif of the white dogs in *El embrujado*; however, since dogs are said to have licked the feet of the crucified Christ, it is believed their tongues have curative powers and their bites are noninfectious, unlike those of wolves. The practice of putting the statue of Saint Peter upside down in a well during a drought in order to bring rain is satirized in *Águila de blasón*. The reference to a person having a bad shadow appears in *Los cuernos de don Friolera*. The evil eye is endemic to Galicia as an explication of otherwise irrational actions, as in *El embrujado*, *Farsa de la enamorada del rey*, and *La marquesa Rosalinda*, the latter full of satirical references to many occult subjects and superstitions.

Tales of the dead and the fear that ghost phenomena evoke are manifest in *Aguila de blasón, El embrujado, Divinas palabras*, and *Las galas del difunto*, while necroemanations and similar apparitions figure in *Aguila de blasón* and *Luces de bohemia*, where they announce impending death. Possession by a demon and its cure, exorcism, are discussed as explanations of otherwise inexplicable states of being in *Sacrilegio* and *Farsa de la enamorada del rey*, but they are not staged. During a drunken binge in *Divinas palabras*, Pedro Gailo claims that he has seen the Devil and that the evil being sat upon him (like Fuseli's incubus), while in *Los cuernos de don Friolera* the Devil is assessed by Don Estrafalario as an intellectual, due to his thirst for knowledge.[6] There are numerous references to the Devil in Valle-Inclán's plays because he is so often in the thoughts and speech of the people Valle-Inclán portrays, as is the case with the ubiquitous witches, held to be devotees of Satan.

What follows is a more detailed view of major esoteric premises, be they purely folkloric or of an occult derivation, from a select group of Valle-Inclán's plays, ranging from *El Marqués de Bradomín* and the first two parts of the trilogy entitled *Comedias bárbaras—Aguila de blasón* and *Romance de lobos*—to *El embrujado*, and the later works *Ligazón, Divinas palabras*, and *Cara de Plata* (the last part of *Comedia bárbaras*), wherein aspects of occultism generally emerge in the plots, with lesser prominence in the early plays to greater prominence in the later ones.

In *El Marqués de Bradomín: Coloquios románticos* (1907; The Marquis of Bradomín: Romantic Colloquies), Valle-Inclán integrates several plots from the four Modernist novels collectively entitled *Sonatas: Memorias del Marqués de Bradomín* (1902–5), and incorporates various occult elements. Early in the first act are presented several folk characters who are associated with occult practices. Madre Cruces is an old crone who acts, Celestina-like, as a lovers' go-between and confidante in amorous intrigues, while Adega la Inocente is described as "*a disheveled girl, with the eyes of one possessed, whose shouts are replete with prophetic terror. . . . She holds a bunch of herbs in her hands, attempting to hide them against her breast with a vague gesture of sorcery*" (I, p. 106–7).[7] Then appears "a red horsefly," which Madre Cruces interprets as a good omen. Her prediction comes true when Bradomín arrives to visit his love of old, the ailing Concha. Adega addresses him immediately, and the point of the herbs becomes clear: "When you see my lady the Countess, place these herbs under her pillow but without her noticing you do it. They will make her well" (I, p. 119).

In the second act, the deathly pale Concha is described as "a white shadow" with "the hands of a ghost" (p. 123), and the words presage her fate. The banter that follows about Hell and the Devil also has future implications:

CONCHA: In Hell they must have always smiled. Isn't there a phrase "Mephistophelic smile"?
BRADOMIN: The Devil has always been a superior being. [II, p. 128]

The warning by the page Florisel that "taking the moonlight" could prove to be dangerous "because of the witches" (p. 135) also bodes ill.[8] Instead of a witch, however, Don Juan Manuel Montenegro, the old hidalgo who is the patriarch of Concha's and Bradomín's family, enters to remind niece and nephew of the supernatural union that gave birth to their lineage: "It goes back to Roland, one of the Twelve Peers (of Charlemagne). Sir Roland did not die at Roncesvalles as histories would have it. . . . Sir Roland was able to escape and, taking a boat, reached the island of Sálvora where, attracted by a siren, he was shipwrecked on its beach. He had a son by the siren and the child, being Sir Roland's, was named Padín, which is the same as Paladin" (II, p. 138).[9] This episode, like so many others in Valle-Inclán's works, shows that magic and its operations are as integral to Galician life as they were to the world that produced the *Chanson de Roland,* an epic work full of supernatural occurrences and superhuman feats.

The third act continues the occult thread as Doña Malvina tells Concha's two daughters and the young Florisel the story of an enchanted Moorish queen held prisoner by a giant: "At her side, on the grass, there is an open silver coffer full of expensive jewels resplendent in the sun. . . . in order to enchant the wayfarers, she attracts them with her beauty and deceives them with the jewels. She asks them which of the jewels they desire the most and they, seeing so many . . . begin to search through the coffer, becoming imprisoned under their enchantment. All that they had to do in order to free the damsel from the spell and marry her was say: 'Among so many jewels, I desire only you, my Queen'" (III, p. 147). In that she guards a treasure and is a victimizer of men, the Moorish queen somewhat resembles the Lamia, which by the Middle Ages had become a being synonymous with a witch, the term having lost its classical connotation.[10] Occult elements are at the very core of such stories and it is their presence that has kept this and similar tales alive in Galicia, where there is a deep-seated need for the marvelous, as Florisel makes clear:[11]

FLORISEL: If only she would appear to me!
DOÑA MALVINA: Poor you! The one who is destined to break the spell has yet to be born. [III, p. 148]

The elusiveness of magic is its charm, what keeps it alive, as in another belief explained to Bradomín by Isabel, his and Concha's cousin: "It's true enough that among the peasants there exists a belief that the blessing given by one's godfather shortens the agony of death" (III, p. 151). And Bradomín explains to her how Concha's mystical bent drove him away years before:

> Do you remember her religious terrors and the celestial apparition granted her while asleep? Concha was in a labyrinth seated at a fountain, crying inconsolably. Suddenly, an Archangel appeared to her . . . and the Archangel spread his wings of light above her and guided her. . . . [A]fter leading her out of the labyrinth, he stood in the doorway and moved his wings for flight. Concha, kneeling, asked him if she should enter a convent; the Archangel did not reply. Twisting her hands, Concha asked if she was about to die; the Archangel did not reply. Dragging herself over the stones, Concha asked if she should let our love be blown away like petals in the wind; the Archangel again did not reply but Concha felt two tears fall on her hands and roll through her fingers like two diamonds. Concha then understood the mystery of the dream. It was necessary for us to part! [III, p.153]

In his interpretation of the religious dream, Bradomín has aptly intuited Concha's fundamental dilemma as one of choosing between the Dionysian and the Apollonian polarities, which in her mind is seen as selecting between selfishness (satisfying her love for Bradomín) and duty (sacrificing herself for her estranged husband, who is dying). And when they do part, the stage directions enfold the final moment of the play within the schema of mythology and unreality: "*the chimerical laughter of the tritons of the fountains bubbles forth and the silvery waters run with a youthful murmur through the turbid beards of the old sea monsters inclining to kiss the sirens captive in their arms. The lady, faltering, reposes on a bench . . . and before her eyes the labyrinth's door, crowned by two chimeras, opens*" (III, p. 157). There is to be no baptism of their love as in the carefree romp through the water by the fountain's denizens. The traditional salutary aspect of the element of water is negated here; the figures in the fountain appear to mock the unfulfilled passion of Bradomín while its waters symbolically drown the sacrificed love of Concha, manifest in her tears.[12] Unlike the labyrinth in her dream, which poses the dilemma of choice, the labyrinth now is marked by two chimeras, mythic beasts that will imprison her within for the evil done by her negation of the Dionysian spirit—doubly so, in that she has denied herself and Bradomín fulfillment in love.[13]

From such genteel mentions of superstition and occult beliefs, Valle-Inclán moves into their more direct, forceful expression in the *Comedias bárbaras*, which have as their protagonist the feudal lord Don Juan Manuel Montenegro. In *Aguila de blasón* (1907; The Emblazoned Eagle), there are distinct references to the Devil, to dogs that become like wolves under the full moon, to blasphemy, to the large old hearths, "*which bring to mind those grotesque peasant stories about witches who scurry under the cauldron-hanger and knock-kneed demons who romp across the hearthpole where the blood sausage is hung to smoke*" (III, p. 60), and to the evil eye and the countermanding of its effect through positive (white) magic:

> GRANDFATHER: I have a daughter who can't have children because someone cast the Evil Eye on her when she was a girl. We've been told that the spell can only be broken by finding a bridge with a wayside cross and baptizing her in the water of the river at midnight. . . . For the spell to be broken no dog, cat or human being can cross the bridge until after the baptism. . . . If witches know a lot, there are others who know more, and a healer told us that in order to frighten the demons and witches away, we had to place at each end of the bridge a small Moorish brass coin, the kind that have King Solomon's circle on them. [III, p. 92]

Other examples include a vision of the child Jesus and the Virgin Mary, the snatching of a witch's buried body and an attempted defleshing in a cauldron by a seminarian, the apparition of a penitent soul, and talk of an enchantment supposedly worked upon Don Juan Manuel Montenegro by his niece and lover Isabel:

> LIBERATA: She must have cast a spell on him to keep his heart captive.
>
> MANCHADA: There are spells against spells, and if one woman knows a lot, two know more.
>
> ROSALVA: Spells can be broken.
>
> MANCHADA: Why don't you visit the healer from Céltigos. She knows how to conjure and prepare remedies for love pangs.
>
> LIBERATA: I've already seen her. . . . She told me that if a spell has been cast it can only be broken by using some item of clothing which Doña Sabelita used for a long time. . . .
>
> ROSALVA: One hears so many stories about the old woman of Céltigos! A young woman from my village went to see her to get a potion with which to win a married man. It was so potent that the very next day the man's wife died of a raging fever. [V, pp. 134–35]

Shortly after Liberata obtains Isabel's handkerchief for the conjuration, the former mistress of Don Juan Manuel attempts suicide by drowning, seemingly drawn to the water by the power of the counterspell, but perhaps seeking the self-punishment appropriate to her sin of incest.

Valle-Inclán also alludes to the Santa Compaña, one of the most pervasive of Galician superstitions, which holds that on certain nights the Holy Company of the dead process along roads and byways, often near cemeteries, and that anyone who encounters the frightful horde, even inadvertently, is taken by them or dies soon thereafter.[14] Also, as in the Irish lore of the Banshee, the Santa Compaña is said to herald someone's imminent death.

It is in *Romance de lobos* (1908; Wolf Song), which closes the trilogy, that Valle-Inclán returns to the Santa Compaña mentioned briefly in *Aguila de blasón*, devoting much of the opening scene of the play to it, giving the supernatural event the serious attention it has for the populace of Galicia:

> *A path. In the distance, the green and fragrant cemetery of a village. It is night, and the emerging moon shines through the cypress trees. Don Juan Manuel Montenegro, returning drunk from the fair, rides along the path on a horse that is jittery and seems unaccustomed to the saddle. . . .*
> MONTENEGRO: Goddamn horse! . . . I don't know what the devil has gotten into you! . . . May lightning strike me dead if I know!
> VOICE 1: Sinner, don't curse!
> VOICE 2: Your soul is as black as coal from Hell, sinner!
> VOICE 3: Sinner, think of the hour of death!
> VOICE 4: Seven devils are boiling oil in a great cauldron to scorch your soul, sinner!
> MONTENEGRO: Who speaks? Are you voices from the other world? Are you Souls in Purgatory, or are you sons of bitches? [I, p. 12]

Don Juan Manuel Montenegro, the grand old feudal lord, puts on his bravado to do battle with the sinister voices as if donning his seignorial armor. The response he receives is a tremendous clap of thunder that makes his horse bolt; but what unnerves the man is what he beholds:

> *Among the corn rows appear the lights of the Holy Company. . . . There are heard cries of agony and the rusty sounds of chains being dragged in the dark night by the suffering souls who have returned to the world to do penance. The white procession passes like a fog through the cornfield. . . . Montenegro feels the chill of death on seeing the quivering flame of a candle in his hand. The procession of dead souls surrounds him and he is dragged along with the*

white phantoms by a cold sepulchral wind as they march to the sound of
chains and intone a hymn in Latin. [I, pp. 12–13]

The tradition of the Santa Compaña, or Hueste as it is sometimes
called, is a strange mixture of often conflicting beliefs. It is evident that
its source lies in the ancient celebration of Samhain, the Celtic festival
that ushered out the old year on October 31, during which ancestors
returned to the world of the living to be welcomed by newly lit fires,
both in hearths and outdoors. But while the visitation was joyous for a
people who saw human existence as a continuum, not an end, Christianity supplanted Samhain with its All Souls Day, bringing a perspective
that was at odds with that of the Celtic festival. In its attempt to eradicate pagan ways, the Church replaced the positive interaction of the
living and the dead, which typified Samhain, with the Christian view
toward death and the dead, which relied on instilling fear of Hell in the
afterlife as an incentive to perform good works in this one. Unfortu-
nately, human nature being what it is, people focused more on the
dreadful aspects of death (and the potential punishment for sin, as in
the cases of the all-too-human Faust and Don Juan Tenorio) than on
the joyous reward awaiting the just in Heaven (the seemingly less
human, divinely touched saints). Likewise, the popular mind too often
failed to distinguish between those damned eternally in Hell and those
doing temporary penance in Purgatory before entering Heaven. That
commixture is responsible for the ironic perception of the Santa Compaña—whose very name is positive—not as a group of souls suffering
in Purgatory, but as *damned* souls:

VOICE 3: You are our brother and we are all sons of Satan!
VOICE 4: Sin is blood and makes men brothers, as does the blood of
   fathers!
VOICE 5: All of us sucked at the hairy teats of the Mother Devil!
... Montenegro feels a blast of air unseating him and sees his horse disappear
in an infernal run. As he watches the flickering candle in his fist, he is hor-
rified to realize that what he is holding is a human bone. Closing his eyes, he
feels no earth beneath his feet as he is carried through the air. When he dares
to look once more, the procession has stopped at a riverbank where witches
murmur while seated in a circle. A funeral can be seen across the river. A
cock crows. . . . The phantoms disappear in a fog, while the witches begin erect-
ing a bridge and seem like bats flying over the river, wide as an ocean. At the
opposite shore, the funeral procession waits. Another cock crows. . . . Only one
stone remains to be placed and the witches hurry because day nears. Immobile
at the other shore, the funeral awaits the completion of the bridge in order to
cross. A third cock crows. . . . The witches fly off as bats. [I, pp. 13–15]

Having crossed the bridge, the funeral cortege also disappears in a mist.[15] Montenegro, as if waking from a nightmare, lies in the field, his horse placidly grazing nearby. He wastes no time mounting and riding away from the haunted site to his estate.

It should be noted that the number three appears in the context of the cocks that crow at crucial moments in their traditional roles as heralds of dawn and dispersers of the evil of night. Not only are they three in number but are of three colors: white, dappled, black. The colors may be seen as symbolic of the range of interrelationships—from the dualism of white (positive) and black (negative), to the blurring of their distinctions, which the motley color represents.[16] Although the number of witches is not stipulated, only three speak, each one reacting to the crowing of one of the three cocks. The number three has a long, complex symbology that has been explicated from Plato, Aristotle, and the Pythagoreans in Greek antiquity through the propounders of Gnosticism, Cabbalism, and Christianity.[17]

Since tradition has it that the Santa Compaña appears in order to herald the death of someone in the vicinity and that those who encounter it accidentally are themselves destined to die immediately or soon thereafter, not only will Don Juan Manuel Montenegro not be an exception, but Doña María, his wife, will pass away before he does. Thus their deaths are in compliance with the dual function of the Hueste, the ghostly horde. Don Juan Manuel knows the lore and believes it, as verified in the scene in which he addresses the old woman who lets him into his house: "Blow out that candle. . . . I have seen the Hueste! . . . After seeing the lights of Death I don't want to see other lights. If I am to be Hers . . . and if I am to live, I want to remain blind until the light of the sun appears. . . . My heart tells me something has happened" (I, pp. 16–17). Soon thereafter the news reaches him of his wife's serious illness, reacting to which he shouts, "She's dead! Tonight I saw her funeral and what I thought to be a river was the ocean that separated us!" (I, p. 21). Doña María's death is attested to in the following scene, thus verifying Don Juan Manuel's encounter with the Santa Compaña, at least insofar as it presaged another's death. The path to his own death is longer but no less assured as he confronts his five rapacious sons, who have plundered their mother's estate immediately on her demise and await the old hidalgo's death to do the same with his. Montenegro, repenting his sins against his wife, incarcerates himself in her bedroom and refuses to eat, his death wish tied to his experience with the Santa Compaña. When he flees the unwanted attentions of his household, he encounters the local madman, Fuso

Negro, who describes Montenegro's sons as the "sons of the Principal Devil. He made each one at a Sabbat, at the stroke of midnight, when he lays with the witches. . . . Taking the appearance of the husband, he goes to the wife and lays with her. . . . My lord, because he knew that you liked the wenches, the Devil made you a cuckold by going to bed with Lady María" (III, pp. 124–25). In the confrontation with his sons that closes the play, not only does one of them die but Don Juan Manuel Montenegro also falls in the struggle. The Santa Compaña has indeed claimed the life of the man who, on encountering the ghostly horde, knew that his death was at hand and resigned himself to his fate, sensing that it could not be avoided.[18] So it is that such folk beliefs attain their verification and are perpetuated throughout the centuries.

In *El embrujado: Tragedia de tierras de Salnés* (1913; The Bewitched: A Tragedy of the Lands of Salnés) there are a variety of occult elements, ranging from such universal beliefs as bewitchment, the evil eye, fortune-telling by cards, and lycanthropy, to numerous references to superstitions native to Galicia. The play opens outside the estate of Don Pedro Bolaño with a host of village women and assorted beggars. In setting and characters, the scene is reminiscent of *Romance de lobos*, while the feudal tribute early in the first act, satirically entitled "Georgics," underscores further the subservience of the masses to the landowner as in that play. But if the conflict in the *Comedia bárbaras* is within the family of nobles portrayed, that of *El embrujado* is centered on the antagonism between the feudal lord and Rosa Galans (La Galana), a common woman who claims that she bore his dead son a child out of wedlock.[19] Gossip has it that the child's father is Anxelo, however, one of Don Pedro's servants and one of Rosa's numerous lovers. Although the hidalgo suspects the truth, he wants to give the child the Montenegro name since he no longer has a legitimate heir. Rosa, playing to his dynastic need, demands an exorbitant payment in exchange for her son. When denied, she reluctantly takes the child in her arms, exiting to the accompaniment of voices ostracizing her as a witch.

The identification of Rosa Galans as a witch prepares the occult revelations that begin in the second act. One of these evolves through the guilty conscience of Anxelo, who wants to free himself of the weight "of the chain of double rings" that oppresses him by confessing a serious trespass so that "having paid for my evil deed, my black soul will turn white" (p. 109). Mauriña, the wife on whom he cheated with Rosa Galans, has no sympathy with his plight when she says, "Salúdate," using the traditional term for a spiritual purgation through magic rites, but the tormented man sees himself as beyond such rescue:

ANXELO: That evil woman bewitched me. I feel a captive spirit beating its
wings and flying around inside me. . . . Light the holy candle and
close the door. . . . Rosa Galans will come for me! . . . Don't let her in
for if she looks at me I must follow her!
MAURIÑA: Now you have me trembling with fear! Is she that powerful?
ANXELO: Just look at my hands full of blood! . . . The soul of the dead
man cannot be redeemed until I confess everything. . . .
MAURIÑA: Your evil is buried under the ground. . . .
ANXELO: I feel remorse at letting a young man grope along facing the
gallows. When the soul of the dead man appears to me, it accuses
me most on that account. More for that than for his spilled blood! [I,
pp. 110–16]

The double theme of witchcraft and murder is thus introduced: the
bewitchment of Anxelo by Rosa Galans has led to his being used by the
seductive woman to kill Don Pedro's son in her avaricious scheme to
claim him as the father of the child she had with Anxelo and thus to get
what she can out of the old hidalgo. When Rosa's new lover enters,
Anxelo tries to warn Valerio of her power by detailing how he became
involved with her:

Returning from harvesting when the sun was already setting, a barking
dog with fiery eyes crossed my path. I kicked him with my clog and it
ran off with a yelping that filled the darkness like the voice of a woman
possessed. Walking a bit further, I came across a wayside inn and she was
sitting at the door. . . . Would that I had never entered! She filled a glass
for me. I drank it and as I did I felt her eyes fix upon me. . . . I noticed
that there was a drop of blood on her forehead. . . . She took a cloth,
wiped her face and showed me that it was white. . . . Holding the lamp
to my face, she asked without moving her lips: "Who did you meet on
the way?" At that moment, I recognized in her voice the yelping of the
dog when I kicked it in the head. After that I was unable to get out of
her circle. . . . Laughing, she hit me with the cloth she had used to wipe
her face, and in a flash I saw it covered with blood. [II, pp. 120–21]

Valerio listens with amusement, but the Blind Man and his mistress,
more attuned to such beliefs, are more attentive; Mauriña, however,
berates Anxelo: "You're always delirious over seeing phantoms and
souls and other things that don't exist" (II, p. 122). Then, as if in confirmation of Anxelo's story, a dog is heard barking, and Rosa Galans
appears almost instantly. She protects the child in her arms, afraid of its
rumored abduction at Don Pedro's hands. Even her plight cannot
stem the concern of the others over Anxelo's condition:

THE MISTRESS: The Evil Eye has been cast on this possesed man. We must take him to the sea to bathe in the waves under the midnight moon.
BLIND MAN: Perhaps at Saint Peter the Martyr!
ROSA GALANS: Or at Saint Justa of Moraña.
BLIND MAN: Better yet at Our Lady of Lanzada! [II, p. 125]

Although the three places mentioned are Galician sites long famed for the kind of miracle Anxelo needs, the bewitched man rebukes the suggestions:[20]

ANXELO: That's enough of litanies! My spell can't be cured by healers or by the waves of the sea.
ROSA GALANS: . . . Look at me and let your eyes be bright! Take a drink of this and you'll get rid of that sucking witch.
ANXELO:: Move back! Get away from me! In Christ's name, remove the chain around my neck!
ROSA GALANS: I order you to stop raving. Now, have a drink with me. [II, p. 125]

Again under her spell, Anxelo *"rises like a shadow. His eyes are feverish, his mouth white and trembling on the yellowed-wax face of a man near death"* (p. 126). As before, he addresses the soul of his victim, stating that he will confess. Threatened by his ranting, Rosa again tries to get him to drink, finally resorting to another ploy: "Let's all have an empanada under the moon, next to the oak tree, like the witches" (II, p. 127). Is it sardonic playfulness or admission of her true calling? Soon, Rosa abandons Anxelo when Mauriña screams that Rosa's child has been taken from her. The act ends with the pursuit of the kidnapper, who has been wounded by Valerio, and with Anxelo lying unconscious on the ground.

In the last act, Don Pedro speaks of the intuitive sense that warned of his son's murder and of the problems the child would bring. Underscoring this is the bad omen of turtledoves that died without apparent cause in his house. Then, when Diana, one of the local women enters the kitchen to ask for flour and is jokingly treated by the women of the household as if she were a witch, she turns to the hidalgo and says, "I have certain knowledge! With it I throw light on people's lives. My lord Don Pedro, would you like me to read the cards and show you the future?" (III, p. 139). Steadfast in his disdain of what he considers witchcraft, Don Pedro looks instead to his dark intuition of what is to come that night. When the blind man and his mistress arrive, Don Pedro calls them birds of bad omen, and their narration of the kidnapper being shot proves that his intuition was right. Shortly, his servant Malvín returns with the child against his chest and falls, critically wounded. The same bullet that pierced his chest also killed the child that he held against it. Dying, Malvín speaks of the white dog of death that pursued him to the estate, and when the bewitched and wife arrive, they too speak of its proximity:

ANXELO: The howling dog! Don't let it enter!
MAURIÑA: Make your confession quickly, Anxelo. We were dragged here by the wind of a soul in Purgatory! The soul of the son for whom you grieve, my noble lord! We both saw it while walking along a path! He embraced us in a whirlwind and brought us here, but I'm not guilty!
ANXELO: The dog is howling! Listen to him howl!
MAURIÑA: It's the woman who bewitched him. Don't let her in. [II, p. 147]

But it is too late. A gust of wind brings the voice of Rosa Galans, who is visible only as a shadow outside the door. Like a Fury wronged, she demands the return of her child, only to learn that it has been killed. Her dead son before her, Rosa now stands accused by Don Pedro of having had his own son killed. It is a scene of retributive justice gone awry, for neither can be verified as responsible: although Don Pedro intuited the tragic events of the night, it is never stated that he had sent Malvín on his ill-starred errand; nor is it ever shown that Rosa Galans plotted her lover's death through the agency of Anxelo. The only certainty is that the two sons have died under ambiguous circumstances. The play comes to a close as Rosa Galans orders Anxelo and Mauriña to go with her "To Hell!" They leave with humiliation and defeat on their faces: "*Rosa Galans's hard black look follows them until they pass the emptiness under the archway. At the threshold, she turns, spits on the tiles and makes the sign of the horns with her left hand. Those in the kitchen bless themselves. A moment later, three white dogs bark at the door*" (III, p. 150). Those who believe in lycanthropy will accept the implied human-to-animal transformation; those who cannot accept such lore will be left with a final ambiguity.

Ligazón: Auto para siluetas (1926; trans., *Blood Pact: A Play for Silhouettes*) employs light and darkness to give the characters the quality of silhouettes, literally making them occult.[21] Against the brilliance of the moon, profiles and figures take on an aura of unreality. The luminosity of moon, stars, and objects reflecting their light contrasts with the dynamic shadowiness of characters moving in the night and the static landscape set blackly against the illuminating elements. In this visual setting words seem like discordant echoes, strangely sensual and menacing. Thus, the three women in the play, two old and one young, talk with relish of the black arts that they practice with apparent success and abandon in their Galician village. They and other characters speak of marital arrangements, of pent-up passions, of love's prostitution, of pacts with the Devil, of blood, and of death. It is the kinetic interaction of light and shadow, though, that paces the play: the dazzle of a necklace held up to the night's light, the knife sharpener's wheel in motion heralding a tragic action as scissors reflect the moonbeams, the ritual cadences of passion as lovers maneuver around each other toward their blood pact in the moonlight, and the final bloodletting brought on by the stroke of the brilliant scissors.

La Raposa (The Old Hag), a Celestina, approaches La Mozuela (The Lass) with a present from an old man who wishes to make her his mistress. The nubile virgin refuses the necklace and the lewd offer of concubinage, despite the practical entreaties of the go-between. La Raposa, realizing that La Mozuela cannot be won over, enters the inn to deal with La Ventera, the innkeeper who is the girl's mother. When she exits, La Mozuela gaily proclaims her victory. Shortly, another figure appears on the scene. El Afilador (the Knife Grinder), another silhouette in the night, proclaims his services and advances toward La Mozuela with the offer to sharpen her scissors in exchange for an embrace. The sensual girl counters with her coquettish wit and and pays for his services with wine. At his insistence, she drinks first and when he quaffs the potion a symbolic pact between them is achieved. He promises to return as he sets out on his rounds. La Ventera and La Raposa reenter together and converse briefly. Before they part company, their words reveal both to be witches:

INNKEEPER: Old crony, we're of the same Art!

OLD HAG: Are you a flier?

INNKEEPER: At midnight on the Sabbat, I mount my broom and I'm off through the heavens. The arc of the Sun! The arc of the Moon!

OLD HAG: You're drunk!

INNKEEPER: You say I'm drunk because I bested you.

OLD HAG: The Devil visits me every night!

INNKEEPER: It's just a dream!

OLD HAG: It's as true as his horns and tail! Show me the way, dear crony. The moon blinds me.

INNKEEPER: The night twists everything around.

OLD HAG: I'll use that big star as a guide.

INNKEEPER: Old friend, I'm at your disposal.

OLD HAG: You're in my soul, sister.
INNKEEPER: Sister, my life is yours for the asking. [SA, p. 9]

The element of witchcraft has been introduced and with it the perception of La Mozuela's role changes. She, like her mother, is a witch, but while the older woman has accepted the necklace, thus giving her approval to the illicit bonding of the lecherous man and her daughter, La Mozuela cannot be bewitched by the bribe, not even when the necklace sparkles in the light of the moon. Mother and daughter part without concert.

The return of El Afilador acts as a counterpoint. The dialogue becomes more impassioned as he and La Mozuela are brought together in a bond as dark as the night that envelops them. Her visionary power traces the recent steps of El Afilador, his thoughts of her, and the fact that he was bitten on the shoulder by a dog. She attributes their second meeting to destiny. The darkening of the moon obscures the two figures, however, and only vocal contact remains. She calls out seductively to El Afilador to receive the embrace he had asked for earlier. He thinks of her first as a siren and then as a serpent. When her mother calls out to her, La Mozuela tells him to wait by her window.

His shadow blends with those of the landscape until La Mozuela, crying from the beating she has received for her obstinacy, opens her shutters, symbolizing her receptivity. She offers herself, and her virginity, to El Afilador, who hesitates, thinking that she is playing a dangerous game. He is right, except that it is not a game. His head swimming, the man of the world watches as she pierces her hand with the scissors he had sharpened. She presses her hand to his lips and orders him to drink her blood; then she drinks blood from the wound on his shoulder. She has completed the blood pact, a pagan ritual as old as humanity.

Tied by the unholy ritual, the lovers are united in the room whose light has been extinguished by La Mozuela. Later, during the darkly silent tryst, another silhouette appears outside the inn, knocks at the door, and is admitted surreptitiously. Shortly, La Mozuela is discerned crossing her room rapidly. Then, raising the scissors, which catch the moonlight briefly, she plunges the instrument into the dark shadow that had moments before gained admittance to the inn. A scream and a thud punctuate the silence of the night. Four arms toss the body through the window as dogs bark in the moonlight, their feral sounds almost like those of wolves. La Mozuela and El Afilador have executed the lecherous pretender to the girl's favors. The pact that had begun with wine and was sealed with the mutual bloodsucking has been bathed in the death blood of a sacrificial victim. The ritual is complete. The Devil has received his due from the priestess and new initiate of his ancient cult.

Ligazón shows the savagery inherent in a context ostensibly Christian; it demonstrates the pagan substratum that lies close to the surface veneer of Christianity in Spain as elsewhere. Elements of paganism come to the fore when normal means cannot provide the desired result in a society governed by Christian tenets. It is a profane pagan ritual instigated by The Lass that binds her own lust and The Knife Grinder's lust in a savage blood pact. Their subsequent complicity in the brutal murder that closes the play so savagely makes the intimate blood pact transcend its personal consequences; a real victim has been sacrificed and the body given to the earth, which receives its fluid, as if it were a libation in an ancient rite of propitiation. It is a yet more savage blood pact with larger implications.

In *Divinas palabras: Tragicomedia de aldea* (1920; Divine Words: A Village Tragicomedy), Valle-Inclán again pits Christian mores against natural instincts. Within a realistic setting in rural Galicia, in which Mari-Gaila, wife of the sexton Pedro Gailo, and Lucero, an itinerant huckster, are highly attracted to each other, the playwright inserts a scene in act two in which the protagonist Mari-Gaila, wheeling the cart bearing the hydrocephalic dwarf in her charge, encounters the Trasgo Cabrío, one of the many names given the Devil in Galicia, as elsewhere in Spain.[22] Valle-Inclán sets up the scene: "*Night of bright stars. Mari-Gaila wheels the cart along a white path full of the sounds of cornfields. The cuckoo sings. When it stops, there is heard the tremulous voice of the Trasgo Cabrío. He is sitting on a boulder, his beard disheveled, made to tremble by a gust of wind. Mari-Gaila conjures him*" (II, p. 90). The "Noche de luceros" obviously refers to Lucero, the male protagonist. No doubt Mari-Gaila's mind is as full of Lucero as the night is filled with the bright stars to which his name alludes. Then, as if her illicit thoughts were brought to life, Lucero's counterpart—Lucifer—materializes before her eyes. Afraid of what she sees, she does what any Galician would do when confronted with the Devil. She attempts to counter the evil presence with spells. Her words are a mixture of formulas derived from Galician folklore and biblical antecedents:

> At one, the light of the Moon!
> At two, the light of the Sun!
> At three, the Tablets of Moses!
> At four, the crow of the Cock!

At five, that which is Writ!
At six, the Star of the Magi!
At seven, the candles of Death!
At eight, the flames of Purgatory!
At nine, three Eyes and three Trivets!
At ten, the Sword of the Archangel Michael!
At eleven, the opened Bronze Doors!
At twelve, the Lord's lightning explodes in the Great Devil's guts.
[II, pp. 90–91]

Throughout her incantation, the Trasgo Cabrío interjects his hooting laughter and taunts her by offering his behind for her to kiss, the traditional rite of witches when pledging their service to the Devil, the act Inquisitors termed the *Osculum infame*. She awaits a positive result to her conjuration, but to no avail: "*Mari-Gaila awaits the lightning, but hears only the laughter of the Trasgo Cabrío. The scene changes again. There is a church at a crossroads. Witches dance all about. Through the door can be seen a reddish glow while the smoke-filled wind carries the odor of sardines. The Trasgo Cabrío, atop the church's weathervane, makes his hooting sound*" (II, p. 91). He continues to tempt Mari-Gaila throughout the Goyaesque scene with offers of pleasurable things, including the witches' sabbat: "Why do you deny knowing me? . . . Come with me to the dance. . . . I'll take you flying, higher than the Sun and the Moon. . . . Do you want me to place you at your destination? It will only take my blowing on you. . . . Or else you will spend the whole night trying and never get there" (II, p. 92). Convinced of his powers and naively believing that all the Trasgo Cabrío wants as a reward is a dance, Mari-Gaila assents. To the accompaniment of demonic laughter, the scene reverts to the original setting but quickly takes on a magical aspect:

Mari-Gaila feels herself carried along by a gust of wind, hardly touching the ground. The momentum increases, she is suspended in the air, and as she soars she sighs with carnal delight. Beneath her skirt she feels the violent thrashing of an animal's hairy rump. When she extends her arms to prevent a fall, they encounter the twisted horns of the Trasgo Cabrío.
CABRIO: Jujurujú!
MARI-GAILA: Where are you taking me, Dark One?
CABRIO: We're going to the dance.
MARI-GAILA: Where are we now?
CABRIO: The arcs of the Moon.
MARI-GAILA: I feel faint! I'm afraid I'll fall!
CABRIO: Press your legs against me.

MARI-GAILA: How hairy you are!
Mari-Gaila loses consciousness and feels herself being borne through the clouds. When, after a very long ride she opens her eyes, she is standing at her door. The Moon, large, round and succulent, lights the cart in which the dwarf makes his eternal grimace. [II, p. 93]

While Mari-Gaila has had her night of unnatural delights, there awaits her the natural encounter with Lucero, the down-to-earth manifestation of the Trasgo Cabrío, the Dionysian spirit. This occurs in the third act when she keeps the assignation with Lucero, and they fornicate in the fields. When some male villagers discover their illicit tryst, Lucero abandons Mari-Gaila. She is left alone to confront the men. When one of them attempts to have his way with her right then and there, she stalls his passion with the promise of a later tryst away from the others.

The play comes to its climax with a scene reminiscent of the Gospel story of the adulterous woman, whom Christ rescued from the mob that was about to stone her. Taken in sin, Mari-Gaila, too, is about to suffer a similar fate. Half-naked, she is wheeled into town in a cart by the same men who found her with Lucero. In this instance it is her husband, Pedro Gailo, the drunk and lecherous sacristan, who pronounces the words spoken by Christ: "Let he who is without sin cast the first stone." Yet the words have no effect because they are in the language of the people. Only when he realizes this and pronounces them in Latin, by then a mysterious, mystical language to the populace, do they become the divine words that give the play its title. Mari-Gaila, like the adulterous woman in the Gospel, is rescued from physical punishment, but instead of a "Go and sin no more" admonition, Mari-Gaila undergoes a rite of passage. Conducted by the sacristan, she is led through the church graveyard, symbolically dying, and into the church proper, to be reborn. The exorcism, which began with the ringing of the church bell, the lighting of a candle, and the reading from the book containing the Gospels, is completed in the rite of passage experienced by Mari-Gaila. She is thus reintegrated into the bosom of the Church.

The final example of a major presence of occult lore in Valle-Inclán's plays is seen in *Cara de Plata* (1923; Silver Face), the last published but first in the chronology of the *Comedias bárbaras*. Returning to the feudal world of Don Juan Manuel Montenegro and, in this case, his six sons, the playwright creates other memorable characters, including the titular one, his son, and the Abad de Lantañón, both his antagonists— the first over the love of Sabelita, whom the father will win, the second over being denied what he perceives as his right-of-way through the Montenegro estate, despite the feudal privilege against such trespass. Since Cara de Plata barred the Abad's way, the priest has labeled him "Lucifer's Soul." Indeed, the first act is full of references to Satan and Hell, from the mouths of the three leading characters.

The opening words in the second act are from street vendors offering wares to satisfy the superstitious needs of the populace. The first one is selling *O Ciprianillo*, the book of Saint Ciprian (or San Cebrán), a fabled magical text of Galicia said to give the reader the power to obtain treasure hidden from others under an enchantment.[23] Among the people in this opening scene, as in the previous act, there is much talk of Hell and the Devil, and thereafter the Abad refers constantly to Cara de Plata as Satan, while the madman Fuso Negro entones his creed: "Satan could govern the world to the satisfaction of one and all. . . . Governed by evil, the world would be something of merit. . . . With Satan reigning, women would walk around naked" (II, pp. 80–81). As the act ends, Cara de Plata has his fortune read by the wanton Pichona, who uses the "book by Vilham." She has him cut the deck three times and then says: "Give me what is secret, book of Villano, if you don't want me to read it in the lines on his palm. Point the way, illuminate destiny, through the staff of Moses, open, cards, that I may read good and evil" (II, p. 105).

In the third act, such is the Abbot's prideful passion in the clash of his and the hidalgo's authority that he resorts to diabolical means in order to have his way; at a crossroads, where witches habitually congregate to conjure up the Devil, the Abad follows suit: "Satan, I'll sell you my soul if you come to my aid now. Even the sacrilege does not terrify me! . . . Today I bet my soul! . . . Satan, help me and I'll give you my soul! Assist me, King of Hell, you who can do all evil!" (III, pp. 117, 120). But only the madman Fuso Negro responds to his call and the Abad is unable to sign the traditional pact with the Devil á la Théophile or Faust.[24] Frustrated in his attempt, during his final confrontation with Don Juan Manuel Montenegro, the fallen Abad runs off terrified at the magnitude of the hidalgo's diabolical act of wresting the sacred chalice from his own tainted hands. The play ends with Montenegro saying, "I fear I may be the Devil!" (III, p. 150). His words recall those of the protagonist in *Don Alvaro, o La fuerza del sino*: "I am the ambassador of Hell; I am the exterminating Devil" (V, p. 244).

From his earliest plays at the start of the century to his later, mature works of the 1920s, Valle-Inclán demonstrates a growing interest in portraying the life of his native Galicia, a large part of it being the lore and occult beliefs stemming from the region's cultural flux, from prehistory to the first quarter of this century. Be it through the sophistication of Concha's household in *El Marqués de Bradomín*, the decaying feudal life of Don Juan Manuel Montenegro and his rapacious sons in the *Comedias bárbaras*, the fright-filled life of *El embrujado*, the feral passion in *Ligazón*, or the hypocritical and grotesque existence in *Divinas palabras*, Valle-Inclán presents a broad range of the indigenous folklore of his own region with deep insights. In so doing, Valle-Inclán parallels the spirit of the Celtic revival in Ireland as manifested in the works of the playwrights Lady Gregory, J.M. Synge, and, especially, William Butler Yeats. And because of his commitment to his people and their traditions, these plays of Valle-Inclán are central to the ongoing current of Pan-Celtism in Europe. The major occult premises in the plays discussed here, as well as lesser references to the esoteric elsewhere in his dramas, are, indeed, true manifestations of what Valle-Inclán said he desired to preserve before its extinction: the ancient ways and lore of Galicia.

V

Toward the Dionysiac:
Pagan Elements and Rites in
Federico García Lorca's *Yerma*

What a terrible loss not to be able to feel the teachings of the ancients!
—Federico García Lorca, *Yerma*

The second play in Federico García Lorca's trilogy of rural tragedies, which includes *Bodas de sangre* and *La casa de Bernarda Alba*, *Yerma* examines human sexuality through a perspective differentiated from that of its companion works. In *Yerma*, Lorca assesses the nulliparous state of his titular protagonist, the attendant frustration brought about by her unfulfilled desire for a child of her own, and the tragic consequences of her despair.[1]

The play is not only a study of maternal instinct gone awry but also a powerful statement on two polarities that govern the characters' lives and effect massive changes in those lives when the contrasting systems are placed in direct and open conflict. Yerma's is a distinctive struggle between two diametrically opposed aspects of European life in general and Spanish life in particular—the veneer of the Christian ethos and the substratum of pagan tradition. García Lorca's protagonist is victimized by the social and religious codes of a Christian milieu, codes that frustrate human drives and are, therefore, *contra natura* in the eyes of the playwright. In sharp contrast is the naturalness of those who follow the old pagan ways, especially in instinctual and sexual matters; theirs is a holistic state, a wellness both of body and spirit, as García Lorca sees it, for they have attained a state of integration in which the Apollonian and the Dionysiac modes are in harmony.[2] Out of this cohesiveness comes the fullness of human potential.

Throughout *Yerma*, García Lorca focuses on the contrasting forces at work on the protagonist, as well as on the means to their resolution. He does so by introducing natural factors that are in obvious opposition to the unnatural state of affairs in Yerma's relationship with each of the three men in her life—her husband, Juan, her dream man, Victor, and her potential lover, the son of La Vieja. Simply put, Yerma rejects all three in one manner or another. She views Juan only as a means to an end—procreation legitimized—and never as a man to be desired for himself; Victor, the only man to have aroused her sexual instinct, was not chosen by her father to be her husband, and she neither protested nor sought him as a lover; and the virile young man who awaits her meaningfully behind the church is never given the opportunity to make love to her. For Yerma, only that which is socially and morally legitimate can be considered as a potential cure for her barrenness. Thus, she spends herself berating Juan for his callous indifference to her maternal need, or envisioning Victor with a child that might have been theirs had she been given to the shepherd in marriage, or indignantly rejecting La Vieja's Celestinesque pandering on her son's behalf.[3] The temptation of that which is illicit cannot overcome her resolve to live within the social and moral bounds of her Christian upbringing.

Yerma comes closest to crossing that barrier when she makes a desperate visit to Dolores the Conjurer. The old crone, who services the more esoteric needs of the villagers, leads Yerma to the nearby cemetery, where prayers are offered and conjurations performed to cure her infertility. This, Yerma's first inclination toward the pagan, is the result of the inevitable surfacing of instincts long suppressed; these emanate from an internal pagan substratum and threaten to erode her Christian bulwarks. Put in other terms, the primal forces of Dionysus are arrayed against the civilized minions of Apollo, and Yerma is to be the battleground.[4]

The most pervasive and, therefore, notable factors that García Lorca marshals against the Christian ethos and its Apollonian counterpart are the four cardinal Elements: Earth, Water, Air and Fire. The lore of the Elements has its origin in antiquity and manifests itself in all inhabited continents of the world, having various and diverse associations with the four seasons of the year, the four "humors" that characterize human temperament, and the four points of the compass, as well as colors, gender, signs of the Zodiac, deities, totems, and the ages of humanity.[5] Wherever they appear, the four Elements constitute the foundation of all that exists. So pervasive was this belief in Europe that it survived in hermeticism, alchemy, and rudimentary sciences until the Apollonian Age of Reason caused the demise of many of the ancient world's concepts. And yet, the Elements survived, even though metamorphosed into symbols of lesser impact.

The four Elements begin to appear in the very first scene of *Yerma*, either singly or in combinations and continue to be a major frame of reference throughout the rest of the play. Through the Elements, García Lorca creates a symbolic pattern that is both ironic (in that it is

Yerma who most frequently and intuitively refers to the pagan Elements, yet cannot assimilate them) and portentous (in that they build toward the full manifestation of the Dionysiac in the final scene of the play).

Earth is the first Element introduced. It is manifested, if somewhat indirectly, in an offstage lullaby at the very beginning of the play:

> For the baby, baby, baby,
> for the baby we will make
> a cute little hut in the field
> and refuge in it we'll take. [11]

"The field" (*el campo*) is the manifestation of the Element Earth. As such, it is the foundation for a "hut" (*una chocita*) that will shelter the child and the singer of the lullaby. If the singer is the mother, then Earth, child, and woman are immediately bound together. This relationship demonstrates the traditional view of this Element's association with birthing and nurturing, of the Earth as the Great Mother out of whose womb came many living things. Earth is, therefore, a feminine Element in ancient systems of belief.[6]

Just as many living things originate in this Element, García Lorca's drama begins with the field and goes on to establish Yerma's relationship to the Earth. Early in the play Yerma herself makes the significant connection when she explains to her friend María: "Often at night I go barefoot into the patio to feel the earth, without knowing why" (20). Although she does not know what motivates her, she follows the instinct that prompts her to tread the ground with bare feet. Yerma senses that she must be in physical contact with the soil underfoot, thus identifying with Earth.

Yerma's husband, Juan, also has an association with the soil. His longstanding commitment to it is evident in the time that he devotes to farming and in the way that he speaks of the fields: "My life is in the fields" (5). Juan fails, however, to recognize in Yerma the other soil that he must fertilize to achieve her personal fruition as a mother; he desires in her only the pleasures of sexual union, abhorring the thought of procreation. Juan also experiences the soil in a physical manner, but his involvement with it culminates in its fecundity. The attention that Juan gives his wife pales in comparison. Unlike the soil that he perpetually tills, plants, and sleeps on, Yerma is uncared for, has not been impregnated, and is frequently left to sleep alone. Thus, she must find a way to attract Juan as much as the soil that he farms if she too is to become fertile. Since Juan is seldom at home, Yerma must go where that productive life is lived, to the fields.

Yerma trudges daily to those fields to fulfill her obligation of bringing her husband his food. What she has yet to learn is that she must also feed his other appetite—for the lover that he craves to find in her. She must give herself wholly, like the earth to the farmer, in order to attain the fulfillment of her potential as a woman. Like La Vieja, who tells her, "I've lain on my back and started to sing" (27), Yerma must willingly lie prone on the earth and let its chthonian powers arouse her senses toward the sexual enjoyment of her husband as a man. For that end to be realized, Yerma must undergo a major transformation: only with her rebirth as an earthy woman capable of satisfying her husband's passion for her earthy body will she find herself as productive as the fields that Juan farms. Only then will Victor's words to Yerma at the end of the first scene—"¡qué ahonde!"—be fulfilled by Juan. The verb *ahondar* means to dig, to deepen, to go deep into, to penetrate; Victor is telling Yerma that Juan must enter her deeply, tilling her into fecundity, as he does the earth. Yerma repeats his words passionately—"Yes! Let him penetrate!" (24)—but immediately returns to the thoughts she had expressed in an earlier soliloquy:

> Oh yes, I would say, my child,
> for you I'd be severed and torn.
> How painful this waist has become
> where first your cradle will be!
> When, child of mine, will you come?
> When jasmine has perfumed your flesh! [24]

Yerma has clearly misinterpreted the intent of Victor's words. Instead of comprehending the sexual connotation of the phrase, which he had underscored with a knowing smile, Yerma has taken it to signify a means to quite a different end—the fulfillment of her maternal desire. What she has failed to recognize is that she must put aside her fixation and yield to Juan; she must become "severed and torn" for her husband, not for the dream child that she addresses. She must become lover before she can become mother. Only when she abandons her egocentricity and accepts this natural state will she possess that scent of jasmine that will herald her body's fecundity. She will only become like the earth when she opens herself to the Dionysiac.

Even so, other factors must come to bear before the natural course of events can follow. Despite Juan's intense attention to the fields, it has been very difficult for him to make them productive. But even if his labor takes its toll on his body, as Yerma reminds him, Juan sees strength rather than weakness in his situation: "When men are dried up [*enjutos*], they become as strong as steel" (12). Yet, if the condition of steel is improved by its dryness, the state of man is not. The word *enjuto* means wizened, shrivelled up, arid, dry; when applied to Juan, *enjuto* indicates a serious lack in his constitution.

What Juan lacks is symbolized by the second Element, Water. The soil that Juan works so diligently must be irrigated by the scant water allotted to him by a community cursed with little precipitation and few rivers. As Juan tells Yerma: "I'll spend the whole night irrigating. What little water there is belongs to me until the sun comes up and I have to keep watch for thieves" (40). Just as he has minimal amounts of water to give the parched soil, so too is he unable to quench the thirst of his wife. It is a situation that Yerma herself brings to the fore when she expresses her concern and proposes a solution to Juan: "I would like to see you go to the river and swim, see you go to the roof when the rain drenches our house" (12). Yerma's invocation of two types of water—river water and rain—harkens back to an ancient conception of this Element's dualistic nature. The water of the river, like all water present on the surface or innards of the planet, was referred to in antiquity as "Lower Water" and symbolized actuality; the water that came down in the form of rain or dew was thought of as "Upper Water" and symbolized potentiality.[7] Dew, furthermore, was symbolic of semen.[8]

Intuitively, Yerma wants these symbols of what exists and what could be to come together in her husband. She wants Juan to swim in the river so that its water may reinforce what is already in his being; she wants him to be exposed to the rain so that its water may stimulate a new vitality in his body. The respective activity and receptivity would construe beneficial rites of passage. Swimming in the river (an immersion) and being sprinkled by the rain (an aspersion) represent two forms of initiation. They also signify both an annihilation (or death) of the old identity by a symbolic drowning in the water of reality and a regeneration (or rebirth) of the life force by a symbolic reemergence through the water of potentiality, as that of the womb. Exposed to these aspects of Water, Juan would no longer be *enjuto*; rather, as Yerma believes, he would be able to impregnate her. Just as lower and upper waters work together to stimulate seeds to take root and thrive, so too would Juan's revitalized semen instigate growth in Yerma's womb.

Victor, the dream man in Yerma's life, needs no such rite of passage. His association with Water is consistent and positive, as evident in

Yerma's encounters with his virility in their youth. This is established in
the first scene when Yerma tells La Vieja of her reactions to Victor's ex-
uberance: "He took me [*me cogió*] by the waist and I couldn't say
anything to him because I couldn't speak. Another time, when I was
fourteen, that same Victor (who was very big) took me [*me cogió*] in
his arms to jump over a water ditch; I was shaking so much that my
teeth rattled" (28). The symbolism of his jumping over the irrigation
ditch with Yerma in his arms clearly associates Victor with Water—his is
the fluid that could flow through the channel that is Yerma, just as
water is intended to flow through the irrigation ditch. Furthermore,
the use of *me cogió* in Yerma's narration of both incidents may refer to
the sexual possession implicit in Victor's embraces if the verb *coger* is
given the prurient interpretation that it has in some areas; to do so
would reinforce the symbolism of Victor's fluid flowing through
Yerma.[9]

Unlike the Earth-Water axis in the Yerma-Juan relationship, the symbolic union of these Elements when Victor carried Yerma over the
irrigation ditch was positive, highly charged, and potentially fruitful.
That these factors are still evident years later is attested by the encounter
of Yerma and Victor in the second scene of the first act. There, having
heard a man singing offstage, Yerma listens intently to his words, but
when the singer emerges, she is surprised to find that it was Victor who
sang so movingly: "How well you sing! I had never heard you. . . . And
what a gushing voice. It's as if a torrent of water fills your mouth" (36).
Her association of Victor with water, and in particular with a torrent of
water emanating from his mouth, reinforces the image that La Vieja had
stated earlier: "We have to have men we like, girl. They have to undo
our tresses and give us water to drink from their own mouths" (29). It
was also La Vieja who had told her that "children come like water"
(27). But it is now too late for Yerma to drink the water from Victor's
mouth. Because she is married, her mores will not permit an illicit dal-
liance even though her need to quench her maternal thirst might be
thought of as justifying the means, particularly when her husband has
"an arid nature" (36), and Victor is water personified. So great is
Victor's affiliation with life-giving Water that the intense silent struggle
between him and Yerma over their natural but impossible love culminates in the crying of a child that only she hears, a child that very close
by "was crying as if drowned" (38). The child that could have been
theirs must forever be drowned in that water that Victor symbolizes.

Since it is impossible for Yerma to become the conduit for his fluid,
the natural flow is impeded. Thus, in the opening scene of the follow-

ing act, Victor's torrent of water is replaced by "the cold brook" (43) in which gossiping women wash the laundry—water having become only a means to a routine end. Significantly, the very first item referred to in their laundering song is "tu cinta," the sash associated with pregnancy (*estar encinta* means to be pregnant), but here it is being washed in the "cold brook" that represents both Victor's inaccessibility and Juan's cold aloofness.

In Yerma's encounters with both men, Water has been dealt with as a masculine Element. However, Water is traditionally, along with Earth, a feminine Element in most ancient religions and mythological systems because of its capacity to bear life. This is encapsulated in a saying attributed to Moses: "Only Earth and Water bring forth a living soul."[10] Earth and Water are also procreative Elements in the *Corpus Hermeticum* and numerous other esoteric writings, where they are frequently interlaced: Water is the fluid of the Earth Mother's womb and the substance of the sea, in both of which life is nurtured; Water is the sustaining life-fluid (sap, milk, blood) of all nature; Water in springs, fountains, and wells is the sacred emanation of the female numen resident in Mother Earth.[11] Seen in the female orientation, the river water and the rain by which Yerma wishes Juan to be bathed are meant to infuse in her husband the feminine Element as a complement to his masculinity. But whereas Juan's present state makes him incomplete, Victor's condition is one of wholeness, for he contains the fecundizing fluid that could engender Yerma's child.

Unable to motivate Juan to perform the ablutions she desires, Yerma must bring the sacred water to him. Her daily task of going to the fountain for water is, therefore, of larger import than that of a mere household task. In her role as water-bearer, Yerma daily re-creates the ancient pagan custom of pilgrimage to places where water rises from the earth; in this case, she goes to the fountain at the center of the village (Water is at the center of life). When Yerma fills the earthen jars with water, the vessels become female symbols of plenitude, for they hold the numinous emanation of the deep, the Water of Mother Earth. Quite in contrast, the same jars filled with the same water become symbols of sterility in the hands of Juan's spinster sisters.

But Yerma's daily rite is to no personal avail because the water in the earthen jars remains only a symbol of potentiality. Earth and Water may be the only Elements capable of bearing life, but in reality the female must be impregnated by the male if procreation is to occur. Yerma may, despairingly, see men negatively—"They are stones that stand before me. But they don't know that if I wanted it, I could become the rushing water that would carry them" (64)—but she cannot conceive without the semen of the male; thus, the water that she says she could become would be as that of the "cold brook," unsuitable for anything more than the menial task of laundering. Similarly, the process of completion cannot occur without the joining of the masculine Elements.

In those cosmogonies that consider it the primary Element, Air is held to be masculine and active because of its association with the "breath of life" (as in the Old Testament, when Yahweh performs the ultimate act of creation by breathing life into Adamic Man), with the dynamics of storms and winds, and with the concept of flight (into the male dominion of a god, such as Saturn or the Gnostic's Unknowable God).[12] Furthermore, Air is the medium through which movement occurs, as well as the Element that surrounds all things in nature, envelopment being suggestive of the male's sexual embrace of the female.

There are many and varied references to Air in the play. In the first scene, Yerma bemoans the irony that even worthless plants are caressed by the pollen-bearing air, flaunting "their yellow flowers in the air" (14), and that "the wind sings in the trees" (15), agitating the numerous leaves. Seeking the same plenitude, Yerma "raises her arms in a beautiful yawn" (15), a ritualistic, deep inhalation of the air that has made nature fertile. Yerma fails, though, to recognize that she cannot be passive like the flowers and trees; in order for her own fruition to take place, she must actively manifest her sexuality. This is the lesson that La Vieja tries to instill in her through example: "I've always been a woman with her skirt in the air" (26); her "free as air" attitude has fulfilled her as a lover, having had two husbands, and as a mother, having given birth to fourteen children. Yerma finds it impossible to follow her lead for she lives by one code and La Vieja "lives on the other side of the river" (26), where the pagan way of life thrives. Nonetheless, when La Vieja tries to end the fruitless conversation, Yerma makes a last effort to arouse the old woman into answering her searching questions—"and you, knowing everything, leave with your mighty airs" (30)—but to no avail.

When, in time, Yerma's unwillingness to change brings increased frustration over her barren condition, Air is cast in a negative role. In a dreamy soliloquy, after an encounter with Juan, Yerma bemoans the fact: "I ask to suffer with child, and the air/offers me dahlias of a sleeping moon" (61). After a later heated conversation with her husband, she alludes to herself as the victim of "the evil airs" (83), comparing her state to that of the good wheat that bad winds have blown to the ground. Ultimately fed up with her lamentations, Juan turns on her and berates her for the fixation "with things that drift in the air" (98), that is, beyond reach.

The most telling function of Air in *Yerma* is described in one of the early stage directions. After a conversation with Victor at the end of the first scene, Yerma "goes to the spot where Victor has stood and breathes deeply, as if inhaling mountain air" (24). This ritualized breathing of air is very distinct from the earlier generalized inhaling of the air that fertilized the flora. It is Victor's specific virility, symbolized in the breath he has exhaled and in the air that has surrounded him, that Yerma inhales so fervently, as if taking into her being the air that touched him could in itself make her fecund.

It is appropriate for Yerma to associate the masculine Element with Victor because he is the embodiment of maleness in the play; as such, Yerma realizes, if too late, that he has always had the potential to satisfy her fully. Such is the power latent in Victor. To breathe in the air of a potent man is, therefore an action full of sexual significance; furthermore, the stage direction refers to Yerma as inhaling "*aire de montaña*", the cold, hard-edged and penetrating mountain air that Nietzsche has termed phallic.[13] This sexual connotation is reinforced by one of the washerwomen, who sings: "And the tents of the wind cover the mountains" (52). The coursing wind covers the mountains just as potent men cover women during coition. Such is the role of any male worthy of the name in the context of the work, as another washerwoman gleefully sings: "Through the air is coming/my husband to sleep" (51). "Sleep" (*dormir*) is the lightly veiled reference to sexual intercourse, and Air is the Element that conveys the male's potency.

But, as with the sterile union of Earth and Water, the joining of Earth and Air is ineffectual here. Yerma may be symbolically united to Victor in their respective associations with Earth and Air, feminine and masculine Elements, but there is nothing to change their inert status into an interaction toward procreation. As in the mixture placed in the athanor, the alchemical furnace, an agent of transmutation must be present; that catalyst is the fourth Element, Fire.

Fire is also a masculine Element. In esoteric traditions it functioned as an agent of purgation (the purifying fire of the ascetic), of transmutation (the alchemical fire that changed base metals into gold), and of regeneration (the consuming fire out of whose ashes rises the Phoenix). Fire also has a traditional association with well-being or ill-health, depending on the fluctuations of body heat between normalcy and extremes beyond or under it. Its relationship to the Sun in ancient religions and mythologies is universal, often being considered as worthy of deification itself as an emanation of the heavenly body.[14] Sometimes, as in Celtic Europe, fire was the focus of major rituals in which bonfires, torches, and hearth fires were lit to propitiate ancestor spirits, to stimulate the fertility of fields, animals, and humans, or to magically attempt to forestall the Sun's departure in winter (as in the festival of Samhaim), or to herald the Sun's return in spring and welcome all its blessings (as in the festival of Beltane). In Christian times many pagan symbols were taken over and adapted, among them Fire, both in its negative aspect (reinterpreted as the fires of Hell) and in its positive aspect (visualized as the inspirational fire-tongues of Pentecost).

Many such symbolic uses of Fire appear in *Yerma*. Passion, of course, is symbolized by this Element, and the lack of passion is an early concern of the protagonist when she addresses her husband: "Now your face is as white as if the sun hadn't shone on it" (12). Juan's face lacks the color of life—the ruddiness of blood—of passion, of fire. He is pale, not having been touched by the fire of the sun's rays, and morose. In contrast, when Yerma sees Victor, she notices a mark on his face that is "like a burn" (37), and he explains that "It must be from the sun." Victor's passionate nature is symbolically evident on his face, as if an inner fire was burning through in an attempt to manifest itself outwardly. Victor possesses the signs of a sanguine personality—the ruddiness, cheerfulness, and hopeful spirit that in early physiology were the outward signs of abundant, healthy blood and an active circulation. Again, Victor epitomizes the potentiality of an Element—in this case, Fire.

Yerma is also involved with the Element, but not in the positive context of Fire's basic symbolism. Her capricious embrace of her husband, "taking the initiative" (14), is not expressive of the fiery passion of sexual desire; rather, it represents her ardent quest to become pregnant, with copulation considered only as the means to that end. Because of Juan's antagonism, Yerma's maternal drive has no proper outlet. Her fixation with fecundization is a flame that sears her very being, as she admits: "I don't think it's fair for me to be consumed here" (20). Yerma's association with Fire, therefore, is as its victim. As one of the washerwomen says of her situation: "With every hour that passes the hell in that house increases. . . . For the greater the dazzle of the household, the greater the burning inside" (47). Yerma would like to exchange that victimizing fire for one that would enliven her womb: "I sense that those who have given birth recently possess something like an inner glow" (76).

The possibility that Yerma has decided to pursue the illicit Fire that would fulfill her maternal need becomes plausible when, at the end of the second act, one of Juan's spinster sisters searches for her with a large candle, itself an ironic symbol of maleness in her hand. When the bells of Victor's flock of sheep are heard offstage, it would appear that Yerma has indeed gone to seek out Victor.

Yerma has not taken that course, however. What she has done is steal away in pursuit of another fire, that of esoteric knowledge. Yerma has taken a direction that, if not illicit, is certainly borderline in terms of her moral stance; she has gone in search of Dolores the Conjurer, the village wisewoman. The ritual to which the hag subjects Yerma in the cemetery is not dramatized but subsequent references to it indicate that it contained a syncretic mixture of pagan incantations ("The laurel petition twice") and Christian orations ("and the prayer to Saint Ann at midday" [79]) that Yerma is to continue daily. The need to placate the pagan gods is emphasized more than the need to pray to the Christian saint. The greater efficacy of the Dionysiac is thus underscored.

After the ritual Yerma explains how the hope of having a child is kept aglow in her being: "Sometimes, when I'm certain that it'll never, never happen . . . something like a surge of fire goes through my feet" (77). Such feelings occur only when she is alone; when in bed with Juan, matters are very different: "When he lies on me, he's doing his duty; yet, his waist is cold against me, as if his body were dead. And I, who have always been disgusted by passionate women, would like to be a mountain of fire at that moment" (78). Juan's lack of passion is pitted against Yerma's flaming desire; the consumption implicit here will be effected in the climax of the tragedy.

Yerma's words unify two of the Elements—Earth (*montaña*) and Fire (*fuego*); earlier, she had similarly brought together in herself Water ("I could be rushing water") and Air ("and breathes deeply, as if inhaling mountain air"). This need to have all the Elements coalesce in her being proceeds from Yerma's view of men as useless in her life and from her subsequent desire to be self-sufficient in the context of childbearing: "Oh, if only I could have them by myself!" (78). But Yerma's androgynous daydream cannot be, and so she must continue to weigh her need against the social and religious constraints that she has chosen to honor. The presence of Victor is ever a reminder of what might have been; it is also a temptation.

First associated with Air and now with Fire, the masculine Elements, Victor combines the maleness requisite to interact with Yerma's femaleness. The natural conjunction Earth-Fire, which the union of Yerma and Victor would represent on one plane, would be enhanced on another level by the conjunction Water-Air, their other axis, thus bringing about that tetralogical unification of the Elements necessary for fecundity. Yerma had longed for this very union in the first scene of the play where, threading a needle (a symbol of sexual integration), she soliloquized in an imagined dialogue with her child:

> O child, what is it you seek from afar?
> White mountains that lie on your breast.
> Let branches wave wildly in sunlight
> and fountains leap high all around! [16]

The soliloquy unifies the Elements—"mountains" (*montes*) and "branches" (*ramas*) are Earth; "wave wildly" (*agiten*) and "leap" (*salten*) are Air; "sunlight" (*al sol*) is Fire; "fountains" (*fuentes*) is Water—but only in Yerma's dream dialogue. In her reality, the integration of the Elements is not actualized because Yerma cannot give herself to the natural course, the Dionysiac, that would end her distress. The Fire of Victor is never permitted to burn in the Earth of Yerma, nor is his Air allowed to permeate her Water.

Having erected the structure and developed the symbolic interaction of the four Elements in the lives of his principal characters, García Lorca proceeds to show the contrasting pattern in the lives of those who follow the pagan, that is, natural, way, by having the Elements cohese in the last scene of the play, where the Dionysiac is dominant in its encounter with the Apollonian. Whereas the pagan substratum of the society in *Yerma* is viewed intermittently during the rest of the play, and primarily through dialogue rather than action, the "Romería" scene is the enactment of a pagan fertility rite within the setting of a Christian pilgrimage. Yearly the barren women of the vicinity tramp to the mountain sanctuary (Earth) of an unnamed male saint to pray for his intercession in attaining the grace of fecundity. After drinking holy water (Water), the women process barefooted, feet in direct contact with the soil (Earth), through the night with the solemnity of candles (Fire) and chants that pervade the air (Air). Each woman brings an offering to the male saint.

Both the trappings of Christianity and the married state of the women are mocked immediately upon the start of the scene in an offstage song that sets the tone and defines the real purpose of the "Romería":

> I couldn't be with you
> when you were a maid,
> but now that you're wed
> I'll take you to bed.

And naked I'll make you,
you pilgrim and wife,
when out of that darkness
the bell tolls midnight. [86]

The lecherous cynicism of the song is reinforced by La Vieja's cutting remarks to the solemn women: "You come to ask the Saint for children and every year more men come alone on this pilgrimage; just what is going on?" (87). Her laughter punctuates the rhetorical question, which, unanswerable, establishes the hypocrisy of the women. The offerings by the women to the male saint will be less efficacious than those to be made to the numerous males present. Another female bystander amplifies the count of males at the "Romería" and in the process reestablishes the symbolic association of men and Water: "A river of single men comes down from those hills" (88). It is this river of unaccompanied males coming down the mountain slopes (Earth) that will fertilize the women, not the grace of God sought through the saint's intercession, for as La Vieja said of God earlier: "When are you going to realize that he doesn't exist?" (30). For the miracle of fecundity to take place, the women must give themselves to that river of men, as do the sierras to the water that runs down their slopes. Yerma had the opportunity to do just that with Victor but realizing that she would not act dishonorably, he has left the village. Under the circumstances, not to take the natural course toward fulfillment—sexual relations outside of the nonproductive marriage—is to court even greater frustration. Such is the case of the woman who "has been coming for eight years without result" (87). For those who only pray, the "Romería" has no miracles and only serves to demonstrate the inefficacy of Christian prayer. Thus, Yerma and her fellow supplicants must help themselves if they are to satisfy their maternal need. The "Romería" provides both the setting and the means for the activity that must precede the fecundity they seek.

The revels of the modern pagan feast are remnants of the Dionysian worship that spread through the Mediterranean world in antiquity. Dionysus was a fecundity or fertility deity and as such was associated with many of nature's manifestations, including the products of the earth, grapes and corn among them; one particularly important affiliation was with the fig tree and its fruit, symbolic of the female. Besides his relationship to flora, Dionysus was also manifested in the form of various fauna, notably the goat and the bull, animals that symbolized his status as a god born with horns.[15] What's more, Dionysus personified the male principle in nature, entering the female (the Earth Goddess) by dying after the harvest, making her fecund again in the spring with his resurrection. Dionysus, therefore, was a fertility deity whose cyclical death and resurrection brought together the male and female principles in a natural bond. The copulation that marked his worship imitated the sacred union and was, therefore, an act of sympathetic magic that sought to ensure the fertility and continuity of all life, even in the face of death.

It is this ancient tradition that permeates the "Romería" scene in *Yerma*. After the staid, funereal Christian procession of the barren women at the opening, the inner scene of the Dionysian love feast bursts upon the senses. Nubile girls enter running, gracefully twirling ribbons symbolic of pregnancy. Their entrance is announced by the ringing of many different animal bells, themselves symbolic of the procreative energy of the fauna. All this commotion heralds the appearance of two unusual figures: "*The noise increases and two traditional masked figures appear. One is male and the other female. They wear large masks. El Macho has the horn of a bull clenched in one hand. Rather than grotesque, they are of great beauty and possess a quality of pure earthiness. La Hembra shakes a neckpiece of large bells.*" (90). The children, with typical Christian ignorance of pagan tradition, misidentify the masks as the Devil and his wife.[16] But El Macho and La Hembra are popular representations of the age-old symbols of fertility associated with Dionysus and his consort, the Earth Goddess; thus, García Lorca identifies them as being "of pure earthiness."

In this powerful dance scene with dialogue, the Elements are finally brought together toward actualization in the women who will follow the pagan way. As La Hembra sings first of the barren wife, her words show that all the Elements are indeed at hand:

> In the river of the mountain
> the mournful wife would bathe.
> Over her body, the spirals
> of water would ascend.
> The sand of the shores
> and the air of morning
> brought fire to her laugh
> and a shiver to her back.
> Oh, how naked was the maiden
> who bathed in the water! [91]

Like Yerma, the woman in the ballad has all the Elements within her reach and needs only the natural inclination to cojoin them in a procreative way within herself. It is during the Dionysian "Romería," which celebrates that most fundamental of human encounters, mating, that the time is propitious for such action; as La Hembra proclaims: "When the night of the revels comes round/I will shred the ruffles of my petticoat" (91). Only by tearing apart her own under-garments (a rending akin to that in the Dionysian rites and, here, symbolic of Yerma's need to shred her oppressive Christian mores) will the woman be able to find the fruition that she seeks. Thus, El Macho sings of her as he moves the phallic horn suggestively: "Poppy and carnation she'll then become/when El Macho spreads his cape on the ground" (92). Just as nature flowers in spring through the rebirth of Dionysus, so will the married woman who gives herself freely to a virile man. Then El Macho, approaching La Hembra with the patent sensuality of the gypsy *tablao flamenco* and the overt sexuality of the Dionysian bacchanale, sings of how the orgiastic spirit must resolve itself into the sexual union of one man and one woman:

> Go by yourself behind the walls
> where the fig trees are densest
> and there bear my earthen body
> till the white whimper of dawn. [92]

The encounter will take place where the fig trees are densest, the fig being symbolic of the vagina ("densest" [*cerradas*] could also be taken literally as closed, thus the closed vagina is to be opened in the sexual union). In that Dionysian setting, El Macho's earthiness (*cuerpo de tierra* could also be earthy body, body made of earth, or body that belongs on or to the earth, as with that of the dying-resurrected Dionysus) will transform the barren wife into a mother. Once again, Fire is the Element that will serve as the agent of transformation. As she undergoes the Dionysian initiation, the woman will respond with the same fiery passion that La Hembra shows in her sexual dance: "Oh, how she glows!/Oh, how she glows,/oh, how the married woman quakes!" (92). The verb *cimbrear* (*cimbrar*) also means to shake, sway, bend, vibrate, tremble, or quiver. The noun *Cimbre* means subterranean passage or gallery. Used with the verb *relumbrar* (to be aglow, to shine brilliantly, to be afire with passion), "*cimbrea*" has an obvious sexual meaning, that of passionate quivering in the woman's innermost recesses during coitus. The power of Dionysus is manifested in the physical union of El Macho, the horn, and La Hembra, the fig.

The act of love simulated in the erotic dance is narrated by El Macho as a numerical extravaganza worthy of the bacchanale's orgiastic ends:

> Seven times she cried out,
> nine she was aroused,
> fifteen times they united
> jasmines with oranges. (93)

The numbers themselves are symbolic of sexuality and fertility. Seven, the most mysterious of numbers to many ancient civilizations and to mystics, in this context is related to the menstrual cycle of women (the lunar month on which a woman's period is based consists of four phases of seven days each); it is the cycle on which all human life depends. The woman's moaning (*gemía*) represents both her sexual pleasure and the pain attendant on her menstruation. Nine is the marker of the transition between simple and compound numbers and is, consequently, the number of initiation (the sexual act is itself initiatory when first performed, as well as integral to entrance in many mystery religions of antiquity); it is also the number of months of the gestation of the human fetus (García Lorca emphasizes pregnancy with *levantaba*, a word descriptive of the pregnant woman's abdomen). Fifteen is a number of marked erotic symbolism and is, therefore, Dionysiac; from it is derived the number six ($15 = 1 + 5 = 6$), the number of harmony (as in the union of *jazmines con naranjas*, with its echo of the earlier "when jasmine perfumes your flesh"). Lastly, fifteen also stands for woman in the role of mother, a state dependent upon her union with man in the sexual act.[17]

All these numbers are odd, which in Numerology represents the male; thus, the seven, nine, and fifteen are male-dominant integers. In the society that García Lorca depicts in *Yerma*, it is the male who instigates the copulative union through his forcefulness and animal lust. El Macho exemplifies this when he states:

> In this pilgrimage
> the male always commands.
> Husbands are bulls.
> The male always commands. [93]

The male principle always rules in a Dionysian rite of fertility. It is *el varón* (he of the rod) who represents both virility and authority, as El Macho does with his symbolic horn. Thus, the sexual reward is for the man who takes the initiative: "And the pilgrim flowers / belong to the one who earns them" (93). The lesson for Juan, who is present at the "Romería" but not participating, is obvious: he must act like a lusty man and arouse Yerma's sensuality. But Juan chooses to remain a bystander while the other males—from the child to the older men—are caught up in the frenzy of the torrid dance, shouting lasciviously to El Macho: "Get her now with the horn! . . . Get her now with the air! . . . Get her now with the branch!" (93). And El Macho replies:

> Come and behold the fire
> of the woman who bathed!
>
> . . . .
>
> Let burn both the dance
> and the glimmering body
> of the chaste married woman. [93–94]

The woman who had bathed alone in the cold water of the stream is now portrayed as being afire, purged of her earlier reluctance by the fire of passion. The Elements, which had been close at hand but inactive, have now been brought together and activated in the crucible of shared passion. It is fitting then that the fertility ritual end with words that herald the procreativity of the woman:

> Heaven has its gardens
> with rosebushes of joy,
> between one bush and another
> is the rose of marvels. [94]

This fruition of nature is symbolic of that achieved by the barren wife who has given herself wholly to the Dionysian spirit. The "rose of marvels" (*rosa de maravilla*) represents the child, the flower that turns a woman into a mother.[18] Such is the reward of those women who follow the pagan way.

What remains is for Yerma to emulate those women. And yet despite the exhilarating rite of passage that she has witnessed, Yerma refuses La Vieja's offer of her virile son as lover. The approaching tragic consequences of her obstinacy are underscored in the ensuing dialogue by the negative use of the Elements as applied to her; Yerma's references to Water are exemplary: "poisoned pond . . . what you offer me is a small glass of well water. . . . ¡*Marchita!*" (95–97). This last word, more negative than her own name, denotes a condition without hope of reversal. In her own eyes, Yerma has withered; lacking the wherewithal for life herself, she sees no possibility of ever giving life to the child she has so ardently desired. Thus, her husband has no further purpose in her life and, when he belatedly tries to make love to her in the sexual spirit of the "Romería," she rebels against his impassioned embrace. Uttering a primal scream, she strangles him with frenzied force until his body lies inert on the ground, as ironic and useless in death as it was to her in life.

Juan's demise is the culmination of a series of rejections. Besides turning his back selfishly on Yerma's maternal hope, Juan has also rejected a natural principle. Like Pentheus in Euripides' *Bacchae*, who went to the Dionysian feast to mock the god and his rites, Juan attended the "Romería" with cynical disdain. Both Pentheus and Juan failed to give Dionysus his due and, as a consequence, each forfeited his life as a sacrificial victim. The death of each represents not only the deletion of the individual in life but, especially, the termination of his line: an irreversible sterilization. Just as Pentheus will be incapable of continuing the male line of his noble family, so Juan can no longer be the potential sire of a child. In contrast with the Dionysian symbolism of the god's death and resurrection, the execution of these males who failed to honor the god will not result in even a symbolic rebirth.

Yerma, of course, has been the most obvious rejecter of Dionysus. In her youth, she accepted as her husband a man she did not love, never revealing that Victor was the one for whom she cared. Consequently, she never wanted Juan as lover, only as the man who could legitimately give her the child she craved. Yet when he failed her, she neither sought out Victor nor La Vieja's son to satisfy her need. Even facing the revels of the god, Yerma stood steadfast against the Dionysian spirit.

In her refusal to cojoin the male and female Elements through the Dionysiac, Yerma becomes her own victim. She has built a series of rejections throughout the play that culminate in this denial. Incapable of loving Juan as a man, she has victimized herself by not allowing him to love her as a woman, thus eschewing the fullness of the marital state. Yerma's rejection of Juan's embrace in the final moments of the play mirrors his rejection of hers earlier; her impulsiveness in that previous encounter, together with her avowed desire to be a "montaña de fuego," can be seen through hindsight as precursor of the deadly "embrace" of the finale. Juan's consumption in the fire of Yerma's manic frustration is more than the victimization of husband by the wife; in killing Juan Yerma has committed the ultimate act against herself—she has exterminated the possibility of ever having a child. With the approaching chorus of the "Romería" as a blatant counterpoint, Yerma rises from the ground and utters the terrible words that denote the end of hope: "I've killed my son; I myself have killed my son!" (101).

Unlike a recognition scene in classical tragedy, Yerma's cognizance of her action does not contain the promise of redemption and renewal. Rather, her words close the play with a finality that indicates a rending of her being akin to the physical dismemberment in the Dionysian rites of antiquity. This rending, as for Agave—who killed her son Pentheus during the bloody feast of the Maenads in *The Bacchae*—is one of the spirit, each woman having to live out her life in the knowledge that she has killed her own son. Such is the punishment meted out by Dionysus to those who have failed to accommodate the libidinal imperative in their lives. Pentheus and Juan may have suffered physical death for mocking the god, but the punishment of Agave and Yerma for their crimes against human nature is that of living death.

The lesson is clear in both Euripides' and García Lorca's tragedies— in the confrontation between the Apollonian and the Dionysian, each must be given its due if the human condition is to attain parity. The lesson from psychoanalysis, derived from clinical experience, is the same; repression of the libido is dangerous to the psyche, for it will force it to recoil upon that which is abnormal in the individual. Therefore, it is fundamental to the well-being of the person that the ego be allowed to function as mediator between the primitive drives of the id and the social and moral demands of the milieu in which that individual lives.

In the symbolism of *Yerma*, the protagonist must cojoin the four cardinal Elements in order to realize her potential as a mother and thus attain the harmonious state of being that results from the integration of the Apollonian and the Dionysiac. But Yerma's excessive adherence to the Christian ethos blocked her pursuit of that end through licit or illicit means. That she recognized the impossibility of that fusion long before the finale was made evident when she exclaimed to Victor, "What a terrible loss not to be able to feel the teachings of the ancients!" (69).

VI

The Devil in the Blood: Genesis and Subversion of the Demonic Pact in the Plays of Alejandro Casona

Demons at times become thoroughly aware of men's dispositions with
the greatest ease, not only from what men say, but also from what they
conceive in their thoughts.
—Saint Augustine, *De divinatione daemonum*

In a brief and little-known article entitled "Don Juan y el Diablo," Alejandro Casona recalls his first encounter with the Don Juan theme, "a little ballad of unknown origin that I used to hear as a child sung by unlettered peasants from my area of Asturias and León."[1] Since the concern here is with other than the donjuanesque, the statement serves primarily as an indicator of a very important root in the works of the Spanish dramatist: the folklore of his region. Just as the large family house of his youth inspired his pseudonym, his native region imbued the child with its traditions, ballads, tales, and popular beliefs (some might say superstitions).[2] Federico Sáinz de Robles, who knew Casona well, indicates how as a child he would crawl inside a hollow tree trunk "to dream of *duendes* and fairies, magicians like Merlin, witches, heaven-sent messengers, dragons out of Hell. . . . He feared none of them; on the contrary, he would have liked to have met them personally in order to take part in their life-or-death, joyous-or-terrifying adventures."[3] So important was this fantasy life that on concluding his studies at Madrid's Escuela de Estudios Superiores del Magisterio in 1926, the young Alejandro Rodríguez Alvarez wrote a thesis entitled "El Diablo en la literatura y en el arte."[4] In a prefatory note to the study, the author explains the subtle but important role of the diabolic as a universal theme: "The Devil incorporates a long series of aesthetic values, which literature has brought together, as well as a concentration of psychological values garnered over centuries and preserved as folkloric elements in legendary songbooks, festivals and popular customs" (*Obras completas*, 2:1267).

Some years later, when he was already signing his works with his pseudonym, Casona united the two venues—the folkloric and the literary—in his dramas, within which can be found a group of four plays wherein the Devil (or one of his cohorts) figures as a character—if not in the crucial role á la Milton, at least as a picturesque entity. He appears in the unexpected setting of Christmas in ¡A Belén, pastores! (To Bethlehem, Shepherds), a five-act play written in 1951 and destined for children's theater; he plays an inferior but notable role as the Archdevil in one of Quevedo's dreams in the 1963 play El caballero de las espuelas de oro (The Knight of the Golden Spurs), and is the principal instigator of the dramatic action in Otra vez el Diablo (1935; The Devil Once More) and La barca sin pescador (1951; The Boat without a Fisherman).

Both Otra vez el Diablo and La barca sin pescador have at their core the pact of a human being with the Devil, each individual hoping to attain through supernatural intervention a desire that is illicit or impossible under normal human circumstances. It is the ancient pagan theme that Christianity continued in the lives of its earliest saints and in the legends surrounding their encounters with the Devil and his wiles.

Casona, who had studied the subject and published his findings, was familiar with Le miracle de Théophile (1261), the French dramatization of the Greek legend surrounding a sixth-century cleric who made a pact with the Devil but later repented, and also with Christopher Marlowe's Tragical History of Doctor Faustus (1588), which was based on the German Das Faustbuch (1587). The French work was the first literary manifestation of the demonic pact, while the English work was its definitive interpretation. Thereafter, the pact with the Devil becomes a stalwart theme in dramatic literature worldwide.

In Spain it is in the Siglo de Oro (the Golden Age, 1492–1680) that the demonic pact reaches its apogee, particularly in the plays of Cervantes, Mira de Amescua, and Calderón de la Barca. Some of their works dealing with this theme, El rufián dichoso (The Fortunate Rogue), El esclavo del Demonio (The Devil's Slave), El mágico prodigioso (The Prodigious Magician), and Las cadenas del demonio (The Devil's Fetters), were well known by the student who wrote "El Diablo en la literatura y el arte."

Nonetheless, in Otra vez el Diablo and La barca sin pescador, Casona achieves a new interpretation of the ancient motif. If in the tradition of the demonic pact the individual is condemned in equitable rigidity (as in the Protestant ethic that informs the work by Marlowe), or is saved through supernatural intervention by the Virgin Mary or some saint (as in the very Catholic emphasis on a merciful God that permeates the works of Calderón), Casona evades both the reformist severity of the former and the deus ex machina propensity of the latter.

Modern dramatist that he was, Casona put in play a third process: the salvation of the individual *through his own means,* exempt from the context of religion. By the mechanism of an autopsychoanalytic process, the individual performs a heroic act of will that eliminates the Devil borne in his blood. It is through the emphasis in the action of the protagonist in desiring to be rid of his encarceration by the Devil and in believing in the integrity of his own person as the fulcrum toward that liberation that Casona eradicates the traditional formula of thunder and lightning that accompany the damnation of Marlowe's Faust to Hell. Casona also eschews the benefic divine intervention that rescues Théophile from the punishment in the nether fires that he has earned in the medieval drama that Rutebeuf conceived. Neither is a solution that could be superimposed on today's human beings, who are no longer haunted by the demons of earlier eras but by the very real horrors of war, famine, pestilence, and other evils that have become the hallmarks of modern life. As evidenced in *Otra vez el Diablo* and *La barca sin pescador,* after Freud and his ideas on psychoanalysis it is no longer necessary, desirable, or even possible to look for the solutions to humanity's problems exclusively in religion (or its negation); it is only in the individual himself that the potential solution to his internal conflicts can be found. This is the venue that Casona explores in his plays.

Thus it is that at the climactic moment in *Otra vez el Diablo* purgation is attained when the protagonist alone overcomes the lust that had been instilled in him by the Devil, with whom he had made a verbal pact. Similarly in *La barca sin pescador,* it is the protagonist who breaks the invisible but powerful "chains" of the Devil through introspection, motivated in part by love, in part by a new social consciousness; astutely, he manages to invalidate the pact, though in writing, accusing the nefarious supernatural agent of having used deceit to obtain his end.

The first of these plays, completed in 1928 but premiered in 1935, marks the introduction of the demonic pact into Casona's dramaturgy. That *Otra vez el Diablo* has been situated in an indefinite time and place—"Antaño" (days of yore), "En un país imaginario" (in an imaginary country)—is indicative that Casona wanted to make the theme universal by removing it from the constraints that a definite time and locale would have placed upon it. In so doing, Casona has underscored the universality of the desire to overcome human limitations, but he has not approached the subject in the traditional way of making a pact with supernatural beings, be they the gods of paganism, the Yahweh of Judaism, or the Devil of Christianity. Recognizing modern man's view of God as alienated from Creation (to some, God is dead to man), Casona has eliminated God from any consideration in the drama of humanity in search for the untenable.

In *Otra vez el Diablo*, the Estudiante (student), who has accepted the Devil as an ally, finally comes to recognize that true personal triumph does not consist in possessing the Infantina (Princess) through infernal aid, but in overcoming his own lust and in exalting his love for her through an act of self-sacrifice. That is why he is able to shout victoriously, "I've killed the Devil! . . . I did it! This very night, right here. He coiled himself around my flesh like a serpent; we struggled until dawn. I was stronger! . . . I disarmed him! . . . I tied his hands! I was stronger, I was stronger! . . . I drowned him (*Gripping his chest*). I drowned him inside here" (*Obras completas*, 1:392–93). In this discovery of an interior power capable of defeating an adversary from the supernatural dimension lies the reason behind Casona's writing of this play. The dramatist wants to exalt the human condition by showing that despite its long inferiority complex before God and his celestial creations (a complex that humanity has had since its expulsion from Eden), human beings possess an internal power that can lead them to triumph over their personal demons. This victory can be achieved without recourse to religion, as Casona posits in *Otra vez el Diablo*.

Similarly in *La barca sin pescador*, it is the individual who must overcome himself in order to defeat the Devil. Ricardo Jordán, a businessman whose personal and professional worlds are coming apart, is approached by the Devil and given a choice between failure and success. The Devil presents a brief but effective summation of Jordán's dual dilemma: "Your lover has deceived you. Your friends have done the same. You're on the brink of being ruined. You might even go to jail. Under the circumstances, I am the only one who can save you" (*Obras completas*, 1:838). The Devil, here named El Caballero de Negro, proffers a type of "salvation" that exacts the highest possible price. But Ricardo Jordán, knowing very well that his previous actions have brought his soul to the brink of the worst possible condition, that of eternal damnation, replies, "I don't think it'll be very difficult for you to damn my soul; the poor thing must be pretty far gone by now" (1:840). In a show of openness rare in the tradition of the demonic pact, El Caballero de Negro speaks frankly: "In point of fact, according to the record I have on it, it's almost ripe enough for picking—for damnation. But it still needs a bit of a push, just one last one" (1:840). But before offering the temptation that he hopes will be that "push," the Devil pronounces the list of past actions that will serve to condemn Ricardo Jordán: "Your list is replete with treachery, spitefulness, scandal and injury. You have never been moved by human suffering, nor have you honored your sworn promises, nor have you respected your neighbor's right to his wife. And insofar as not coveting the goods of others, I think it's best not to mention that. Don't you agree? . . . In short: whatever the law demands that you respect, you have trampled; whatever has been prohibited, you have done" (1:840). Like Don Juan Tenorio, his countryman and predecessor in sociopathic behavior, Ricardo Jordán has transgressed all human considerations, offending everyone and mocking everything. And, like Don Juan, he lacks something to complete his list of crimes, if not the same thing. El Caballero de Negro informs him that "up to this moment, only one Commandment has stopped you in your tracks: 'Thou shalt not kill'" (1:840).

El Caballero de Negro—who "wears a cut-away suit and is holding a briefcase under his arm"—has all the trappings of a petty salesman, but what he offers Jordán is the greatest, most imposing business deal that can be made: the exchange of his soul for success in his personal and business affairs, eternal damnation in exchange for temporal "salvation." According to the Devil, Jordán only needs to make "a simple effort of the will and all your fortune and power will suddenly come back to you. . . . I only require your signature. Here . . . Sign it now!"(1:844). As in *Otra vez el Diablo*, the will is the key to good and evil.

The demonic pact in *La barca sin pescador* is not used in its traditional sense. Casona does not employ the ritual of signing in human blood a parchment made in Hell, as is the practice in the cases of Théophile and Faust. Rather, El Caballero de Negro—adhering to the business format in which Ricardo Jordán functions—presents a document that is not unlike the many commercial transactions the protagonist has signed over the years once a mutually satisfactory agreement has been reached over terms. And, as in business contracts, whose end is to assure that the parties thereto comply with its stipulations, the demonic pact that El Caballero de Negro puts before Ricardo Jordán makes no reference to God nor requires any sacrilegious act as part of the bargain. Jordán's signature on the demonic pact is treated only as another earthly transaction.

If, however, Casona has excluded God and his intervention (as in the congealing of Faust's blood before he signs the pact), the contract signed in ink by Jordán is no less efficacious. At the very moment in which he pens his signature, the "accidental" death of a fisherman takes place in a distant Scandinavian country. Ricardo Jordán believes that he has caused the death through the will to kill manifested in the signing of the demonic pact. He is convinced that he has broken the only Commandment requisite to the damnation of his soul: the "bit of a push" has taken place.

Full of misgivings after having seen its immediate repercussions, Jordán travels to the site of the crime and spends two weeks in the house of the dead fisherman's family. When he and the widow fall in love, Jordán decides to confess his misdeed to her before he departs. Before he can do so, however, her brother-in-law confesses to murdering her husband, with whom he had competed as a fisherman and with whose wife he was enamored.

On hearing the tale, Ricardo Jordán realizes that he has not caused the death of the fisherman after all, but that it was ordained to happen when it did by the man's destiny. He also realizes that the Devil cannot alter natural law and only used his precognition of the death to deceive Jordán. Thus, when El Caballero de Negro reappears to remind him of the business arrangement, Jordán confronts him with his new knowledge. The Devil responds calmly: "I told you that it was only an experiment. . . . I agree that you didn't kill. But you wanted to kill. And for me that's the only valid truth. I also told you that day that the material deed was not important to me. My only world is that of the will. . . . your contract is still valid. Here is the signature agreeing to the crime. When 'the time' comes, I will tender this bill" (*Obras completas*, 1:882–83). But Jordán is no longer the same individual who had pacted with the Devil. He let his impulse guide him to the scene of the "crime" and his instinct draw him to the fisherman's widow. In her he sees both a beautiful woman and the keeper of a wholesome life. He falls in love with her and with an existence unlike any he has known before. He tells El Caballero de Negro of his metamorphosis and of how he intends to keep to the letter of the demonic pact: "Very Well. The best way to liquidate a contract is to comply with its terms. I've promised to kill and I shall kill. . . . The person who signed that piece of paper. . . . I've been struggling with that man since I came here; I'll struggle with him the rest of my life. And on the day when not a trace of what I was is left in my soul, on that day Ricardo Jordán will have murdered Ricardo Jordán" (1:883). Recognizing the new and strong direction in Jordán's willpower, and being true to his own code ("My only world is that of the will"), El Caballero de Negro does something totally out of keeping with the tradition of the demonic pact: he hands over the document to the man who has bested him. Later, Estela, the woman whose love has empowered Jordán, innocently burns a paper that was lying on the table. It is the discarded demonic pact. The egoism that had given rise to that contract is also consumed in the fire of the hearth.

In *Otra vez el Diablo* and *La barca sin pescador*, Casona has expressed his "irresistible propensity for putting himself in contact with the supernatural world, with a transcendent world nurtured by magic."[5] It is out of his childhood meanderings in folklore and from his student research in literature that Casona created the characters, situations, and themes of his dramaturgy.

In the case of the plays here, Casona has added his own creative imagination to the traditional aspects of the pact with the Devil. If in medieval and Renaissance drama the Devil could be foiled through the intercession of the Virgin Mary or a saint, Casona toys with the expectations of reader and public alike by providing a wholly modern twist: the "salvation" of a human being through his own means—the power of the will, that internal force that everyone possesses. What is most original in Casona's treatment of the old theme is that he provides a new definition of "supernatural forces," transforming what was once superstition into a basic aspect of the human condition. We all have demons within ourselves. For Casona, it is the individual himself who must purge the inner evil, as in an existentialist condition in which God has no place, and each human being is responsible for his own actions.

VII
Illuminati, Witches, and Apparitions: The Unholy Plays of Domingo Miras

The will to put Apollo to flight has become more conscious, more lucid daily.
—Domingo Miras, *Primer Acto*

The world that the contemporary Spanish dramatist Domingo Miras (b. 1934) brings to the stage in many of his plays is more often than not peopled by historic and fictitious beings associated in one way or another with occult practices and beliefs, sometimes in their most extreme manifestations. His inspiration for these plays is generally the culture of sixteenth- and seventeenth-century Spain, the nearly-two-hundred-year period known as the Siglo de Oro, in which the new openness to the classical world inspired some to explore astrology, mythology, and occultism, among other esoteric traditions, at the same time that rational concerns occupied others. In the case of the former, the ways of Dionysus were of greater personal import than those of Apollo.

The pursuit of the esoteric is notable in the dramatic works of that era in that numerous plays delve into occult lore, either seriously or employing it for comic effect.[1] Whereas Lope de Vega, Ruiz de Alarcón, Tirso de Molina, and Calderón de la Barca, among many other playwrights, had to work under the watchful eye of Catholicism's Holy Office of the Inquisition, and within the limitations of the stage of their times, Domingo Miras writes in a society recently freed from such external controls and, empowered by the capabilities of modern staging techniques, suffuses his plays with human characters that appear and disappear magically, that fly or levitate, or that participate in other fantastic or grotesque occurrences, as well as with demons and angels who are the agents of the supernatural happenings on stage. Whereas Golden Age playwrights usually dealt with the occult themes in the context of Christianity in order to enhance the doctrines of the Church vis-à-vis pagan and heretical ideas, Miras uses irony and satire to point to the absurdity of society, be it the monarchy, the nobility, or religious institutions. Aberrations in human conduct on all social levels become the focus of Miras in many plays, and the portrayal of moral corruption shows that he mastered the lessons learned in the grotesques painted or etched by Goya and in those plays of Ramón del Valle-Inclán termed *Esperpentos*.[2] Four of Miras's major plays demonstrate his continuity both of the Golden Age's fascination with occult lore and of the later aesthetic of the grotesque as a means of interpreting heterodoxy.

The first case in point is that of *Las alumbradas de la Encarnación Benita* (1979; The Illuminati of the Benedictine Convent of the Incarnation), whose title speaks directly to the occultist theme of the play.[3] Set in Madrid during the seventeenth-century reign of Philip IV (1621–65), the cast of characters includes members of the Church and of the state, with the king himself making an appearance late in the final act. The religious setting and mystique serve as foils to the playwright's vision of superstition, egoism, and corruption at the very core of the Church—its nuns, priests, cardinals, popes—and of credence in the secular sector, including the high-born.

The play opens on a dark chapel. Doña Teresa Valle de la Cerda, prioress of the Benedictine convent, is seen in contemplation of Velázquez's evocative painting of Christ crucified, a gift to the convent by its patron, the Conde Duque de Olivares, not only the most important nobleman after the king but also at one time accused of being a sorcerer.[4] The painting created by Velázquez is one in which the firm-muscled, nearly bloodless figure of Christ belies the suffering he had undergone during his Passion and Crucifixion; it was that tortured image painted and sculpted by so many others that had become the norm.[5] Perhaps because of its semblance of quietude, the Prioress becomes ecstatic as she prays before the dimly lit image when, suddenly

> Her head is raised as if by an invisible thread; thereafter, her torso undergoes the same movement, incorporating itself slowly but energetically; her knees unbend and her whole body rises yet it is impossible to see if her feet have left the ground. But her whole body is in such a precarious equilibrium that it appears as if nothing is supporting her. She is surrounded by an unreal light while the organ can be discerned playing some not quite definable music. . . . In the dark doorway of the cloister appears the radiant habit of Sor Luisa María de Ribero who, upon seeing the levitation of her Prioress, lets out a hysterical scream and runs off shouting. [I, pp. 21–22)

Within the tradition of mysticism, levitation is a welcome physical manifestation of the soul's intense attempts to be with God by rising above the limitations of the body, which is perceived as a "cárcel de barro" (prison of clay). The ecstatic levitation of the Prioress is the first of many supernatural events in the play, and the only one whose occurrence might have its origin in the miraculous workings of God. She is soon seen by her nuns and noble visitors as another gifted Teresa, like her famous namesake Saint Teresa of Avila, the sixteenth-century mystic.

While the Prioress's ecstasy looms large as a sign of God's grace, other events call that into question. Later in the first act the young Sor Luisa María becomes hysterical and falls to the ground; shortly, the stage becomes totally dark and silent. Then, there appears a grotesque apparition: "*In the dark background, a strange and nebulous shape becomes more and more visible in a red glow that seems to come from within it. It is a centaur-like figure whose human part resembles Fray Francisco, his torso naked and two large horns atop a crown of ivy, while his animal half is that of a cow with prominent udder and a huge belly on which are projected great movements and fluxes of blood filled with emanations and gurgling bubbles*" (I, p. 47). And Sor Luisa María, the same nun who saw herself as privileged in witnessing the ecstatic levitation of the Prioress (and who enhanced the details of the event when reporting it throughout the convent), now describes to her companion, Sor Anastasia, the new phantasmagoric vision á la Hieronymus Bosch that is evolving in the belly of the cow: a surreal panorama of unsavory bishops, archbishops, cardinals, and a pope. She adds, "I have had this dream on three consecutive nights and in it you always tell me that the animal is a dragon, that it is the Devil giving birth to the Princes of the Church, and that the process takes a long time, and when they are born, after he has given the world everything he has in him, the dragon will swallow the Earth" (I, pp. 48–49). Described in the vision as "centaur-like," (a true centaur would be part horse), and in the dream as a "dragon" (traditionally, since Sumeria, the primordial adversary— later, the Devil), the half-human, half-beast figure of Fray Francisco symbolizes the negative qualities of discord, animality, and heresy. Yet, under the circumstances in which she describes the shape-shifting creature of her vision and dreams, the impressionable (some might say gullible) Sor Luisa María is declared possessed by the Devil. And the very Fray Francisco whose grotesque image she had seen in the vision, inexplicably carrying the cross, attempts to exorcise her with the Latin phrases of the Roman rite. But when this process fails, he immediately mounts her: "*He sits on the abdomen of Sor Luisa María. . . . He presses his weight against the body of the possessed woman, moving against her, holding her tight with his knees while she tries to contract her muscles at the same time that she screams. . . . He smacks her face several times*" (I, pp. 62–63). His intent now, as earlier when embracing, kissing, and fondling the nuns, is clearly to satisfy his own lasciviousness, and thus his ranting of formulaic prayers in Latin as he stradles the young nun leads not to her liberation but to his own sexual exaltation. The religious rite of exorcism becomes yet one more sacrilege by the wayward friar, who has taken the "galanteo de monjas" (art of paying homage to nuns), so typical of the courtly ways of the era, to sexual extremes. Yet, so prevalent was the practice among his peers that a decree forbidding friars from speaking to nuns could not be published.[6] Ultimately, Fray Francisco's aggression against the nun will contribute to Sor Luisa María's mental deterioration.

The situation evolves into a more complex pattern when, as the raving Sor Luisa María had disclosed during the exorcism, the Prioress and Sor Anastasia also show signs of being possessed.[7] The latter is under the control of Peregrino Raro (Rare or Strange Pilgrim), the strongest of the demons present in the confines of the convent. His revelations through the agency of Sor Anastasia confound Fray Francisco and the nuns: "It is important that you know, and you will, that the Lord God has ordered that a handful of devils be His ambassadors and ministers, possessing the nuns of this convent to make them instruments of His revelations and marvels, which will be edifying and glorious for you, bring fame and honor to this convent, salvation to the world, and punishment for us. . . . we are here by the order and mandate of God in order to accomplish a very important mission, and so exorcisms have no power over us" (I, pp. 68–69). Thereafter, Sor Anastasia makes a series of predictions, among them that the Church will undergo many radical changes in order to conform to the plan of the Almighty. In an attempt to verify God's presence, Fray Francisco gives the possessed Prioress Communion. When he refuses it to Sor Anastasia, however, she "*takes the ciborium from the altar. . . . She gets on her knees at the same time that she puts her mouth into the chalice, devouring all the consecrated hosts that she can*" (I, p. 73). It becomes clear, as the adage has it, that God works in strange ways. He has allocated the most powerful demon to possess not the Prioress, as logic would have it, but Sor Anastasia, who has resented her secondary position in the convent and who now relishes her newfound power over the Prioress, who is posessed by the lesser devil Ganalón. Perhaps none of the predictions is as strange as the series that Sor Anastasia's devil offers subsequently to the friar: "in less than five years Pope Urban will give up his soul to God and he will be succeeded by a Cardinal who will be your close friend since this convent and its principles will have become famous in Rome by that time. And that new Pope will make you a Cardinal. And when he dies, God has ordained that you be crowned Roman Pontiff" (I, p. 74). That the unholy Fray Francisco will become Pope is shocking enough, but the incredible revelations continue to issue from the mouth of the possessed Sor Anastasia: "during your pontificate, the soldiers of Spain . . . will conquer Jerusalem with the aid of the pontifical army, led by the Pope himself—you. . . . Your Throne will not be in Rome because you will transfer the Apostolic See to Jerusalem when the Prioress Doña Teresa Valle dies there as a martyr; you will preside there for thirty-three years, when you will die and everyone will see the Child Jesus emerging from your mouth" (I, pp. 74–75). The Prioress becomes jubilant at the news of her predicted martyrdom (wishful thinking on the part of Sor Anastasia?) while Fray Francisco acts as if he cannot believe that he has been chosen by God to play such a major role in the Church's destiny, but he accepts his future readily enough. As if these marvels were not enough, the first act ends with the convocation of a chorus of nuns brought onstage in a miraculous manner to sing God's praises in the "Te Deum." Shades of the ancient's deus ex machina technique, it would seem, but the agent here is a demonic power now firmly ensconced in the convent.

Strange events continue to occur in the second and final act, which takes place two years later. First, there is the shocking revelation that the proper and religious Countess, who has been barren, is fornicating with the Conde Duque, her husband, in the convent's chapel behind curtains while the nuns and Fray Francisco fill the area with incense and hymns to ensure that God would bless the exotic doings. The sexual ritual has been choreographed by Sor Anastasia's devil to fulfill another part of the earlier prognostication, as she explains to the Conde Duque: "it was Peregrino who spoke through me and decreed that you had to fornicate here with the Countesss so that your son could be born, and that your son would become a Benedictine monk and that he would suffer martyrdom in Jerusalem, and that he would become a great saint" (II, pp. 80–81). The efficacy of the sexual act performed in the chapel remains unknown at the moment, although the belief is strong that the Countess will become pregnant through the grace of God.

Second, it is revealed that the number of possessed nuns in the convent has grown to twenty-two, each having a devil and a guardian angel with a name, and, curiously, that the demon who possesses Sor Luisa María has ordered portraits depicting several guardian angels to be painted. Third, the Prioress has a premonition that the Inquisition will enter the convent and put an end to their privileged existence in the convent: "I have seen or felt in some unknown way the Inquisition enter the convent, the members of the Holy Office throw all our bedding on the floor, search for papers, books, search for anything, overthrow everything, the doors wide open, the house empty" (II, p. 92). Fourth, a case of miraculous translocation is discussed when Sor Luisa María was said by another nun to have been talking outside her cell while in fact she was onstage during that exact time.

Again, at the instigation of a demon, this time the one who possesses Sor Anastasia, the body of a nun dead a year is exhumed to verify that the corpse has been preserved from physical corruption, as the demon claims. When the grotesque process has been completed, however, he is proven wrong. Sor Anastasia exclaims, "Peregrino Raro did say it! I swear to God that he said her body would be uncorrupted! If he lied, all the devils have lied! They are still lying to us!" (II, p. 102). Fray Francisco rationalizes the turn-around as a change in God's will of which Sor Anastasia's devil was not informed. The nuns are momentarily calmed after the shock, but doubts persist. Only Sor Luisa María, however, questions all the promises and prognostications of the demons, shouting that the nuns have allowed themselves to be deluded, but she is held to be deranged. Saint Teresa's comments in *Las Moradas* should be considered in light of the offhanded manner in which Sor Luisa María's accusations are dismissed: "I have known more than one sister, of the highest virtue, who has passed seven or eight days in a state which they thought to be ecstasy. The faintest spiritual exercise completely possesses them in such a fashion that they allow themselves to be paralysed, obsessed by the idea that they must not resist Our Lord. . . . From this, little by little, they die or become idiots, or go mad unless a remedy can be found for them."[8] But is the case of Sor Luisa María an apt example of Saint Teresa's observations? In the situation here, where the tenets of Christian charity have given way to personal gratification and engrandizement, no "remedy" will be attempted for Sor Luisa María, the one voice of open dissent; she is taken to her cell at the instigation of Fray Francisco to wallow in her "madness."

Sor Luisa María's protestations are soon joined by those of another nun. When King Philip IV arrives at the convent in the company of the Conde Duque, he is accosted by Doña Catalina. Throwing herself at his feet, she informs the sovereign that "my heart is bleeding over the many offenses against God and the many heresies that are present in this house. . . . The heresy of the Illuminati, brought here from Seville by Fray Francisco, has infested the convent and made it decay" (II, p. 113). The nun reveals to the king how the friar has kissed many of her companions on the mouth and touched their bodies intimately, and how, prior to his departure to reform other convents along his lines of Christian charity, he had been bathed by his three favorite nuns, the Prioress among them. Then she adds: "My Lord, I have never believed the business of the devils nor that the nuns are possessed, nor anything similar. Those 'devils' are nothing more than mental disorders and wild imaginings. I know this for a fact because the nuns say the same things when the devils speak through them as when they speak for themselves" (II, p. 115). When the king learns from her that she and others have reported Fray Francisco to the Holy Office, he himself refuses to stop the inevitable investigation, reminding the Conde Duque, who pleads with him to restrain the Inquisition, of the devil's failed promises regarding the Countess's pregnancy and the Spanish victory at Maestrich. When pressed to reconsider, the king admits that he himself denounced the perpetrator of the tainted miracles to the highest ecclesiastical authorities prior to visiting the convent, hoping that the Church would ascertain whether the nuns have been contaminated by the heresy of the Illuminati.

The play ends with the arrival of the delegates of the Holy Office, the Inquisitors, who, finding that the heresy has indeed been introduced into the convent by the corrupt Fray Francisco, take the fallen nuns into custody and later capture the fleeing friar. While the prolonged "dark night" of their souls is over, the possibly dire fate of their bodies is to be determined in Toledo beyond the time of the play's action.[9]

Las alumbradas de la Encarnación Benita is one of the works in Domingo Miras's dramatic repertory most concerned with occultism, but his preoccupation with folkloric beliefs, esoteric practices, and the strange personages out of the heterodox history of Spanish religious life is also influential to a greater or lesser degree in other of his major works, among them *De San Pascual a San Gil* (1980; From St. Pascal to St. Giles), based on historical events during the reign of Isabel II, first under the regency of her mother María Cristina and, after coming of age, as the notorious queen of Spain who was besieged on various occasions until deposed in 1868 after a long tenure of immorality, corruption, and despotism.[10]

De San Pascual a San Gil dramatizes the story of that turbulent period of Spanish history, focusing on María Rafaela Quiroga (b. circa 1810), who on taking the veil in 1829 and becoming Sor María

Cipriana del Patrocinio de San José, began to have mystical experiences—ecstasies and revelations—upon which followed the replication
on her body of the wounds of Christ, the stigmata.[11] With these signs of
sanctity came widespread fame and Sor Patrocinio, as she came to be
called, took on the role of prophetess both within her convent and in
the political arena. In the latter, rumors that she had prophecied the
downfall of the very young Isabel at the hands of her uncle Don Carlos,
pretender to the throne, were promulgated by the Queen's enemies.[12]
Sor Patrocinio, therefore, became politicized and was soon under the
scrutiny of the monarchy. Disgraced when discovered to have faked her
wounds and miracles through the duplicity of a friar, she was ordered
into a convent far from Madrid. Yet, years later, she was allowed to
return. Ultimately, she became a fixture at the Isabeline court, as influential over the Queen as Rasputin was to be in the Romanov Russia of
Czar Nicholas II.

The two-part play begins with a long scene wherein, as stated in the
stage directions with the satirical and ironic tone typical of Miras in all
his plays, the occult is introduced: "*As is inevitable in those damnable
nights of Madrid, the Devil prances across the housetops, breaking the roof
tiles of honest people with his sinful cloven hoofs, while he flits about assisted
by his large bat wings*" (I, p. 15). Despite physical appearance and rowdy
manner reminiscent of the medieval period, this Devil, whom Miras
calls El Maligno (the Evil One), wears modern trappings: a morning
coat, no less. He is not wholly cast in a modern image, however, as can
be seen in the stage directions that describe his flight with the nun,
where he acts like the Devil of old: "*his black arms sustain and imprison
the body of Sor Patrocinio, which is modestly covered by a very demure white
nightgown. The Nun of the Stigmata, who has bandages on her hands and
feet, is writhing energetically. The Evil One grasps her with his huge hands,
without any chaste concerns*" (I, p. 15). Although the "flying nun" had
been known as Lolita, the Devil's intimate, prior to entering the religious life, in her reincarnation as Sor Patrocinio she has acquired the
nickname "the Nun of the Stigmata" and attained a position of privilege
and influence. It is this new respectability that prompts her negative attitude toward El Maligno's sexual advances and attempts at her political
realignment .

When the Devil deposits her on the roof of the convent on being
unable to convince her to partake of his physical love or his Progressive
politics, the nun is discovered there by others, who interpret the event
as miraculous.[13] When she verifies it, Sor Patrocinio presents her true
face: "There will be some, no doubt, who will deny it. There will be

some! But this time it will be useless since all my daughters have seen me on this rooftop and are witnesses to the miracle. . . . Dear, dear daughters, have you any idea of who has brought me here? . . . It was the Prince of Darkness! Satan himself!" (I, p. 20).

As in *Las alumbradas de la Encarnación Benita*, demonic intervention in the context of miracles, or what is perceived as miraculous by human beings, is the norm. What's more, because it is deemed acceptable for priests and nuns to traffic with the Devil, his intervention is openly avowed, even with glee. And although the Evil One does not reappear in the rest of the play, his curious relationship with the nun is again brought to the fore when, in a conspiratorial meeting of the most important Progressives, one of them, Olozaga, is identified with him not only by the familiar political slogans he mouths but very especially by physical description—"*He bears a terrifying resemblance to the Evil One who took Sor Patrocinio on her flight across the rooftops*" (I, p. 40)— and by name, when Olozaga is addressed as "don Salustiano," the very name that Sor Patrocinio had called the Devil when flying in his arms. This identification is further underscored when Olozaga speaks warmly to his colleagues of his relationship with Sor Patrocinio before she became a nun: "If only you had known her when she was Lolita!" (I, p. 41). Since evil is imputed to the Progressives by the Queen, her ministers, and religious advisors, it is evident that Sor Patrocinio sees her previous life as Lolita, in which she had an illicit relationship with Olozaga, as evil; in her fanatically religious mind, she has associated Olozaga with the Evil One and turned her lascivious (and sinful) dreams of the politician into the fantasy visualized in the tableaux of flight at the beginning of the play.

Such is Sor Patrocinio's abhorrence of Progressives and their liberal cause that she "appears" in front of the Queen in order to frighten her out of toying with the idea of seating leftist politicians on her governing council. First, she manifests herself "with a great shout":

The Nun of the Stigmata gives credence to her nickname: she has no bandages on her wounds and shows her hands dripping with blood, as well as her bare feet. Likewise, under her headdress, the wounds of the Crown of Thorns drip blood unto her face; the front of her habit is stained by the blood from the wound in her side. Intensely enraptured, her arms are in the form of the cross, her mouth is agape, and her eyes are bulging out of their sockets. The Queen, thunderstruck by the vision, falls to the floor. [I, pp. 34–35]

Then, showing her power over Isabel II, Sor Patrocinio (taken to be an apparition by the Queen), accuses Isabel of having committed the great sin of playing at being a Progressive. Finally, hammering home the accusation, she adds a shattering judgment: "There's no forgiveness. . . . You are condemned! You belong to Satan! . . . You will burn in Hell! You have damned your soul!" (I, p. 35). With the terrified Queen facedown on the floor, not daring to look at Sor Patrocinio, Padre Claret enters. It becomes evident at this moment that the priest is the nun's accomplice in maneuvering the Queen politically and religiously, for when Isabel tells him of Sor Patrocinio's apparition, which she still sees, Padre Claret says, "Where? There's no one here but you and me. . . . I am not so fortunate as to see your Saint. No doubt it is God's will that only Your Majesty have the joy of seeing her beatific vision. *He approaches the Queen and covers her with his cape. He signals Sor Patrocinio to leave*" (I, p. 36). The duplicity of Padre Claret and Sor Patrocinio is clear, as are the spurious deeds that the Queen and other gullible people take for miracles. Like Saint Teresa who castigated the false ecstasy of certain nuns, Saint John of the Cross denounced those who took on the trappings of sanctity in a blatant, self-promoting manner, á la Sor Patrocinio, as well as those who believe too readily in their fraudulent acts: "I can well speak here of certain women who have simulated false stigmata, wounds, crowns of thorns, and images of Christ on their breasts, since in our epoch one has seen all these things. . . . People who are sensible and versed in the spiritual life will take no account of these chimeras; but simple folk think that such things are the mark of sainthood. And because some woman has swooned four times, these people extol her saintliness."[14]

The play has other occult elements as well. In the second part, with the background of the open revolt against the monarchy, the Queen and Sor Patrocinio experience some unnerving events while lying prostrate before two baroque altars:

> *Out of the Penumbra of both altars emerges the Phantom of Democracy, in duplicate form, one belonging to the Queen and the other to the Nun. They are exactly alike, with terrifying masks and enormous black trappings. . . . [They] point to the approaching revolutionary hordes. Out of the dimness emerges a compact group of strange, grotesque beings; they drag themselves along, snakelike, as a surging pile. Their heads are Mongoloid, chameleon- or lizard-like, with bulging eyes and hanging tongues; their webbed hands rest on the floor or on their neighbors' backs; they have the tails of reptiles and the calloused asses of monkeys; they wear the dribbling cloths or hospital shirts of the insane asylum and make noises like those of a swarm of insects mixed with the grunts and squeals of rats. The vanguard, crouching along, advances until becoming visible and stops to see the prostrate women. The*

rest of the army of larvas and succubi remains in the shadows, allowing its presence to be known but without revealing its numbers. [II, p. 66]

The Phantom of Democracy and the grotesque figures, in dialogue with each other in a choral mode reminiscent of Greek tragedy, are manifestations of the fears latent in the subconscious of both women.[15] These repulsive shapes come out of the dark pit of each woman's psyche when the long-feared rebellion of antimonarchical and antireligious forces begins. The terror of Queen and Nun is unabated until another vision— the form of General Serrano, who heads the Queen's troops— announces that the rebellion has been quelled. Only then do the fears subside: *"With weak whimpers, yelps and laments like those of sick little beasts, the horde of insects and reptiles starts to fall back until reentering its black hiding place. The double phantom does not retreat but does become visibly smaller while covering its head with its arms. . . . General Serrano bows ceremoniously, becoming evanescent as he does so. . . . The double phantom has been reduced bit by bit to the smallest possible size"* (II, pp. 70–71). But the plot has yet another disclosure, a literal one: *"Triumphantly removing masks and trappings, the phantoms provoke a happy anagnorisis. . . . The phantom that faced the prostrate Queen reveals itself to be Sor Patrocinio, while that which faced the Nun is the Queen herself"* (II, p. 72). The use of Aristotle's anagnorisis makes possible the revelation that each woman has been haunted by the other. The unexpected discovery of their mutual doppelgänger is felicitous because it has resolved the tension between the Queen and Sor Patrocinio. The entire experience has been an effective psychodrama performed by their projected selves.

But there is one more occult card to be played—death. Having declared that O'Donnell, the former head of the Queen's government, is Satan because he removed his troops from the palace during the revolt, Sor Patrocinio convinces Isabel that he should oversee the executions of the rebels before himself being banished from the court in disgrace. It is then that Death, personified, appears on the scene: *"Death . . . is extremely diligent in gathering the dead and arranging the bodies beautifully on a well-centered, careful heap. . . . Death has finished making the pyramid of corpses"* (II, p. 79). Symbolizing how her rule has been empowered through the bodies of those who have died on her behalf or of those her armies have crushed, Isabel ascends the throne that Death has erected atop the gruesome pyramid; Padre Claret and Sor Patrocinio, meanwhile, take positions at her back—powers behind a throne built on corpses. The scene is an *Esperpento* worthy of Valle-Inclán, not only because it depicts the grotesque result of past abuses of power but also because it promises more of the same through the re-maining years of Isabel's reign.

Domingo Miras also embarks on a personal mission of representing the world of the Spanish witches—or, at least, some of them—from a perspective that he sees as distinct from that of previous dramatists: "Sooner or later, there has to be written the first dramatic work on witches from their own point of view or, at least, from one which ap-proximates theirs to the extent possible. As for me, I feel disposed to attempt it."[16] *Las brujas de Barahona* (1978; The Witches of Barahona) is the result of that commitment. The play takes place during "the last months of 1527 and the first days of 1528," in the small-town environs north of Cuenca. There are fifteen female witches ranging from young to old, a male witch (warlock is an erroneous term), a dancing frog, the Great Goat, Astaroth, two incubi, and two succubi, among other "male and female fiends," all under the scrutiny of the Holy Office of the Inquisition and the administrators of secular justice. The period of the action lies in the century in which Spain and other European na-tions experienced what would be a lengthy crisis of faith during which thousands of individuals would be accused of the great heresy termed "witchcraft" and executed under the mandate of the Holy Office of the Inquisition in Catholic areas or that of a parallel group in Protestant venues.[17] Some have termed the lengthy event, which extended well into the following century, "the Witchcraft Panic."

The two-part play opens with a group of witches at a forest cross-roads tending a cauldron that will serve as the focus of their outdoor ritual. When the cauldron begins to smoke

> *The three women gather around it, cover their faces with their veils, and lose their individuality, becoming three black silhouettes which are exactly alike. They lean over the mouth of the cauldron as if breathing the smoke; their voices are directed to its depths.*
> THE THREE: (*In a rhythmic and solemn tone . . .*)
>   Our Dark Father, our Dark Father,
>   Who art in Hell!
> *Two of them kneel while the third, pridefully standing next to the hanging hen, is unrecognizable now because of the phantasmagorical lighting, the black veil covering her face, and the smoke that distorts her profile. . . .*
> STANDING WITCH: (*Removing a knife from within her clothing*)
>   Let your dead come
>   to this crossroads
>   and drink the blood
>   that I shall spill

from this black hen
whose neck I sever.
[I.1][18]

The incantation and ritual to petition Lucifer for their own future well-being continue as the three witches join hands in a whirling dance around the cauldron until they fall exhausted. But all too soon their satanic revels come to an unexpected end as four men enter the clearing. The two older witches lose themselves quickly in the forest, but La Pajarera is taken prisoner by the local constabulary.

This first scene presents a traditional view of witches and their unsavory doings, not unlike the three hags toiling over their cauldron in Shakespeare's *Macbeth*. But in the following scene, the play's protagonist, Quiteria, gives a different dimension to the ancient craft. First, she is seen effecting a love spell for a young married woman who wants to win another man to her bed. The witch works over the fire reading its ashes. Second, she traces a circle on the floor, entering it with salt and coriander for her long conjuration. It is in the third ritual, taught her by a priest, that her role as a provider of illicit solutions to social needs takes a turn that would surely condemn her to death if discovered by the Inquisition. This ritual involves a huge crucifix the priest gave her and is a very dangerous operation. Quiteria instructs her client on what to do: "Pay close attention to what I'm about to tell you since you have to do it: When I scream as if I'm hurt, you must extinguish those two candles and close your eyes. You musn't look or speak, no matter what you hear. Even if you hear me say things that astound you or if I speak nonsense, keep your mouth shut; if you say anything, even one word, the spell will be broken and can never be repeated again for you, not on this night or any other as long as you live" (II.2). Placing the huge crucifix on the ground, Quiteria removes her shirt and, bare-breasted, kneels by it. Her fingers stroke the figure of Christ as she intones her unholy incantation:

> We must fall in love and make love to each other;
> you're a strong young man who should take me for his own.
> Make a miracle through love, as you've done so very often:
> unnail your two hands and grasp these two breasts.
> Then take me, possess me, as I lie upon you
> the better to kiss you and feel your whole body.
> Ay! Now I have you fully taken,
> now I have you firmly grasped,
> with my arms tightly wrapped,

with my legs wholly seized,
with my lips madly kissed,
with my teeth amply bitten,
with my breasts duly pressed
with my thighs tightly harnessed.
[II.2]

Then, when in the way of sympathetic magic, Quiteria transfers the identity from Christ to the man her client desires, the woman reacts with jealousy and, on berating the witch, breaks the unique spell that would have satisfied her desire. She is sent home with the promise that Quiteria will work other spells for her.

The third scene, wherein Quiteria and her mother Juana despoil the body of a hanged man for his teeth (an important ingredient in their sorcery), returns to the traditional conception of what witches "do" and thus completes the "frame" around the sacrilegious second scene. Subsequently, the mother of a dead child accuses Quiteria of her murder through witchcraft, but when the witch is taken for public punishment it is ostensibly for whoring, since only the Inquisition can judge the practitioners of the heresy called witchcraft. The first part ends with the indifference of the guard as Quiteria is hit by stones thrown amid the produce hurled at her by the citizenry inflamed by the mother of the dead child. Among them is Ansarona, one of her companions in witchery not yet initiated, who is trying to avoid being identified as a witch. Ansarona is not alone in her fear of public recognition as a witch. There are moments when one or another of the witches attests to being an "old Christian," that is, one of untainted blood, and abhors any association with Judaism (with whom deviants from orthodox ways were identified), but their self-serving declarations are more on the basis of lineage than of religious belief. The pose serves to ensure personal safety, or so the witches believe, but when one of them is flogged publicly, as was Quiteria, their confidence is shaken.

In the second part of the play, Quiteria has recovered from her ordeal of a week before and tries to win over Ansarona, the companion who had sided with the crowd against her, offering her the magic ointment that will permit her to fly to the Devil's festival that closes the calendar year.[19] As Quiteria undresses, Ansarona becomes enflamed by her beauty and begins to make love to her. Quiteria reciprocates and undresses her as well, her plan being to force the still-reluctant woman to be anointed for the encounter with the Devil. Having done so, Quiteria has her join her rhythmic incantation to the Devil: "*The beat has become increasingly faster. Ansarona, falters and falls to the ground, remaining immobile. Alone, Quiteria continues the incantation and the clapping, but with demonic speed, as if the fall of her companion had stimulated her. She tosses her hair like a black flag, while her Bacchic dance—primitive and brutal—becomes violently delirious to the accompaniment of percussive sounds*" (II.1). Shortly, Quiteria too is overcome by the heightened rite, swooning in a state akin to ecstasy. The results are seen in the next scene, where the misty night is full of owls, black cats, dead children, and witches flying to the gathering in Barahona—one on the skeleton of a horse, another on a white goat, a third on a broomstick; Ansarona is mounted on a naked devil and Quiteria sits atop a black goat. A pair of women appear riding a broom, the older witch in front while the younger woman holds on fearfully to her hair, as in Goya's famous etching.[20] Later, at the witches' meeting, succubi and incubi are seen astride monstrously large insects as they intone a hymn descriptive of the midnight ritual, which is presided over by the larger-than-life He-Goat.[21] The Devil crowns Quiteria his queen and places her on the throne next to his, probably on his left (the sinister side), although Miras does not stipulate it. The Devil's aide, the androgynous Astaroth-Astarte, functions in the capacity of initiator of Ansarona into the cult of Satan, of confessor of witches who have "sinned," and of celebrant of the Black Mass. The satanic mockery of the Catholic Mass is sung in Latin in Gregorian chant by Astaroth, while at the offertory the witches place gifts in Quiteria's basket and then kiss the He-Goat's anus. Thereafter, the Devil orders that the drinking, eating, and dancing revels begin. In time, devils and witches fornicate, performing all kinds of sexual acts from incest to sodomy to bestiality, all at a frenetic pace, leading to a mass of entwined bodies in orgiastic ecstasy. But the unholy gathering of the Devil, his minions, and his disciples comes to a halt when the cock crows; the approach of dawn brings an end to night, the realm of the Devil.[22]

In the brief scene that follows, Quiteria, Juana (her mother), Ansarona, and the incestuous father and daughter, among others who participated in the Sabbat, are incarcerated as witches and undergo torture during questioning by the local authorities. After this initial process, they learn, they are to be taken before the Holy Office of the Inquisition in Cuenca to be tried as heretics. Quiteria's mother, rather than face the certainty of being burned at the stake, hangs herself. In the final scene, the other witches of Barahona face their dreaded fate. Put in a cart and dragged into the chapel of the convent in which they have been held,

they attack each other verbally, one blaming the other or proclaiming innocence. The witches of Barahona are reduced to sniveling wretches. In
their self-demeaning condition, they are led off to Cuenca amid ominous smoke and the dire sounds of the "Dies Irae," the death chant that
accompanies the Catholic funeral service.

Miras's desire to voice the point of view of the witches of Barahona is
attained only insofar as he understands witchcraft to be a Christian
heresy—indeed, the attitude of the Church. Both Church and laity hold
that women (and men) who perform such unholy rites in honor of the
Devil as the infamous Black Mass are practitioners of Witchcraft and, if
baptized, are liable to prosecution as heretics. As such, they are under
the jurisdiction of the Holy Office of the Inquisition, whose principal
function was to root out heresy in the Catholic world.

In fact, the practices that Miras's witches perform are as those un-
dertaken by Satanists, who hold their deity to be the true, if displaced,
God. Miras, however, attaches pagan concepts to satanic practices, as in
adding to the ancient fertility ritual of the Sabbat the blasphemous
Black Mass; in so doing, he perpetuates the misconception of Witchcraft promoted by the Church and accepted by its credulous laity since
the Middle Ages.

The problem lies in part on the misappropriation of the term *Witchcraft*. Church tradition and popular belief to the contrary, Witchcraft is
not Satanism. The Old Religion, as Witchcraft is sometimes called, was
the pagan worship of deities affiliated with nature, among them the
Goddess (the Female Principle, manifested as the Moon) and the
Horned God (the Male Principle, manifested as the Great Goat or another horned animal), whom cultural historians find to have been
prominent in the belief systems of the Middle East and Europe, Spain
included, in pre-Christian times.[23] In many instances, these deities were
feted in what came to be called the Sabbat, a large ritual often held
outdoors around a bonfire. Sabbats recognized humankind's intimate
relationship with nature and were celebrated in a manner that mim-
icked the fertilization and productivity of land and animals; they also
recognized the need to propitiate earth and sky deities with rituals appropriate to their cults.[24]

While Miras intends his witches' festivity to be a Sabbat, he has
created only a satanic gathering that preempts traditional Witchcraft
practices, making the focus of the event the mockery of the most fundamental Catholic ritual, the Mass. Since Witchcraft has nothing
whatsoever to do with Satanism (except in the public's misconception),
using the term Sabbat not only is inappropriate but militates against

the real perception of what Witchcraft is. Furthermore, there is no Sabbat on December 31, as Quiteria proclaims in *Las brujas de Barahona*; in referring to the Feast of Pope Silvester I as she seduces Ansarona—"A major feast! The Night of Saint Silvester, the witching night at the end of the year!" (II, 1). Perhaps Quiteria's words show a misunderstanding of the calendar of Witchcraft, in which the year's end falls unequivocally on October 31, the major Sabbat, called Samhain.

Miras's witches do not protest the accusation that they are affiliated with the Devil in light of the pre-Christian origin of their faith and practices. Although they proclaim their innocence, even among themselves, they never discuss the real origin of their faith or see themselves as its martyrs. The reason is that Miras either is unaware of that pre-Christian lineage or purposely eschews its mention to serve his own purpose. Had his witches espoused the Old Religion, Quiteria and her cronies would have been seen as martyrs for their faith, not as Christian heretics.

In another treatment of magical operations and persecution, the accused is the titular protagonist of "El doctor Torralba" (1982; Doctor Torralba). In this play Miras deals with the age-old confrontation between reason (represented by science and its practitioners, some of whom were thought to be magicians) and faith (with emotion as its ally). The protagonist, a physician in the court of Cardinal Volterra in Rome, is the same Torralba of whom, according to Don Quijote, people say that "the devils took him flying through the air, . . . the very one who said that while in the air the devil ordered him to open his eyes, and when he did that he saw that he was so extremely close to the body of the Moon that he could have touched it with his hand, and that he did not wish to look at the Earth for fear of fainting."[25] Yet Miras flies in the face of that august tradition when, in the second act, it isn't a devil but the Angel Zaquiel who takes Torralba through the ether toward Rome, both aboard a pole or staff (some would suggest a phallic significance in the conveyance, as in the case of the witch's broomstick).[26] Eyes tightly shut until he dares to behold his elevated state while going through the regions of Earth, Water, Air, and Fire without suffering personal harm, Torralba is able to perceive "the harmony of the Spheres, the first music of Creation" and to express his desire to continue in his exalted position—"If only this flight could last forever!"—a sentiment paralleling that of the mystic during ecstasy.[27]

In the opening scene of "El doctor Torralba," Doctor Morales sings the praises of Eugenio de Torralba, with whom he has just shared the bed and favors of a courtesan: "What wouldn't I give to resemble my lord Torralba and possess his reputation! Such a great and true necromancer, warlock, sorcerer and magician!" (I). And shortly the opportunity presents itself for Torralba to merit the recognition of his esoteric talents. He is willing to conjure the apparition that daily torments the prostitute in her bedroom, but the specter becomes invisible when approached by the doctors; the much-awaited proof of Torralba's magical prowess is frustrated, at least for the time being.

When next on stage, the famed doctor is seen discussing the curious case in the enlightened court of Cardinal Volterra, his patron. Torralba explains his views with a sceptic's perspective: "As for me, my lord, to tell the truth, I am not certain of anything. . . . It could have been that my eyes saw only an image projected by my mind, your Eminence, or simply some concoction out of my delirium. As of now, I can't say for certain; I can't say anything at all. . . . I'm not wholly convinced" (I). Despite his seemingly candid statement, Torralba is lying. Later, when he discusses the matter with Fray Pedro, the Dominican alchemist who was once his mentor, he tells the truth: "I saw a ghost at midnight." The old friar, wishing to help the young thaumaturge, introduces him to another ethereal being, the angel Zaquiel. The benevolent spirit is described as "a kind of androgynous being, an adolescent with a femenine aspect." Zaquiel, Torralba learns, will be his protector and counselor during the rest of his life. Yet again, Torralba doubts what he sees and hears. His is the conflict between faith and reason á la Calderón or, in a more modern context, á la Unamuno. Only when he and Zaquiel fly to Rome to witness the ruthless sacking of the city by the Spanish and German soldiers of Holy Roman Emperor Charles V (Charles I of Spain) does Torralba accept as fact all that his Guardian Angel has revealed to him.

The play also features a judge of the Holy Office of the Inquisition, which was so active in rooting out the heresy of the period in Catholic Europe. Torralba becomes one more victim of its proceedings. Upon returning to Spain, where the intellectual liberalism of the Italian Renaissance had limited application, and certainly not in matters religious, he is exposed to the fanatical Catholicism typical of the Spain of that era. His principal adversary is Don Diego de Zúñiga, who denounces him as a heretic to the inquisitorial tribunal of Cuenca. Having suffered torture, Torralba "confesses" that Zaquiel is a malevolent being and repents the life of "sin" that he has led. Ironically, confession and repentance led to a lesser punishment than the death mandated for those who protested their innocence. Torralba is left destitute of position and possessions. A broken man, he leaves the city like a beggar, abandoning even his Guardian Angel, to seek only peace and forgetfulness in the years left to him.

Domingo Miras is not the only contemporary Spanish playwright who deals with the occult. Alfonso Sastre has treated various aspects of the multifaceted theme in *La sangre y la ceniza* (1965; Blood and Ashes), which concerns the heretic Miguel Servet, and in three brief plays collected in *El escenario diabólico* (1973; The Diabolical Stage): *Frankenstein en Hortaleza* (Frankenstein in Hortaleza), *El vampiro de Uppsala* (The Uppsala Vampire), and *Las cintas magnéticas* (The Magnetic Tapes). For his part, Francisco Nieva uses the Illuminati in *El rayo colgado* (1952; The Hanging Ray), vampires in *Aquelarre y noche roja de Nosferatu* (1961; Witches Sabbat and the Red Night of Nosferatu), as well as witchcraft and magical machinations in *La carroza del plomo candente* (1971; The Carriage of the White-Hot Lead). Agustín Gómez Arcos, in *Diálogos de la herejía* (1964; Dialogues on Heresy), deals with demonic possession and Illuminati. José Martín Recuerda, in *Las conversiones* (1985; The Conversions), dramatizes the persecution of Jews "be they converts (to Catholicism) or not" in fifteenth-century Salamanca and reintroduces to the Spanish theater the genial witch Celestina, along with "*a choir of Jews seated on the floor . . . which has a varied mission: it will sing and dance, become transfigured into Portuguese revolutionaries, change into prostitutes left destitute by the war, into witches and infernal spirits, into ecclesiastical and royal retinues*" (13–14). And Maribel Lázaro, in *Humo de Beleño* (1982; Henbane Smoke), sets her play in Galicia during a period of witchhunting by the Inquisition.

The occultist works of Domingo Miras and other contemporary dramatists do not represent a new line of endeavor in Spanish drama. There exists a fertile panorama of plays from the Middle Ages (*Auto de los Reyes Magos* [The Play of the Magi]), through the Renaissance (*Tragicomedia de Calixto y Melibea* [The Celestina]) and the Golden Age (works by Cervantes, Lope de Vega, Calderón, among many others) to the present, which belong to the thematic lineage of the occult in Spanish drama.[28] This lineage has its apogee in the Siglo de Oro, experiences a decline with the eighteenth-century's Enlightenment, the so-called Age of Reason, and begins a resurgence in the Romanticism of the nineteenth century. But it is in our own century that occultism again finds a rich and abundant life in the theater, from the *Comedias bárbaras* (Savage Plays) of Ramón del Valle-Inclán, passing thereafter into the plays of Alejandro Casona (*Otra vez el Diablo*, *La barca sin pescador*) and Federico García Lorca (*Yerma*), and the plays of Domingo Miras and other contemporary dramatists. Domingo Miras is, therefore, both promulgator and renovator of the theme of occultism, a long and fascinating tradition of the Spanish theater.

VIII

The Orishas of Ifé: African Deities in Cuban and Brazilian Drama

The gist of it is that due to the virginity of the landscape, to its for-
mation, to its ontology, to the splendorous presence of the Indian and
the black man, to the Revelation that constituted its recent discovery, to
the fecund crossbreeding it engendered, America is very far from ex-
hausting its cache of mythologies.

Alejo Carpentier, "Prólogo," *El reino de este mundo.*

Modern Latin American culture is replete with indigenous and foreign
elements, having become an amalgam as a result of Indian, European,
Asian, and African customs, beliefs, and practices that found their way
into daily life in colonial times and have remained a part of the social
construct. The impact of the cultures of Africa in historical times, especially on the Caribbean and Atlantic South America, is a major example of modern diffusion.

The transmission of African lore to the Americas was not the result
of conscious planning but of unforeseen necessity. Religio-mythological
beliefs from many sectors of Africa came to the two continents between
1517 and 1873 with the enslaved peoples, largely the Yoruba-Lucumí
of western Africa, as well as others from the Gulf of Guinea and the
Congo River basin (among them, the Ibo, Efik, Mahi, Fon [Daho-
mey], Bantu, Bambara, Foula, and Wolof).

Despite the adversities suffered by these peoples through their di-
aspora, which brought about a separation in time and space from the
matrix, Africa, as well as through the oppressiveness of those who enslaved them, particularly in regard to the forced suppression of their
religious practices, their culture persevered. Those of their traditions,
often so ancient that their origin may be in prehistory, that survived the
shock of transplantation and the subsequent break in continuity, did so
first through the preservation of their deeply rooted indigenous oral
traditions by the slaves themselves, and, in due course, through the
adoption of written expression for their lyrical and narrative literature,
old and new, both by educated slaves or freedmen and white folklorists.
All kinds of African-rooted traditions came to the fore in the process

and survived alongside the cultures of the several European and indigenous peoples encountered in the New World.

Among the fittest survivors were the Yoruba deities, termed Orisas in Nigeria and its environs, where they are still worshipped.[1] They consist of a vast hierarchy of spiritual entities, who range from the aloof Supreme God (variously, Olofi, Olorum, or Olodumare), through the hermaphroditic creative force (Obatalá, Orisalá, or Oxalá) and the Mother of the Orisas (Yemayá or Iemanjá), to those associated with specific aspects of nature (Sàngo, Shango, Changó, or Xangô for one). These and other ancient gods of the religion the Yoruba call the oldest extant in the world, still figure prominently in the life of the Hispanic Caribbean, where they are called Orishas, and in Brazil, where they are known as Orixás.[2]

The Yoruba belief system in the Hispanic Caribbean and Brazil has not been diminished in its vitality or its impact despite its long separation from its roots. The form of worship in each region, however, has undergone changes that, on the surface, appear to be drastic. Spanish-speaking countries of the Caribbean and some areas of Brazil have come to call the Orishas *Santos* and their worship *Santería,* terms that signify the syncretic nature of the religion in those regions, the result of dressing the African gods in Christian garb in order to circumvent the prohibition of their worship under Spanish and Portuguese Catholic strictures in place since colonial times. Rather than abandon their deities when priest and master demanded conversion to Christianity, the slaves associated the African deities with saints whose colors, accoutrements, functions, or other aspects were the same as or resembled those of the Yoruba Orisas, gender notwithstanding. Thus, in Cuba, for one example, Changó, Orisha of Thunder (the music of the heavens) and Lightning (and, in Cuba, of the drum, the "thundering" instrument), whose weapon is the double-headed axe, became manifest in the figure of Saint Barbara, patron saint of the Spanish artillery who is pictured with a two-edged sword alongside a cannon. So powerful was the association with their Orishas, and so impelling the need to preserve them at all costs, that the slaves throughout the Caribbean and Brazil resorted to this syncretizing process independently, admirably manifesting thereby the functioning of what Jung has termed "the collective unconscious" in the creation of archetypes.

Yet the Yoruba faith persevered largely intact, due to a large degree to the existence of a body of its incantations, tales, recipes, myths, sayings, charms, and pharmacopeia known in Brazil as *Odú* and in Cuba as *Patakín*.³ This traditional African knowledge has been in continuous use through both oral transmission and handwritten communication by the priesthood of the various Afro-Cuban and Afro-Brazilian cults.⁴

In Brazil, the most traditional African-derived religion is known as Candomblé, whose etymon is "Candombé," which is both the name of a slave dance from colonial times and of the ritual drums that accompany it. Candomblé is the Brazilian worship of the Orixás. It is the "purest" of the extant African traditions brought to Brazil by slaves from the area of present-day Nigeria, although it has a syncretic factor, here entwining Portuguese Christian saints and Tupi Indian spirits with the African deities.⁵

Paralleling Santería in many ways, as in such syncretism, but especially in the identities and functions of the deities, whose names vary only in the way they are spelled in Spanish and Portuguese, Candomblé nonetheless has its own individuality in its temples, ritual practices, dress, and chants. There are even Orixás extant in Candomblé with no comparative Orishas in Santería, and vice versa. Yet, the similarities between Santería and Candomblé outweigh their differences.

Most Candomblé worship services and rites of initiation occur in the *Terreiro* (the interior place of worship, literally, "the earth place," although many have wooden or cement floors nowadays). Some ceremonies, however, are at outdoor shrines, sacred trees, waterfalls, or at seaside, depending on the Orixá being honored. All rituals are led by a *Mae do Santo* ("Mother of the Saint," the priestess) or *Pai do Santo* ("Father of the Saint," the priest), or by both in some instances. The closeness of the believers to their deities is demonstrated in the individual's desire to be as one with the Orixá with whom he or she is identified through initiation, wherein the individual manifests external aspects of a particular deity, the Orixá who has become "Master of the Head" of that person and who may "mount" (possess) the body, making the bearer "the horseman of the Orixá." When "mounting" occurs, the possessed acts much as his or her counterpart in Santería, with dancing in a trance state as the principal manifestation of the Orixá's presence. The identification with one's Orixá is fundamental thereafter in one's life, and private liturgies are required to acknowledge the special relationship; most homes have a special shrine with an altar and statuary where offerings are placed and prayers are directed daily.

The elevation of select practitioners to sacerdotal status occurs over a long period of training, during which the *Iawo* (also *Iao* or *Yaõ*, "female novice") or a male initiate experiences both physical and mystical effects until considered to have been accepted by the Orixás through the manifestation of certain signs, which the priest or priestess recognize. Thereafter, three emergence rites are held, at each of which the community recognizes in turn the completion of a different stage in the initiation process, finally welcoming the new *Filha* or *Filho de Santo* ("Daughter" or "Son of the Saint") upon confirmation of the new identity. It is, in effect, a rite of passage.

Such rites and lore, many of them found in the *Odú* and *Patikín* and preserved in manuscript form, have been accessed over the centuries in one way or another by writers, since many of the notebooks (called *libretas* in Cuba) have been printed and sold by unscrupulous individuals or otherwise disseminated outside the cult, as by writers who are informed of privileged information due to their participation as initiates in the religion. Since literature often reflects reality, those works of Hispanic and Lusophone America manifest many motifs from their diverse heritage. The long history and pervasiveness of the Yoruba religion in the daily life of peoples in the Caribbean islands and other sectors of the Americas have given those nations a large measure of their distinctiveness. Such Afrocentricity has prompted numerous writers in many genres to make the legends and worship of the African deities integral to many of their creative works, if often in the syncretic form attained after centuries of exposure and subservience to Western culture and ongoing contact with Amerindian beliefs.[6] This is most evident in Cuba and Brazil. The literatures of the two nations are replete with plays, poems, stories, and novels whose focus, themes, and motifs manifest how integral to Cuban and Brazilian life is the religio-mythological system of belief brought to the Caribbean and parts of South America from Africa. In particular the genre of drama has been notable in this regard. The body of Cuban and Brazilian drama contains many accretions from African sources. Among the most important of these is the presence of the ancient deities from the Yoruba pantheon, the Orisas.

To the *Patikín* and oral continuity is due the prevalence of one particular motif in modern Cuban literature, the legends of the Orishas, as seen in works by such noted writers as the playwrights Carlos Felipe (*Tambores, Réquiem por Yarini*), José R. Brene (*La fiebre negra*), and Pepe Carril (*Shango de Ima*), the poet Nicolás Guillén (*Sóngoro cosongo, West Indies, Ltd.*), the novelists Alejo Carpentier (*El reino de este mundo*), Guillermo Cabrera Infante ("En el gran Ecbó," *Tres tristes tigres*), José Lezama Lima (*Paradiso*), and Severo Sarduy (*De donde son los cantantes*), as well as in tales collected by the late folklorist and short story writer Lydia Cabrera (*Cuentos negros de Cuba, El monte*).

Among the major Orishas whose identities are evident in these and other works are Babalú Ayé, Changó, Echú, Ecué, Eleguá, Obatalá, Ochosi, Ochún, and Yemayá; others in the huge and complex pantheon appear with greater or lesser frequency. In the process of examining the modern literary treatment of these deities, variants in names and roles vis-á-vis the Yoruba-Lucumí Orisas emerge due to differences in the dialects and customs of the peoples brought to the island in the colonial period from those who came in the nineteenth century, as well as in the adoption of the dominant Yoruba system by slaves from other parts of Africa with different languages and cultures. Likewise adding to the complexity is the giving of different names to the same deity according to its manifestations (a process akin to that in Catholicism of giving Mary many titles, as in her litany). In viewing the works of Cuban playwrights, novelists, poets, and writers in other genres, it is impossible to deny that the exalted place of African deities in their writing is due to the importance in Cuban society, both on the island and abroad, of the Yoruba religion.

Several plays are representative of the integration of the Orishas in Cuban literature, both in their African and syncretic guises. In *Shango de Ima* by Pepe Carril, the title signifies the deity's importance as king of Ima, an African land, and as the central character of the plot.[7] Subtitled *A Yoruba Mystery Play* in its English translation, it presents selected segments of Nigerian legends about Shango. The playwright derived his version of the seminal myth in part from the folktale narrated in Rómulo Lachatañeré's *¡¡Oh, mío Yemayá!!*[8] There, the child of Obatala (Father-Mother) and Agayu-Sola (the Ferryman), Shango is raised by three sisters, the Orishas Yemaya (Sea), Oya (Cemetery), and Oshun (Love), his rescuers from a fiery death at the hands of his male progenitor, who refuses to admit his fatherhood. Yemaya then arranges for Shango to marry Obba, a beauty who humbles herself before him and caters to his voracious appetite for food. When she cuts off her ears to provide him additional sustenance in his endless battle with Ogun Arere (Warrior), Shango no longer finds her appealing and deserts her. So great is her sorrow at the loss occasioned by what proved to be a worthless sacrifice, that her endless tears fill ruts in the earth, and she is metamorphosed into the river that bears her name. Now wifeless, Shango's great sexual drive seeks new conquests, and he ravishes Yemaya, Oya, and Oshun, thus incurring the wrath of the powerful Ogun Arere. Shango is then brought to trial before Olofi (Creator, the Sun) for his many transgressions. He is tried and sentenced to undergo recurring cycles of birth and death; in the process, he is destined continuously to seek his origins and to probe for answers about his own nature. In his transgressions, punishment, and search, Shango is Everyman. And his story is, in one respect, a Yoruba version of the fall of man, albeit one told in terms of deific beings.

Carril's play, however, selects out many elements of the traditional tale, opting for those that emphasize Shango de Ima as the victim of circumstances rather than as perpetrator of his own downfall. If he is guilty of any sin in the play, it is of abandoning Obba after her sacrifice. Turning to other women in itself is not seen as sinful. Indeed, the female Orishas with whom he sleeps are not forced into the sexual union; rather, they are willing participants: Oshun gives herself to fortify him for battle, Oya coquettishly allows him to remove her clothing, and his stepmother Yemaya openly welcomes his passion for her. It is Iku (Death) who looks upon all these sexual liaisons with deep-seated hatred because Shango's passion symbolizes Life, and it is Iku who brings Shango to trial. Olofi does not pass judgment in the play, however; the deity, Shango is told, has turned away from creation to remain aloof in his heaven. Like an oracle, Obatala acts in Olofi's stead, but Shango is not cowed by the power she represents. He defends his actions as emanating from the powerful sexual nature given him by Olofi: "This gift of light, of birth, of fire and flame is as it is and if Olofi orders my punishment for using what he himself has given me, then I reject that punishment" (p. 89). Reason cannot intervene where Fate is concerned, however, and Shango is put under the dictum of the eternal cycle of light and darkness, birth and death eternally repeating themselves: Shango as Life, represented by the color red, Iku as Death, represented by white, must forever be entwined. Even the Orishas must fulfill the roles assigned them in what the Greeks termed *heimarmene*, universal Fate.

Changó's role is quite different in José R. Brene's *La fiebre negra* (Black Fever), in which the disappearance of a white girl in 1919 in small-town Cuba is maliciously laid at the feet of the blacks, who are seen as practitioners of black arts by white society. A large group is rounded up and brutally questioned by the police and the military. The circumstantial evidence against them is made to appear conclusive, and a mentally deficient black man is coaxed into verifying the guilt of the *curandero* (healer) and his cohorts in the killing of the girl. The only recourse of the oppressed blacks is to pray to Changó to save them from certain death; their drums are heard incessantly invoking the mighty Orisha, but to no avail. Their fate sealed by an antagonistic society that will not accept their religion as other than witchcraft, many of the black townspeople commit suicide. After the rest have died as a result of torture or execution, the child returns unharmed. The truth of her disappearance is revealed (she had been kidnapped by her natural father, a white), and those involved in the accusations and killings decide to cover up their grave actions. The play ends with the irreversible genocide of the blacks and the contemptible hypocrisy of the whites. Looming even larger is the indifference of the Orisha to the plight of his people, perhaps because he cannot alter their fate, perhaps because their distance from their African roots has weakened the ties to the deity.

Set in 1910, Carlos Felipe's *Réquiem por Yarini* (Requiem for Yarini), depicts vividly Havana's world of prostitution (in which blacks, mulattoes, and whites participate) in terms of Greek tragedy, Spiritism, and the syncretic Yoruba tradition of Cuba. Santería is evident from the beginning, if only in verbal references. Jabá, an aging prostitute who runs Yarini the pimp's brothel, calls upon Changó, in his personification as Saint Barbara, to protect her man from the lures of another prostitute and from physical danger at the hands of powerful political enemies. When Bebo the *santero* enters, her conversation with him regarding Yarini's well-being is full of Lucumí (i.e., Yoruba) references such as the *Potencias* (African Powers, the major Orishas), Santa Bárbara (Changó), Elegguá (Orisha of crossroads, i.e., life and destiny), the *caracoles* (the sixteen cowrie shells used in divination), *despojos* (ritual cleansings), *batá* (the sacred drums, here dedicated to Changó), *bembé* (a religious feast), *enyoró* (chants to the dead), and the like.[9]

Although neither Changó nor Elegguá appears, Jabá's prayers are answered. Bebo, having undergone a trance during which Changó addressed him, returns to inform Yarini of what he must do to ensure the protection of the Orisha against his enemies. Yarini agrees to undergo a *despojo* and follow the instruction to refrain from looking behind him and turning his body around until the next day; this, Bebo tells him, will guarantee his life. But, in a parallel to the classical legend of Orpheus and Eurydice, Yarini breaks the charm when Santiguera (the woman Jabá feared) calls his name repeatedly, and her alluring voice, like that of a siren, makes him turn to face her. Shortly thereafter, Yarini is killed in a duel over the woman. Jabá, who had foreseen it all and had called on Bebo to intercede with Changó, is left to mourn the tragic outcome. The Orisha had indeed answered her prayer, but Yarini had heeded a call stronger than the instinct for the preservation of life itself. Fate, as in Greek tragedy, has proven implacable.

In the expressionistic prologue to Carlos Felipe's *Tambores* (Drums), set in the eighteenth-century Africa of the slavers, anguished groups of blacks from different parts of the continent are brought together to be auctioned to Europeans. Left in shackles to cry in the night, they are unaware of the presence of a beautiful long-haired woman dressed in animal skins. Her name is Africa, and she symbolizes the continent and its peoples. Pained by the suffering she has witnessed, which she calls seven daggers piercing her heart, she cries out to the Great Power for help in freeing her enslaved children, whose moans accompany her chant.[10] Her entreaty is answered first by thunder and lightning, the manifestations of Changó. Suddenly, the grave voice of the Great Power himself addresses her: "Why do you invoke me with the provocative rhythm of your hips, O Africa, you savage mare? Why do you stir the phallic power of the Cosmos to make me aware of your seven daggers? Your children are going to the Antilles, islands in a distant sea. Let them go. Let them take to other lands the vigorous passion of the African sun" (p. 122). To her further pleas, he replies, "There's no recourse to this evil." As in the other plays, it is universal Fate that dictates his words. He offers only the consolation of the African drums, which the slaves will take on their journey. The drums begin to sound as the Great Power speaks. Then, the Soul of the African Drum becomes manifest in a circle of light; it is personified as a strong, seminude young black man seated majestically on a regal ceremonial throne, from which he addresses Africa: "I am the Soul of the African Drum. My voice can sing out in various tones, from those of life to those of death. I will be the ancestral consolation to your children. Their sorrow will be eased by my beat. When the wise hands of a black musician strike my drumhead, I will speak in words of life and hope, of joy and love to whoever will listen. . . . I will go with your children across the sea, to the colonies, through the centuries. They will find their salvation in me, Africa" (pp. 122–23).

The rest of the play is set in pre-Castro Cuba, the year unspecified. The beating of the drums heard in the prologue continues in the background, now associated with the preparations for Carnival that are taking place in the Havana *barrio* where the action is set. Although the plot centers on the frustrations of a young white playwright who has failed to win applause for his stage interpretation of indigenous life (the Siboney culture of Cuba), the presence of a huge drum in the patio of the boarding house insinuates itself into the action. At first absorbed by his grief, Oscar begins to realize that a "musical voice" is speaking to him through the beat of distant drums. Then, the Soul of the African Drum manifests itself, addressing him as it had Africa in the prologue: "I am the Soul of the African Drum. . . . It was centuries ago that I left the jungles and coast of the mysterious and bewitching continent to take on the mission of giving life to the dying. . . . The slave needs me. You, a slave with white skin, need me. I take pity on you because you're young and you're suffering. . . . Place your hands on me; caress my hide; beat out my sounds" (pp. 141–42). Apparently possessed by Changó, the Orisha of the drum in Cuba, Oscar pounds the sacred Batá drum frenetically, eliciting the sounds of Africa. What he has had revealed to him, leading to the playing of Iyá (the name of the largest of the Batá drums), is his salvation, both as man and as artist. Magnanimously, the Soul of the African Drum has taught him to pursue his ideal (the Siboney culture of the island rather than Cuba's African heritage) in order to truly comprehend it. In the last act, Oscar sets out joyously to discover for himself the roots of the indigenous culture he had depicted only superficially before. The play ends with the convulsive rhythms of the conga drums, the spirit of Changó overcoming even the ignorant American tourists who have come to the *barrio* to see "strange things." The point is well taken that the power of the Soul of the African Drum is all pervasive, no matter what the race or the nation or the era.

If *Shango de Ima* enfolds the mythological exclusively, without an application of its outcome to that human society influenced by the Orishas, it is because the origin of the deities, their place in the cosmos, and their symbology are mysteries that must be celebrated in and of themselves. They cannot be comprehended and so are articles of faith to be held as sacred by the believers. Therefore, *Shango de Ima* is to Santería what a Mystery Play such as the Passion is to Catholicism: the representation in human terms of a divine action. It is up to other works to show how the Orishas have been integrated into the daily lives of blacks, mulattoes, and whites alike in Cuba; thus, the plays by José R. Brene and Carlos Felipe present, to a greater or lesser degree, the impact of Changó, in particular, on the hybrid society of the island in different periods of its history.

In Brazil, as in Cuba, there is a large body of literature in many genres whose primary concern is the Afrocentric culture. Among the outstanding authors in this context are the poets Jorge de Lima, Solano Trindade, and João da Cruz e Sousa, and the novelists Lima Barreto and Jorge Amado, the latter internationally known for works written largely about his native state of Bahia, one of the centers of Afroethnicity in Brazil, most particularly the capital city of Salvador, as in *Tenda dos miraclos* (*The Tent of Miracles*).[11]

The body of Brazilian drama also contains many accretions from African sources. Reflecting the beliefs of numerous Brazilians, black and white, in the African gods, there are also many instances in the genre of drama in which the Orixás have central roles. This is seen to a greater or lesser degree in some works of the well-known playwrights Pedro Bloch, Abdias do Nascimento, and Alfredo Dias Gomes, among others.

One particular dramatist who has concentrated on the Candomblé motif is Zora Seljan, a native of the state of Minas Gerais, who has been writing dramas on the Orixás since the 1950s, yet is little known.[12] Her important works in this context include *Historia de Oxalá, Oxum Abaló, Iansan, Mulher de Xangô*, and *A Orelha de Obá*, all of which appeared in print in 1958, and three earlier plays collected under the title *Os Negrinhos: O Negrinho do Pastoreio, Negrinha de Iemanjá*, and *Negrinhos das Folhas*, the latter two dealing specifically with various Orixás, but in a lighter vein.

To begin at the beginning of the story of the relationship of the Orixás, Seljan wrote *Historia de Oxalá*. The play centers on Oxalá, the Father of the Orixás and head of the Yoruba deities, whose Christian counterpart in Bahia is Jesus Christ, under the title Senhor do Bonfim (Our Lord of the Good End), and whose church in Salvador, Bahia, is the center of the Festa do Bonfim, when the faithful come from far and wide to wash the pavement on the Thursday preceding the third Sunday every January.

The steps in front of the church are the setting for the play, all action occurring with the building in the background or before a curtain placed across its façade to provide for African locales such as the courts of Oxalá and Xangô. Seljan's intent is to maintain the relationship between the ancient African god Oxalá and his modern counterpart, Senhor do Bonfim, represented by the church named after him. The entire play evolves on the same set therefore and is further unified through the narration of Baba, the old Bahian woman who also has the role of the Ekede, the nurse in the household of Oxalá, in the play within a play.

Against the advice of the soothsayer Babalorixa, who had cast the cowrie shells and read a warning from the oracle Ifa against Oxalá's intended journey, the old Orixá sets out to bring back Nanan Burucu. Oxalá's wife has deserted him because the two sons he has given her displease her: Omulú, the Orixá of cemeteries, is grotesquely deformed and must wear straw over his entire body, while the handsome Exú, Orixá of sickness and healing, is a devilish trickster.

As Oxalá walks to the court of Xangô, where his wife resides, Exú tricks him three times, leaving him so dirty and dishevelled after the last encounter that he is taken prisoner and beaten by the servants of Xangô, who believe that the distraught old man has stolen their master's steed. Oxalá remains stoically silent throughout the ordeal and does not complain, for the oracle Ifa had warned that he would die if he did so. Oxalá is a victim of fate, but in disobeying the first prohibition, that of taking the journey, he became responsible for his undoing.

Oxalá is not the only victim, however. His treatment by Xangô's servant, although unknown to that Orixá, brings about negative repercussions. During Oxalá's imprisonment, the kingdom of Xangô suffers plagues and privation. Not knowing why but suspecting that the reason lies in Oxalá's disappearance, Xangô and the other Orixás look for him everywhere. When seven years of futile searching have passed, his whereabouts are revealed by the oracle Ifa to Aira, son of Xangô, and the long plight of Oxalá is ended, although his beatings have left him lame. He is cleansed of the accumulated filth he has had to endure, robed in the white color he has chosen for his new life, and restored to his former splendor. The kingdom of Xangô is relieved of the pestilence it had suffered, and it, too, regains its earlier utopian state. Aira insists, however, that justice must be served and sets a trap for Oxalá's tormentors; and so, when the three servants reappear, they have become cripples in atonemement for their brutal acts against the god. Oxalá, however, is not responsible for their punishment since it is Aira who has prepared the trap for the servants, and it is their avarice that brings about their physical impairment.[13]

The aspects of Oxalá's original deific state, his suffering, and restoration to grandeur offered sufficient parallels to the preexistence in Heaven, suffering on Earth, and apotheosis of Jesus Christ to motivate the syncretic identification of the African Orixá and the Christian deity by the slaves in Bahia when they were being catechized by Portuguese priests. Both deities had left their elite abode and undergone a difficult journey on the road of life, a process culminating in the death of the old ways. Oxalá, the Son of Olodumare, and Jesus Christ, the Son of God, experienced human life and attained enlightenment through the rite of passage each endured. Oxalá henceforth will be worshipped in a different manner: "In memory of my suffering all those who dedicate themselves to my worship will from now on wear only white clothes. . . .

To pay homage to my sufferings they must cultivate the virtue of patience. They must suffer with dignity and always forgive their enemies" (p. 46). Christ, too, brought about a new worship of God by man through his example of patient suffering and forgiveness. However, just as the Yoruba religion posits the need for justice, Christianity threatens sinners with the fires of Hell.

Oxalá is tempted three times by Exú and resists using his power to punish the trickster; this motif has its counterpart in the three temptations of Christ by Satan. Furthermore, both deities are "grounded," Oxalá having been soiled by Exú's three demeaning deeds, Christ by having been buried for three days. Each deity in his own way rises above ignominy to triumph over adversity and reign again.

The efficacy of the bonding of the two deities is manifest in the ritual washing of Christ's church in Bahia during the Festa do Bonfim, a ritual that commemorates the cleansing of Oxalá after his ordeal and the ministrations to the body of Christ after his crucifixion and death. The cleansing symbolizes the resurgence of each deity.

There are other cultural and religious traditions at work in the play alongside the African and the Christian. For one, the emphasis on destiny is akin to that in the theater of ancient Greece, wherein gods and mortals alike are subject to the mandates of Fate. Here, as there, can be seen the participatory culpability of the protagonist Oxalá who, not heeding the warning of the oracle, causes all the ills that befall him and those around him, as in the deeds of Oedipus and the subsequent mishaps at Thebes in Sophocles' tragedy. Too, as with the seer Tiresias, is the oracle Ifa who opens the eyes of the sufferers to the cause behind the punishment. Unlike *Oedipus the King*, however, the *Historia de Oxalá* has an ending that conveys the message that "God is in His Heaven and all is right with the World." It is an optimism based on the security of the divine order and thus distinct from that of Greek tragedy, which celebrates the restorative power of the human will.

Another touchstone is the Old Testament, for the seven years of suffering that Xangô's kingdom undergoes may be seen as analogous to the biblical blight of the seven years of famine. Furthermore, Oxalá's downtrodden state is caused by the demonic Exú, while that of Job, his parallel victim in the Bible, is instigated by Satan; both the Yoruba and Old Testament protagonists suffer loss and pain patiently, ultimately to be recompensed if not wholly restored to their previous state of well-being.

The complex system of belief known as Gnosticism presents still other parallels with the Yoruba faith and its Brazilian extension. The supreme deity of the Gnostic speculation is variously called the Unknown God, the God of Light, or the Alien God, but whatever the descriptive phrase, he is aloof from Creation, which was the act of the lesser deity, the Demiurge, who in turn proceeded from Sophia, the feminine emanation of God. Candomblé and its African progenitor also possess an alien, aloof deity who, although he created the Orixás, does not concern himself with the affairs of mankind; he is Olodumare. Oxalá is akin to the Demiurge in his role as maker, as his statement to his son Oxaguian in Seljan's play makes evident: "I have been charged with the task of procreation. Olodumare—the Lord—sculptures men and women in their roughest form. I improve on them. I give them their eyes, their noses, their mouths, their arms, their hair, so that Olodumare can finish up by breathing into them the fire of life. Thus I have the privilege of molding my own sons. . . . I made you after my own image and likeness" (p. 5). Additionally, Iemanjá, who is the Mother of the Orixás, parallels the Gnostic Sophia, the "mother" of the Demiurge. The Orixás fulfill functions similar to those of the Archons, rulers of the ethereal spheres in the Valentinian system of Gnostic belief.[14]

These relationships demonstrate yet again the similarity of human beliefs about the supernatural order. Be it coincidental or derivative, the Yoruba view of theogony is as complex and sophisticated as its counterparts in Egypt and Greece, among others. Consequently, in Seljan's view, the legends of many of the Orixás merit separate treatment, as her other plays make clear.

Oxum Abalô tells the story of the Yoruba Goddess of Beauty.[15] It is Exú, here in his role as messenger of the gods, who opens the dialogue by announcing the arrival of Oxosse, the Orixá of the Hunt. He enters dancing in the company of two *caboclos,* indigenous Indian spirits who serve him, but he is soon reprimanded by his consort for arriving late and not remembering their anniversary.[16] Oxosse blames Xangô, his brother, who, having just returned from a war, kept him with his tales of derring-do. Oxum is angered further when told that the Orixá of thunder has been invited to dinner without her previous consent. Oxum plots with the mischievous Exú to keep Oxosse away from the feast as punishment for his oversights.

As befits his stature among the Orixás, Xangô is greeted with great pomp and circumstance by Oxum. Song and dance accompany the regal repast, which is served without Oxosse, who, bedeviled by Exú, has failed to return with the lamb for the feast. But losing face is not the real punishment for Oxosse—that comes at the hands of his brother, who is so taken with Oxum's fabled beauty that after dinner he asks to sleep on the floor next to Oxum's bed. Oxum takes him in, unwilling to deny her handsome, exalted guest the unusual hospitality he craves.

Subsequently, Oxum is seen dancing before mirrors in the palace of Xangô; she has become a consort of the Orixá because Oxosse threw her out on finding his brother asleep next to her bed. Nonetheless, Oxum plots to free herself of the insatiable Xangô by having her innocent sister Iansan, Orixá of the winds, unwittingly tempt him with her youthful charms. Meanwhile, the Muçurumins, recently defeated by Xangô, begin a new war against the Orixás. The enmity between them noth-withstanding, Oxosse refuses to side with Xangô's enemies and remains neutral despite Oxumarê's pleas, but Ogum, the Orixá of Iron and War, sides with his brother Xangô, as do the Orixás Iemanjá, Nanan Burucu, and Omulú. Oxum, however, refuses to leave the palace to join Xangô in the battlefield, but Iansan accompanies the Orixá to war, as does Obá, his oldest consort.

The division of the Orixás continues to motivate the action. Exú has come to detest Oxum because the Supreme Deity has granted her the messenger's services whenever she needs to divine the future, a role he had previously given up to Ifa. Oxum then learns of Xangô's scorn over her abandonment and his admiration of Iansan for her devotion to him. Needless to say, Oxum has also earned the opprobrium of Oxosse over her adulterous behavior.

The closing of the rift begins when Oxosse is confronted by the Eguns, the ancestor spirits of the deities, and is convinced by the weight of family tradition to aid his brother Xangô on behalf of the cause of all Orixás. As the war then turns in favor of the Yoruba deities, Iansan begs Xangô not to repudiate her sister, but he is adamant that Oxum must be made an example of upon his return. Unknown to Xangô, however, Fate has led Oxum to participate in the war in order to avoid capture by the Muçurumins. She and her women have left Xangô's palace, which they emptied of provisions to deprive the enemy of food and then en-tered the forest, where Oxum turned herself into a river. From its waters she plotted the defeat of the pursuing enemy. The famished soldiers are poisoned by the food Oxum has had placed in open view, and she re-joices with her women in having helped win the war.

Music and dancing greet Xangô's triumphant return to court; Obá and Iansan are crowned by the Eguns, while the other Orixás—Ogun, Nanan, Oxosse, Iemanjá, Omolu, and Oxumarê—each enter to the re-sounding *atabaques*, the ritual drums. Exú, who again favors Oxum in return for his freedom from his subservient role, enters too, but only to tell Xangô that the Eguns consider his repudiation of Oxum a grave injustice in light of her brave part in the war. Informed of her valor, Xangô relents. When Oxum returns, she too is crowned by the Eguns to the beating of the drums, receiving the greatest acclamation of all.

The tale of Oxum is one of heroic actions and petty quarrels in which the principal characters seem more like the human beings they rule than the exalted gods the people venerate. But such has always been the way of ancient narratives of the deeds of gods and heroes, from Babylonian, Egyptian, Hindu, and Greek myths, through Roman, Celtic, Teutonic, and Nordic legends. As in those and other traditions, the supernatural world is an integral part of life, with the commingling of living gods, their ancestor spirits, and the humans who render them worship. Consequently, the events that take place on the supernatural level have a direct impact on the natural order.

Oxum, like Oxalá in *Historia de Oxalá,* has had her restoration and apotheosis. And like Seljan's previous play, *Oxum Abalô* posits that the once chaotic realm of the Orixás is again in a utopian state of order. Implied in this conclusion is that the rest of life, that is, the world of human beings, can now carry on without concern. Even the Orixás cannot exist forever in a state devoid of conflict, however. As in the case of their human worshippers, the natures and roles of the gods demand activity; often this creates tension and confrontation. This is even more evident in the next play in the sequence, *Iansan, Mulher de Xangô,* in which the story of Xangô's household continues with Oxum's sister as the focal figure.

The play *Iansan, Mulher de Xangô,* opens with the revelation by Carneiro, a mythological ram, that the council of the Orixás has been convened in the palace of Oxalá, always a momentous event. Babalorixá the soothsayer berates his daughters, Iaô and Ebomim, for listening to the gossip and threatens Carneiro, who hides nearby. Soon Exú and his consort Bombonjira enter in pursuit of Martim-pescador, a messenger of the Orixás who has incurred their wrath, supposedly for revealing the secrets of Oxalá's household.[17] Martim avoids capture by crossing "a fronteira da vida" (the frontier of life). Now in the human world, he tells his woes to Carneiro and then to Babalorixá, the latter divining Iansan's instructions that the messenger protect himself by staying in his own house. When Martim leaves, Iansan materializes, brandishing her sword and ordering the winds to level everything in the world because mankind has defamed her. She has been denied revenge by the council of the Orixás, and now she takes matters into her own hands with wind, lightning, fire, and the dead—the Eguns—at her service.

Iansan has erred by protecting Martim from the ire of Xangô and by disobeying the council's mandate. Carneiro, who covets the position of messenger, tells Iaô and Ebomim that he would betray both Martim and Iansan if Xangô wished it, when, suddenly, the thunder of the Orixá is heard. Xangô appears, and Carneiro wins the god's approval, but a world-weary Xangô muses on Fate: "We are mere details in the passage of time. Men, insects and gods, we live together, for without roots there is no trunk, and without a trunk fruit cannot ripen" (p. 142). As Xangô sleeps, Egum, an otherwordly ancestor spirit, enters to thank the frightened daughters of Babalorixá for their defense of Iansan against the defamations of Carneiro. He shows them the suffering of humanity and the inability of other Orixás to countermand Iansan. Oxalá enters next, seeking a way to solve the crisis brought about by his daughter's ire without offending her further; he calls her, and she appears. When she hears his advice to win over Xangô through wifely wiles rather than through confrontation, Iansan accedes to his wise counsel and proceeds to where Xangô sleeps to put good thoughts of her into his dreams, symbolized by the flower petals she strews over him.

Iansan then orders Babalorixá to remember the story she is about to tell and to communicate it to humanity in remembrance of her. There follows a play within a play in which Babalorixá and his daughters act as Muslims who refuse to acknowledge the power of Xangô. The voice of Iansan then narrates her relations with the Orixá, the marriage of her lightning and his thunder, and how their unified power overcame the reluctance of Allah's followers to acknowledge the Orixás as their true gods.

The narrative over, Iansan and Xangô are reunited. The goddess tells her husband how humans no longer worship her as before, giving her due to other Orixás. But Xangô reveals that in the future the River Niger will be revered as the tears she has shed. Consoled and emboldened, Iansan makes a final request of Xangô: that he forgive Martim. The Orixá becomes indignant, however, and the happiness Iansan had just experienced is sundered by his ire. Carneiro, now a messenger of the Orixás, pursues Martim on behalf of Xangô. Believing Carneiro to be his friend still, Martim allows him to enter his sanctum, thus breaching the protection of Iansan. Carneiro tricks him into a basket and drags his captive away, but Iansan frees Martim without Carneiro's awareness.

Tired of cowering in his house, Martim decides to "live" and calls everyone to a feast. Meanwhile, Carneiro opens the basket before Xangô only to find Iansan's sword inside. Xangô allows Iansan to punish Carneiro by cursing him with all the evil he had desired for Martim for having been a traitor to friendship and an opportunistic liar. Carneiro is to be sacrificed to Xangô and his species is thereafter to become the sacrificial victim of the Orixá. In his magnitude, Xangô pardons Martim while Iansan orders her followers never to eat mutton, nor sit on or wear anything made of lambskin.

Iansan, Mulher de Xangô does more than narrate the story of the goddess of the wind who is also the River Niger. It unites her power and that of her consort, Xangô, into an invincible force, which brings justice and unification into the realm of the Orixás and into the world of humanity. The first is achieved through punishment and pardon, the second through the abolition of the worship of Allah. Seljan has wedded legend and history in tying the Yoruba tale of Iansan and Xangô to the reality of the invasion of Islam. While in fact the "new" religion replaced the polytheism of the Orixás with the monotheism of Allah, Seljan's deities are shown to be victorious in reestablishing the traditional worship of the Yoruba gods. And she is right, if not in the context of Africa, certainly in that of Brazil.

A Orelha de Obá again brings together Xangô, Oxum, and Iansan, but the play is structured around the story of Obá, the first consort of the Orixá of thunder, who cut off her own ear. One version of the story is that told in Carril's *Shango de Ima,* in which Obba is moved to the dire action by Shango's need for sustenance in his struggle with Ogun Arere. There, hers is a study of self-sacrifice for love and subsequent rejection by the beloved. Seljan's play has a different perspective, and is in three parts. In the first, the chorus asks who cut off Obá's ear as they see Iansan, but she denies the implied accusation, despite the fact that she is named "in the books" as responsible for tricking her sister into self-mutilation. Seljan does not pursue this accepted version, choosing instead to posit others.

In the scenes that follow Seljan develops two other stories of how Obá lost her ear. In one, Obá's curiosity about Oxum's success with their shared husband leads her to seek her sister's secret. Oxum, tired of Obá's insistence, lets her believe that she has put a special ingredient in his food: her right ear. Since Oxum is wearing a turban that hides her ears, Obá thinks that her conclusion is true and exits overjoyed. When Xangô is in the arms of Oxum, Obá rushes in, blood seeping through the bandage on her head, and offers her husband her right ear as food, but the Orixá, shocked, scorns her for spoiling his appetite and sends her out of his sight. Obá's fury is not directed at Xangô but at Oxum, whom she pursues. Xangô's ire, manifested in thunder, puts an end to the battle between the two wives.

When the fickle chorus now shouts that Oxúm is guilty, Obá's voice is heard offstage denying the story. The next version of the incident then begins to unfold as Obá enters in her role as leader of her troops poised for battle against the Muçurumins, who threaten Xangô's realm. When she steps in to settle an armed argument between several of her soldiers, one of them defies her and manages to cut off her ear before he is vanquished by the Orixá. All-knowing Xangô sends for Obá and gives the messenger a balm for his consort's ear. On arriving at Xangô's court, Obá's ear has grown back miraculously.

Seljan's play puts aside the accepted version of the story, the one blaming Iansan for Obá's plight, in favor of the two lesser-known versions. The episode with Oxum, which substitutes her for the Iansan of the original legend, makes Obá appear in a bad light—a goddess who is gullible. The last version, however, presents Obá, the Orixá of war, as a soldier who is wounded honorably. Obá emerges not only with her honor upheld but also with her ear restored; furthermore, she merits the admiration and love of Xangô. The story that puts Obá in a superior light has been saved for last, the better to serve the deity.

Zora Seljan has written plays that transcend national or continental boundaries, masterfully interpreting through dialogue, music, and dance the age-old Yoruba religion in terms of its germinal myths. Like Carril's *Shango de Ima,* Seljan's *Historia de Oxalá, Oxum Abalô, Iansan, Mulher de Xangô,* and *A Orelha de Obá* tell the stories of the Yoruba deities from the perspective of the Orixás themselves. Yet the tales—myths or legends—come across in terms that followers of the Candomblé can readily understand, for as Seljan says of the Yoruba deities in the stage directions of *Iansan,* "They exist in the imagination of the people, but the people do not know where their myths originated" (p. 114). Thus the passions, pettiness, and other human traits that the Orixás manifest in their dealings with each other, as well as the settings for their actions, exist in the stories in human terms comprehensible to all. In the process of personifying in the Orixás the forces of nature, the Yoruba religion is again shown to be similar to other ancient belief systems, where the gods have human form and their actions replicate those of the followers of their cults, if often enlarged to communicate the supernatural context in which ritual practices and beliefs originated.

Abdias do Nascimento's *Sortilégio: Mistério Negro,* on the other hand, has a modern-day setting and human characters. Belief in Macumba-Candomblé is not only a vital aspect of the society in which the play is set but also an important, if secreted, part of the psychological makeup of its protagonist. *Sortilegio* is a drama about human beings, not about the gods, but the belief in the Yoruba deities is the dominant element in the play. Even if invisible, the Orixás are almost palpable therein.

The play opens at night in an ominous forest with three *Filhas de Santo* ("Daughters of the Saint") completing a ritual *despacho,* an offering of a black cock to Exú. Afterward they talk of Exú, lord of the forest and the crossroads, who will appear at midnight, his hour, to claim Dr. Emanuel, a black man who married the white woman Margarida, whom he has assassinated in a moment of blind passion. When Emanuel enters, driven into the forest by the pursuit of the police, he mocks the "ignorance" of the blacks who believe in the Orixás. To him, Exú is not a god out of Africa but another name for the Christian Devil, whose power can be countermanded by God. Raised a Catholic and well educated, Emanuel has sought to live like a middle-class white man. All too soon, however, innate fears begin to surface in the strange night of Exú. Emanuel beholds apparitions from his past who disturb his thoughts until he begins to doubt his senses and reason. His former lover, the prostitute Efigênia, appears and disappears, taunting him with memories of past encounters and accusations of his abandonment of her (and his heritage) for a white woman. Margarida also materializes before his eyes but remains silent during most of her brief appearances. The air is filled with *pontos,* ritual songs associated with different Orixás, that mark the envelopment of Emanuel's psyche by the mantle of the Yoruba deities. In the end, recognizing his multifaceted guilt and seeing that his prayers to the Christian God are unanswered, Emanuel abandons his foster faith and gives himself to his traditional religion. He accepts the Fate that he knows intuitively awaits him at the hands of Exú when he enters his *pegí* (shrine) and vests himself in the colors of the Orixá. The spear of the deity in hand, his voice has a triumphant note in it as he proclaims, "I killed Margarida. I am a free black" (p. 197). And so he is executed by the three Filhas de Santo, who surround him and pierce him with the spear of Exú. The final *ponto de Jubiabá* is a chant of death.

Nascimento's play has parallels in works outside the Yoruba culture.[18] The most pertinent, however, is in the context of ancient Greece. The three Filhas de Santo function like the chorus in Greek tragedy, annotating the present action, revealing the past, hinting at the tragic future of the protagonist. Like Oedipus, Emanuel at first fails to recognize his own culpability in the death of Margarida and in the abandonment of his traditional culture; he cannot understand why Fate has brought him to his low state. Although Oedipus puts out his eyes when he discovers the truth, he has opted for life; Emanuel has his eyes opened by his experience in the forest but has opted for death. Each has sought freedom from his demons by his choice. Emanuel's lover Efigênia bears the name of the daughter of Agamemnon and Clytemnestra who became a priestess of Artemis and saved her brother Orestes from death but she could not save Emanuel from the charge of murdering his wife because she instigated his action out of jealousy; nor could she assuage his culpability in abandoning his roots. In her taunts, she pursues him like a Fury or a Harpie. No doubt there is a syncretic bonding in this literary context as on the religious level.

The plays analyzed here are but examples of a larger current of African religious influence in Cuban and Brazilian literature. One of several genres in which the Orishas and other religious motifs appear, theater (i.e., drama in performance) permits the figures, gestures, and voices of the African deities to become manifest to the spectator with some of the awesome power they have for the faithful of the Yoruba religion in their intimacy with the deities during the state of possession, be they followers of Caribbean Santería or Brazilian Candomblé.

It is obvious that when Changó, Oxalá, Exú, Oxum, Oxosse, and other Yoruba gods perform roles in these plays they are central to the action, but even when they are not visible, their very "presence" as a crucial point of reference makes them central to the development of the plot, to the understanding of the psychology of the characters, and to the quality of life of those individuals in the works who hold the Yoruba beliefs termed Santería in Cuba and Candomblé, Macumba, Quimbanda, Umbanda, or Batuque in Brazil.

PART THREE

Bibliography

IX
Drama of the Occult:
A Bibliography of Spanish and
Latin American Plays

The intent in this bibliography is to list as many as possible of the works of Hispanic drama through the twentieth century that focus on one or more of the numerous manifestations of what is termed occultism: alchemy, angelology, asceticism, astrology, demonolatry, magic, divination, ecstasy, magic, necromancy, possession, santería, seances, voudoun, witchcraft, and the like, whether feigned or "real." The first section, subdivided into Spain and Latin America, lists playwrights alphabetically with their dates or century. Whenever known, the year of performance or publication is given after the title, as is information on the subject matter of the play. The second section groups the plays under headings referring to characters and motifs that recur with some frequency.

Among the numerous sources for this bibliography are: Germán Bleiberg and Julián Marías, eds., *Diccionario de literatura española* (Madrid: Editorial Revista de Occidente, 1953); Mario N. Pavia, *Drama of the Siglo de Oro* (New York: Hispanic Institute, 1959); Robert O'Brien, *Spanish Plays in English Translation: An Annotated Bibliography* (New York: American Educational Theatre Association–Las Américas, 1963); S. Griswold Morley and Courtney Bruerton, *Cronología de las Comedias de Lope de Vega* (Madrid: Gredos, 1968); *Catálogo bibliográfico y biográfico del teatro antiguo español* (Madrid: Gredos, 1969); Angel L. Cilvetti, *El demonio en el teatro de Calderón* (Valencia: Albatros Ediciones, 1977); Henryk Ziomek, *A History of Spanish Golden Age Drama* (Lexington: University Press of Kentucky, 1984); Javier Huerta Calvo et al., eds., *El teatro español a fines del siglo XVII: Diálogos Hispánicos de Amsterdam*, 3 vols. (Amsterdam: Rodopi, 1989); Germán Bleiberg, Maureen Ihrie, and Janet Pérez, eds., *Dictionary of the Literature of the Iberian Peninsula*, 2 vols. (Westport, Conn.: Greenwood Press, 1993); Carlos Solórzano, *Teatro latinoamericano del siglo XX* (Buenos Aires: Editorial Nueva Visión, 1961); Matías Montes Huidobro, *Persona, vida y máscara en el teatro cubano* (Miami: Ediciones Universal, 1973); Luis Ordaz and Erminio G. Neglia, *Repertorio selecto del teatro hispanoamericano contemporáneo* (Caracas: Editorial Giannelli, 1975), and

numerous other books, bibliographies, and articles on the inclusive
periods and dramatists.

DRAMATISTS AND THEIR WORKS

SPAIN

Agramont y Toledo, Juan de (1700s)
  Recobrar por una letra el tesoro de los cielos, y mágica de Nimega
    (1750) [Magic motif]
  Los sacristanes al pozo [Magic motif]
Alarcón, Juan Ruiz de. *See* Ruiz de Alarcón, Juan
Alarcón y Rojas, Andrés de (d. 1636)
  La hechicera (1581) [Comedia. Magic motif]
Alberti, Rafael (1902–)
  El adefesio (1944)
  Noche de guerra en el Museo del Prado (1956) [Paintings come to
    life. Witch]
Alvarez Quintero, Serafín (1871–1938) and Joaquín (1873–1944)
  Don Juan, buena persona [Don Juan motif]
Anonymous
  Acaso de un anillo
  El Alcides de la Mancha y famoso Don Quixote (1750)
    [Enchantments]
  El arca [Entremés. Cave of Salamanca motif]
  El astrólogo tunante [Cave of Salamanca motif]
  A un tiempo rey y señor, y mágico africano (1728) [Magic motif]
  Auto de los Reyes Magos (1100s) [Only known play of the early
    Spanish Middle Ages. Magi; astrology]
  Aventuras verdaderas del segundo Don Quixote (1600s) [Enchanted
    castle]
  Baile de Celestina (1600s) [Celestina motif]
  Las beatas (1600s)
  *Brancanelo el herrero o Nadie más grande hechicero que Brancanelo el
    herrero* [Magic motif]
  Brujas fingidas [Entremés. Feigned witchcraft]
  El caballero encantado [Enchantment]
  Comedia Clariana (1522) [Celestina motif]
  Los diablillos locos (1600s) [Entremés. Attributed to Polop]
  Egloga pastoríl (1519–20)
  El encanto de un abanico [Entremés]

Los encantos de Amenón [Marqués de Villena motif]
Entremés cantado: El mago [Magic motif]
Entremés de la hechicera
Entremés del astrólogo borracho [Astrology]
Entremés del nigromántico (1600s) [Necromancy]
Entremés de los dos Juan Ranas
Entremés de un viejo ques casado con una mujer moza [Cave of Salamanca motif]
Entremés duodécimo de la endemoniada (1609) [Possession]
Entremés famoso del cuero o botero mastranzos
Entremés famoso del duende (1635) [False duende]
Entremés sin título . . . Sacristán, Filipina, Qurcio y Albertos [False duende]
El esclavo por amor del más infeliz dueño, y mágico lusitano
Farça a manera de tragedia (1537) [Celestina motif]
El fariseo [Entremés. Cave of Salamanca motif]
Fortunilla [Entremés. Cave of Salamanca motif]
La guitarra (1600s) [Entremés]
El gusto en la variedad, y mágica florentina (1739) [Magic motif]
El jardín de Apolo y estatuas con alma (early 1700s) [Sainete. Magic motif]
Jasón o la conquista del Vellocino (1768) [Mythology. Medea]
La mágica chasqueada [Magic motif]
El mágico Brocario (1739) [Magic motif]
El mágico de Astracán [Magic motif]
El mágico de Ballecas [Magic motif]
El mágico de Eriván [Magic motif]
El mágico por vengarse [Magic motif]
El mago de Inglaterra, y príncipe Sergio [Magic motif]
El mago de Palestina (1742) [Magic motif]
El milagro de Teófilo [Based on the play by Rutebeuf. Demonic pact]
El Misteri d'Elx (c. 1300s) [Assumption of Mary into Heaven. God. Angels]
El molinero [Entremés. Sham conjuration]
El pasmo de Inglaterra, y mágica Margarita (1746) [Magic motif]
Lo que por rey no se alcanza, por la mágia se consigue, y mágico de Candahar [Magic motif]
Lo que vale una amistad, y mágico Federico [Magic motif]
El sacristán hechicero [Entremés. Cave of Salamanca motif]
Tan largo me lo fiáis [Attributed to Tirso de Molina. Don Juan theme]

Tragicomedia alegórica del Parayso y del Infierno (1539) [Adaptation of Gil Vicente's *Auto da barca do inferno*. Celestina motif]
La universidad de amor [Baile. Astrology]
Añorbe y Corregel, Tomás de (1700s)
    La encantada Melisendra y Piscator de Toledo [Enchantment]
Arce de los Reyes, Ambrosio de (c.1621–61)
    El hechizo de Sevilla (c. 1653) [Enchantment]
Armesto Quiroga, Manuel Francisco de (1700s)
    Las proezas de Esplandían y deshacer encantos (1729) [Magic motif]
Arrabal, Fernando (1932–)
    Jardín de delicias (*Les jardin des délices*, 1967)
Arroyo y Velasco, Juan Bautista de (1700s)
    Entremés del astrólogo burlado [Astrology]
Artieda. See Rey de Artieda, Andrés
Avendaño, Francisco de (1500s)
    Comedia Florisea (1551) [Allegory. The Dead One, a character]
Azorín (José Martínez Ruiz, 1873–1967)
    Angelita (1930) [Auto sacramental. Supernatural elements, magical characters]
    Cervantes, o La casa encantada (1930) [Enchantment]
    Doctor Death, de tres a cinco (1927) [Death]
Badajoz. See Sánchez de Badajoz, Diego
Bances Candamo, Francisco Antonio de (1662–1704)
    El astrólogo tunante [Entremés. Astrology. Cave of Salamanca motif]
    Como se curan los celos y Orlando Furioso (1692)
    El entremés de las visiones (1691) [Feigned visions]
    El esclavo en grillos de oro (1692) [Alchemy. Astrology]
    Fieras de zelos y amor (1690) [Circe motif]
    El gran chimico del mundo (1691) [Auto sacramental]
    La piedra filosofal (1692) [Continuation of Calderón's *La vida es sueño*. Alchemy. Legend]
Baroja y Nessi, Pío (1872–1956)
    La leyenda de Jaun de Alzate [Pagan myths. Fantasy. Witchcraft]
Belmonte Bermúdez, Luis de (1587?–1650)
    El diablo predicador, o Mayor contrario amigo (1653) [Lucifer]
Benavente, Jacinto (1866–1954)
    La cenicienta (1920) [Magic motif]
    La copa encantada [One-act zarzuela]
    Don Magín el de las magias (1944) [Magic motif]
    Mefistófela
    La noche iluminada (1927) [Magic motif]

Benavente, Luis Quiñones de. *See* Quiñones de Benavente, Luis
Bretón de los Herreros, Manuel (1796–1873)
   La pluma prodigiosa (1841)
Buero Vallejo, Antonio (1916–)
   El sueño de la razón (1970) [Fantasy. Visions. Witchcraft]
Calderón de la Barca, Pedro (1600–1681)
   Los alimentos del hombre (1676) [Auto. Devil]
   A María el corazón (1664) [Auto. Devil]
   Amar y ser amado y divina Filotea (1681) [Auto. Devil]
   Andrómeda y Perseo (1652) [Hell motif. Devil]
   El año santo de Roma (1650) [Auto. Devil:Luzbel]
   El año santo en Madrid (c.1650) [Auto. Devil]
   Apolo y Climene (1661) [Astrology]
   El árbol del mejor fruto (1661) [Auto. Devil:Baal]
   El arca de Dios cautiva (1673) [Auto. Devil:Belfegor]
   El astrólogo fingido (pre-1637) [Astrology]
   Las cadenas del demonio (1635–36) [Devil:Astarot. Demonic Pact]
   El castillo de Lindabridis (1661–63)
   Celestina [Lost. Celestina motif]
   El conde Lucanor [Magic motif]
   El cordero de Isaías (1681) [Auto. Devil]
   El cubo de la Almudena (1651) [Auto. Devil]
   La cura y la enfermedad (c.1658) [Auto. Devil:Lucero]
   La dama duende (1629) [Pseudo-ghost. Popular superstitions]
   La devoción de la misa (1637) [Auto. Devil]
   El diablo mudo (1660) [Auto. Devil]
   El dia mayor de los dias (c.1678) [Auto. Devil:Lucero]
   El divino Jasón (pre-1630) [Auto. Devil]
   El divino Orfeo (c. 1634) [Auto. Devil:Aristeo]
   El divino Orfeo (1663) [Auto. Devil. Harrowing of Hell]
   Los dos amantes del cielo (c.1636) [Auto. Priestess of Diana]
   El dragoncillo (c.1670) [Cave of Salamanca motif]
   Los encantos de la culpa (1649) [Auto. Circe and Ulysses]
   Los encantos del Marqués de Villena [Magic motif. Marqués de
      Villena]
   El encanto sin encanto [Magic motif]
   Las espigas de Ruth (1663) [Auto. Devil:Lucero]
   La fiera, el rayo y la piedra (1652) [Gods and goddesses from
      mythology]
   El galán fantasma (pre-1637)
   El gran duque de Gandía (c.1639) [Auto. Devil]

El gran mercado del mundo (c.1635) [Auto. Devil]
El gran Príncipe de Fez (1669) [Devil]
Hado y divisa de Leonido y de Marfisa (1680)
La hidalga del valle (c.1640) [Auto. Devil]
La iglesia sitiada (c.1630) [Auto. Devil]
El indulto general (1680) [Auto. Devil]
La inmunidad del sagrado (1664) [Auto. Devil]
El jardín de Falerina (1648) [Zarzuela. Enchantment episode in
   Boiardo's *Orlando innamorato*]
El jardín de Falerina (1670) [Auto. Devil:Lucero]
El José de las mujeres [Devil]
El laberinto del mundo (1677) [Auto. Devil]
El laurel de Apolo (1658) [Zarzuela. Astrology]
La lepra de Constantino [Auto. Devil]
El lirio y la azucena (1660) [Auto. Devil]
Llamados y escogidos (c.1649) [Auto. Devil]
El maestrazgo del Toisón (1659) [Auto. Devil]
El mágico prodigioso (1637) [Devil. Demonic pact. Version of the
   Cipriano and Justina motif]
La Margarita preciosa [In collaboration with Juan de Zabaleta and
   Jerónimo de Cáncer. Devil:Egeo-El Mayor Dios]
El mayor encanto, amor (1635) [Circe and Ulysses]
Mística y real Babilonia (1662) [Auto. Devil]
Nadie fíe su secreto (c.1623–24)
La nave del mercader (1674) [Auto. Devil]
No hay instante sin milagro (1672) [Auto. Devil]
No hay más fortuna que Dios (1653) [Auto. Devil]
Las órdenes militares (1662) [Auto. Devil]
El Pastor Fido (1678) [In collaboration with Antonio Coello and
   Antonio de Solís. Devil:Luzbel]
La piel de Gedeón (1650) [Auto. Devil]
El pintor de su deshonra (c.1645) [Auto. Devil:Lucero]
El pleito matrimonial del cuerpo y el alma (c.1631) [Auto. Devil]
Polifemo y Circe [In collaboration with Juan Pérez de Montalbán
   and Antonio Mira de Amescua. Circe motif]
La primer flor del Carmelo (pre-1650) [Auto. Devil:Luzbel]
Primero y segundo Isaac (c.1659) [Auto. Devil:Lucero]
El primer refugio del hombre (1661) [Auto. Devil]
La protestación de la fe (1656) [Auto. Devil:Lucero]
Psiquis y Cupido (c. 1640) [Auto. Devil]
La puente de Mantible (1632)

El purgatorio de San Patricio (1636) [Devil]
Lo que va del hombre a Dios (c.1640) [Auto. Devil]
La redención de cautivos (c.1672) [Auto. Devil. Harrowing of Hell]
La segunda esposa y triunfar muriendo (1649) [Auto. Devil]
La semilla y la cizaña (c.1651) [Auto. Devil]
La serpiente de metal [Devil:Belfegor]
La siembra del Señor (c.1650) [Auto. Devil]
El tesoro escondido (1679) [Auto. Devil]
La torre de Babilonia [Auto. Devil:Membrot]
Los tres mayores prodigios (pre-1637) [Magic motif. Medea]
Tu prójimo como a ti (c.1670) [Auto. Devil]
El valle de la zarzuela (c.1655) [Auto. Devil]
El veneno y la triaca (pre-1634) [Auto. Devil:Lucero]
El verdadero dios Pan (1670) [Auto. Devil]
El viático cordero (1665) [Auto. Devil:Baal]
La vida es sueño (c.1631–32) [Astrology]
La vida es sueño [Loa. Devil]
La vida es sueño (1673) [Auto. Astrology. Devil]
La viña del Señor (1674) [Auto. Devil:Lucero]
Campo
 El mágico mejicano [Magic motif]
Cáncer y Velasco, Jerónimo de (1594–1655)
 El gigante [Entremés. Cave of Salamanca motif]
 La Margarita preciosa [In collaboration with Pedro Calderón de la
  Barca and Juan de Zabaleta. Devil:Egeo–El Mayor Dios]
 Los putos [Entremés]
Cañizares, José de (1676–1750)
 El anillo de Giges, y Mágico rey de Lidia [Parts 1 and 2 of the
  tetralogy are his. Magic ring. Invisibility. Zoroaster]
 El asombro de la Francia, Marta la Romarantina [Parts 1 and 2 of
  the tetralogy are his. Marthe Brossier. Feigned possession]
 El Dómine Lucas
 Don Juan de Espina en Milán [Part 2. Magic motif]
 Don Juan de Espina en su patria (1713) [Part 1. Magic motif]
 Introducción para danzado (1716) [Magic motif]
 La mágica Cibeles [Magic motif]
 Los mágicos encontrados (1710) [Magic motif]
 Mojiganga de la casa del duende
 El talego encantado [Entremés]
 La vida del gran tacaño
Cardona, Antonio de (1623–94)

El más heróico silencio
Casona, Alejandro (Alejandro Rodríguez Alvarez, 1903–65)
   La barca sin pescador (1945) [Devil pact. Devil]
   El caballero de las espuelas de oro (1963) [Devil. Witch. Specters]
   La dama del alba (1944) [Death personified. Superstition]
   Otra vez el Diablo (1935) [Devil]
Castelao, Alfonso R. (1886–1950)
   Os vellos non deben namorarse (1953) [In Galician. Devil]
Castillo Solórzano, Alonso de (c.1590–c.1649)
   Alivios de Casandra (1640) [The Sybil Cassandra]
   Los encantos de Bretaña (c. 1634) [Magic motif]
   La fantasma de Valencia (c.1634)
Castro, Francisco de (1618–c.1679; or 1700s, according to *Catálogo*, 79)
   Entremés de la burla del sombrero (pub. 1702)
   Entremés de la Fantasma (pub. 1702) [Astrology. Specter. Devils]
   Entremés de las brujas [Witchcraft. Sabbat]
   Entremés del hechizo de los cueros (pub. 1742) [Enchantment]
   Entremés del mundinovo
   Entremés del órgano y el mágico (pub. 1702) [Magic motif]
   Entremés de los diablillos
   Entremés de los gigantones (pub. 1702) [Celestina motif. Conjuring]
   Entremés de Pedro Grullo y Antón Pintado
Castro y Bellvís, Guillén de (1569–1631)
   Algunas hazañas de las muchas de don García Hurtado de Mendoza, Marqués de Cañete (1622) [In collaboration with Antonia Mira de Amescua, Juan Ruiz de Alarcón, Luis Vélez de Guenara, and others. Araucanians]
   El conde de Irlos (pre-1621)
   Engañarse engañando (pre-1625)
   Las mocedades del Cid (1618) [Astrology. Imitated in Corneille's *Le Cid* (1636)]
   El prodigio de los montes y mártir del cielo, o Santa Bárbara [Devil pact. Variant on Cipriano and Justina motif]
Castro y Matute, José de (1700s)
   Los triunfos de encantos y amor, y Pitonisa Cibeles (1720) [Magic motif]
Cepeda. See Romero de Cepeda, Joaquín
Cervantes Saavedra, Miguel de (1547–1616)
   El cerco de Numancia (c.1585) [Tragedy]
   Comedia famosa de la casa de los celos y selvas de Ardenia (c.1615)

[Magic motif. Merlin and Malgesí]
Entremés de la cueva de Salamanca (c.1611) [Supposed conjuring]
El retablo de las maravillas (c.1598–1600) [Entremés. Feigned in visibility]
El rufián dichoso (c.1615) [Devil. Demonic pact. Succubi]
El trato de Argel (c.1585)
Chamizo, Luis (1888–1944)
Las brujas (1930)
Claramonte y Corroy, Andrés de (1580–1626)
El dote del rosario (pub. 1655) [Auto. Devil pact]
Coello, Antonio (1611–82)
El Pastor Fido (1678) [In collaboration with Pedro Calderón de la Barca and Antonio de Solís. Devil:Luzbel]
Coello de Portugal y Pacheco, Carlos
La magia nueva [In collaboration with Miguel Ramos Carrión. Magic motif]
Coello Rebello, Manuel (1600s)
El enredo más bizarro y historia verdadera [Entremés. Magic motif. Cave of Salamanca motif]
Concha, José de (1700s)
Marta imaginaria, segundo asombro de Francia ... y mágico gaditano [Magic motif. Marthe Brossier. Feigned possession]
Vence un error a un favor por conseguir un amor, y mágico gaditano (1775) [Magic motif]
Cruz, Ramón de la (1731–94)
Marta abandonada y carnaval de París [Marthe Brossier. Feigned possession]
Cubillo de Aragón, Alvaro (1596–1661)
El invisible príncipe del baúl (c.1637) [Invisibility]
Cueva, Juan de la (1543–1610)
Comedia de la constancia de Arcelina (c.1588) [Zoroaster—Zarathustra]
Comedia del infamador (1581) [Celestina motif]
Comedia del príncipe tirano (c.1588)
Comedia del viejo enamorado (c.1588)
Tragedia de los siete Infantes de Lara (c.1588)
Diamante, Juan Bautista (1625–87)
El caballero de Olmedo (c.1651) [In collaboration with Francisco Antonio de Monteser. Parody of Lope de Vega's play]
Loa humana del árbol florido (pre-1676) [In collaboration with Francisco Antonio de Monteser]

El negro más prodigioso (c.1674) [Magic motif]
Diez, Antonio (1500s)
    Auto de Clarindo (1535) [Celestina motif. First three-act play in Spanish]
Duque de Rivas. See Saavedra, Angel de
Echegaray, José (1832–1916)
    En el pilar y en la cruz (1878) [The Inquisition]
    El hijo de Don Juan (1892) [Suggested by Ibsen's *Ghosts*. Don Juan motif]
Enc[z]ina, Juan del (c.1468–c.1534)
    Egloga de Fileno y Zambardo (c.1505) [Celestina motif]
    Egloga de Plácida y Vitoriano (c.1514) [Egloga decimocuarta. Flugencia and Eritea discuss their *hechizos*; Venus and Mercury appear. Celestina motif]
Estrada y Bustamante, Antonio de (1700s)
    El asombro de Argel, y mágico Mahomat (1742) [Magic motif]
Faria, Pedro. *See* Hurtado de la Vera, Pedro
Fernández, Sebastián (1500s)
    Tragedia Policiana (1547) [Witches. Celestina motif]
Fernández Ardavín, Luis (1892–1962)
    Doña Diabla (1925)
Fernández de Ribera, Rodrigo (1579–1631)
    Los anteojos de mejor vista (1625) [Magic lenses]
Fernández-Guerra y Orbe, Aureliano (1816–91)
    Entremés de la hechicera [Enchantment]
Fernández y González, Manuel (1600s)
    Los encantos de Merlín [Magic motif. Merlin]
Ferrer, Alejandro (1700s)
    El poeta y los duendes
    También habla lo insensible, o encantos de Rosimunda y aventuras de Perseo [Enchantment]
Flores, Antonio (1700s)
    También la ciencia es poder, y mágico de Ferrara (1749) [Magic motif]
García Gutiérrez, Antonio (1813–84)
    El Trovador (1836) [Gypsy witchcraft]
    El vampiro (1834) [Translation of the play by Scribe]
García Lorca, Federico (1898–1936)
    Bodas de sangre (1933) [Death personified. Supernatural elements]
    Yerma (1934) [The Elements. Dionysian revels]
Gil y Carrasco, Enrique (1815–46)

El señor de Bembibre (1844) [Based on the novel. Templars. Fake
   necromancy]
Gil y Zárate, Antonio (1793–1861)
   Don Carlos II el Hechizado (1837)
Gómez Arcos, Agustín (1939–)
   Diálogos de la herejía (1964) [Illuminati. Demonic possession]
   Interview de Mrs. Muerta Smith por sus fantasmes [Ghosts]
Gómez de Avellaneda, Gertrudis (1814–1873)
   El donativo del diablo (1852)
   Oráculos de Talia o los duendes en el palacio (1855)
Gómez de Toledo, Gaspar (1500s)
   Tercera parte de la tragicomedia de Celestina (1536) [Celestina
   motif]
González Martínez, Nicolás (1700s)
   *A falta de hechiceros lo quieren ser los gallegos, y asombro de
   Salamanca* [Magic motif]
   No hay encanto contra amor, y mágica Arcelinda [Magic motif]
   También se ama en el barquillo y mágica siciliana [Magic motif]
   La traición más bien vengada, y mágica Eritrea [Magic motif]
Grau, Jacinto (1877–1959)
   El burlador que no se burla (1928) [Don Juan Tenorio]
   La casa del diablo (1942) [Judgment before God]
   Don Juan de Carrillana (1913) [Don Juan motif]
   El señor de Pigmalión (1921) [Puppets come to life]
   El tercer diablo (1908)
Grimaldi, Juan de (1796–1872)
   La pata de cabra (1829) [Magic]
Hartzenbusch, Juan Eugenio (1806–80)
   Las batuecas (1843)
   El doctor Capirote o los curanderos de antaño (1846) [One-act. Fake
   magic.]
   Los polvos de la madre Celestina (1840) [Celestina motif]
   La redoma encantada (1839) [Marqués de Villena]
Hoz y Mota, Juan de la (1622–1714)
   El castigo de la miseria (1650–60) [On Don Carlos Gil de
   Almodóvar]
   El encanto del olvido
   El entremés del invisible [Feigned invisibility]
Huete, Jaime de (1500s)
   Comedia Tesorina (1531) [Celestina motif. Prohibited by the *Index*
   in 1583]

Comedia Vidriana (1525) [Celestina motif]
Hurtado de la Vera, Pedro (nee Pedro Faria, 1500s)
  Comedia intitulada dolería del sueño del mundo (1572) [Celestina motif]
Jiménez de Urrea, Pedro Manuel (c.1486–c.1535)
  Egloga de la tragicomedia de Calixto y Melibea (1513) [Celestina motif]
Lanini y Sagredo, Pedro Francisco de (1600s, 1700s)
  Colegio de los Gorrones [Magic motif. Don Juan de Espina]
  Entremés de la Tataratera [Magic motif. Don Juan de Espina]
  La pluma (1676) [Entremés. Invisibility]
Lanuza, Marcoa de (1600s)
  Las Belides o Fábula de Hipermenestra y Linceo (1686) [Magic motif. Mythology]
Larra, Mariano José de (1809–37)
  Macías (1834) [Marqués de Villena]
Laviano, Manuel Fermín de (1700s)
  No se evita un principio si se falta a la deidad, y mágico Fineo (1760) [Magic motif]
Lázaro, Angel (1900s)
  La hoguera del diablo (1932)
Lázaro, Maribel (1900s)
  Humo de Beleño (1982) [Witchcraft. Inquisition]
Llamosas, Lorenzo de las
  El astrólogo [Sainete]
Lope de Vega Carpio, Félix (1562–1635)
  El acero de Madrid (c.1608–12) [Astrology]
  Angélica en el Catay (c.1599)
  Arauco domado (1625) [Araucanians]
  La Arcadia (1598) [Astrology]
  El ausente en el lugar (1604–12) [Astrology]
  El caballero del sacramento (1620–25) [Astrology]
  El caballero de Olmedo (c.1615–26) [Witchcraft. Celestina motif]
  Circe (1624) [Magic motif]
  La Circe angélica [Circe]
  Las Cortes de la muerte [Auto. Devil. Possibly the play mentioned in *Don Quixote*, part 2, chap. 11]
  Dineros son calidad (1620–23)
  Don Juan de Castro I (1604–8)
  Don Juan de Castro II (1608)
  El duque de Viseo (1608–9)

El encanto en el anillo [Enchantment]
Entremés de la hechicera
La gran columna fogosa, San Basilio Magno [Devil pact. Proterius motif]
El gran duque de Moscovia, y emperador perseguido (1606?) [Astrology]
El hospital de los locos [Auto. Devil]
La imperial de Otón (1597)
El infanzón de Illescas [Attributed]
El marqués de las Navas (1624)
La maya (1585) [Devil]
La mayor desgracia de Carlos V y hechicería de Argel (1625–27)
El mayor rey de los reyes [Astrology]
El mejor alcalde el Rey (c.1620–23) [Astrology]
El mejor mozo de España (1610–11)
La niña de plata (1610–12) [Astrology]
La niñez del Padre Rojas (1625) [Astrology]
El nuevo Pitágoras
Las paces de los reyes (1610–12)
El pastor lobo y cabaña celestial [Auto. Devil]
Porfiar hasta morir (1624–28) [Marqués de Villena]
Quien más no puede (1616) [Astrology]
Los ramilletes de Madrid (1615) [Also *Dos estrellas trocadas.* Astrology]
Roma abrasada (1598–1600) [Astrology]
Sembrar en buena tierra (1616) [Astrology]
La serrana de Tormes (c.1604)
Servir a buenos (1620–25) [Astrology]
Sin secreto no hay amor (1626) [Astrology]
La sortija del olvido (1610–15) [Magic ring]
El sufrimiento del honor (1604–8) [Astrology]
El Vellocino de Oro (1620) [Medea. Mythology]
Ya anda la de Mazagatos [Astrology]
López de Ayala, Adelardo (1828–79)
El conjuro
El nuevo don Juan (1863) [Don Juan motif]
López Medina, Emilio (1946–)
Faustino (1984) [Faust motif]
Machado, Antonio (1875–1939) and Manuel (1874–1947)
Don Juan de Mañara (1927) [Don Juan motif]
Marquina, Eduardo (1879–1946)

Jesús y el diablo (1899)
Martín Recuerda, José (1922–)
    Las conversiones (1985) [Celestina motif. Witches. Demons.
    Inquisition]
Martínez de la Rosa, Francisco (1787–1862)
    El español en Venecia o la cabeza encantada
Martínez Olmedilla, Augusto (1880–1965)
    El despertar de Fausto (1931) [Faust motif]
Martínez Ruiz, José. See Azorín
Martínez Sierra, Gregorio (1881–1947)
    Don Juan de España (1921) [Don Juan motif]
    Sueño de una noche en agosto (1918) [Apparition]
Maura, Honorio (1886–1936)
    Cuento de hadas
Merano y Guzmán, Antonio (1700s)
    En vano el poder persigue a quien la deidad proteje, y mágico Apolonio
    (1749) [Magic motif]
Millán Astray, Pilar (1892–1949)
    La casa de la bruja (1932)
Mira de Amescua, Antonio (c.1574–1644)
    Algunas hazañas de las muchas de don García Hurtado de Mendoza,
    Marqués de Cañete (1622) [In collaboration with Juan Ruiz de
    Alarcón, Luis Vélez de Guevara, Guillén de Castro, and others.
    Araucanians]
    El esclavo del demonio (1612) [San Gil de Santarem. Devil. Demonic
    pact]
    El pleito que tuvo el diablo con el cura de Madrilejos (1632) [In col-
    laboration with Luis Vélez de Guevara and Francisco de Rojas
    Zorrilla. Devil]
    Polifemo y Circe [In collaboration with Juan Pérez de Montalbán
    and Pedro Calderón de la Barca. Circe motif]
    Lo que puede el oír Misa [Devil]
Miranda, Luis de (c.1510–65)
    Comedia pródiga (1554) [Celestina motif]
Miras, Domingo (1934–)
    Las alumbradas de la Encarnación Benita (1979) [Possession.
    Inquisition]
    Las brujas de Barahona (1978) [Witchcraft. Inquisition]
    De San Pascual a San Gil (1980) [Devil. Stigmata. Prophecy]
    El doctor Torralba (1982) [Alchemy. Spectre. Inquisition]
Molina, Tirso de. *See* Tirso de Molina

Montalbán. *See* Pérez de Montalbán, Juan
Montaner, Joaquín
    El hijo del diablo (1927)
    Los iluminados
Monteser, Francisco Antonio de (c.1620–68)
    El caballero de Olmedo (c.1651) [In collaboration with Juan Bautista Diamante. Parody of Lope de Vega's play]
    Loa humana del árbol florido (pre-1676) [In collaboration with Juan Bautista Diamante]
Moreto y Cabaña (also Cavana), Agustín (1618–69)
    Entremés famoso de las brujas [Feigned witchcraft and necromancy]
    El licenciado Vidriera [Adapted from Cervantes's work]
Muñón, Sancho de (1500s)
    Tragicomedia de Lisandro y Roselia llamada Elicia y por otro nombre cuarta obra y tercera Celestina (1542) [Celestina motif]
Nanclares, Antonio de (1600s)
    La hechicera del cielo [Astrology. Saint Eufrasia]
Natas, Francisco de las (1500s)
    Comedia Tidea (1550) [Celestina motif. Prohibited by the *Index*, 1559, 1583]
Navarro de Espinosa, Juan (d.1658)
    Entremés famoso de la Celestina (c.1643) [Celestina motif]
Nieva, Francisco (1929–)
    Aquelarre y noche roja de Nosferatu (1961) [Vampirism. Witches]
    La carroza del plomo candente (1971) [Magic motif. Witchcraft]
    El rayo colgado (1952) [Illuminati]
Ortíz, Agustín (1500s)
    Comedia Radiana (1530) [Celestina motif]
Palau, Bartolomé (1525–?)
    Farsa llamada salamantina (1552) [Entremés]
Pedraza, Juan de (1500s)
    Auto que trata primeramente cómo el ánima de Christo descendió al infierno (1549) [Harrowing of Hell motif]
    Farsa llamada Dança de la Muerte (1551) [Dance of Death motif]
Pérez de Montalbán, Juan (1602–38)
    Encantadora Lucinda, Palmerín de Oliva (c.1636)
    Para con todos hermanos, y amantes para nosotros, don Florisel de Niquea (c.1638)
    El Polifemo (1628) [Auto]
    Polifemo y Circe [In collaboration with Antonio Mira de Amescua and Pedro Calderón de la Barca. Circe motif]

Los Templarios (c.1635) [The Templars motif]
Vida y purgatorio de San Patricio (1627) [Devil]
Pérez de Oliva, Fernán (1494–1533)
Hécuba triste [Tragedy. Freely adapted from Euripides]
Piña, Juan de (1600s)
　　Casos prodigiosos y cueva encantada (1628) [Magic motif. Don Juan
　　de Espina]
Pina Domínguez, Mariano (1800s)
　　Embajador y hechicero (1849)
Polop y Baldés, Pablo (also Pablo Polope y Valdés) (c.1655–89)
　　Los diablillos locos [Entremés. Attributed to Polop]
　　La profetiza Casandra o el leño de Meleagro (1685) [Astrology. The
　　Sybil Cassandra]
Quevedo y Villegas, Francisco de (1580–1645)
　　Entremés de la ropavejera [Celestina motif]
　　Entremés famoso de la endemoniada fingida y chistes de bacallao
　　[Feigned possession]
　　El marido fantasma [Entremés]
　　Las sombras (pub. 1643) [Entremés]
Quiñones de Benavente, Luis (1593–1651)
　　Entremés de la hechicera (post-1645)
　　El mago (1645) [Entremés. Magic motif]
　　La paga del mundo (1645)
　　El retablo de las maravillas (1645)
　　El talego niño (1645) [Entremés]
Ramos Carrión, Miguel (1845–1915)
　　La bruja (1887) [Zarzuela, with music by Ruperto Chapí.
　　Witchcraft]
　　La magia nueva [In collaboration with Carlos Coello de Portugal y
　　Pacheco. Magic motif]
Rey de Artieda, Andrés (1544–1613)
　　Amadís de Gaula [Comedia. Attributed. Magic motif]
　　Los encantos de Merlín (c.1603) [Comedia. Attributed. Merlin
　　motif]
Reyes, Matías de los (c.1575–c.1640)
　　El agravio agradecido (1629) [Comedia. Dedicated in 1622]
　　Los enredos del diablo (1629) [Comedia. Dedicated in 1622. Devil]
Ridruejo, Dionisio (1912–75)
　　Don Juan (c. 1946) [Don Juan motif]
Ripoll Fernández de Ureña, Francisco Antonio (1700s)
　　Marta aparente [Marthe Brossier. Feigned possession]

Rodríguez Alvarez, Alejandro. *See* Casona, Alejandro
Rodríguez de Villaviciosa, Sebastián (1618–c.1672)
  El bobo enamorado
  Los poetas locos
  La sortija de Florencia
Rodríguez Díaz Rubí, Tomás (1817–90)
  La bruja de Lanjarón (1843) [Witchcraft]
  El diablo cojuelo (1842)
  La fuente del olvido
Rodríguez Florián, Juan (1500s)
  Comedia llamada Florinea (1554) [Celestina motif]
Rodríguez Méndez, José María (19
  Isabelita tiene ángel (1976) [Witch. Angel. Queen Isabel]
Rojas, Fernando de (c.1474–1541)
  Tragicomedia de Calixto y Melibea (1499; 1502) [Also known as *La
    Celestina*. Attributed. Witchcraft. Incantations to Pluto]
Rojas Alarcón, Andrés de. *See* Alarcón y Rojas, Andrés de
Rojas Zorrilla, Francisco de (1607–48)
  Los encantos de Medea (1645) [Medea. Witchcraft. Magic motif]
  La esmeralda de amor
  El pleito que tuvo el diablo con el cura de Madrilejos (1632) [In col-
    laboration with Luis Vélez de Guevara and Antonio Mira de
    Amescua. Devil]
  Lo que quería ver el Marqués de Villena (1645) [Marqués de Villena.
    Magic motif]
Romero de Cepeda, Joaquín (1500s)
  Comedia salvage (1582) [Celestina motif]
Rosete Niño, Pedro (1608–59)
  Los gigantes [Entremés. Cave of Salamanca motif]
Rueda, Lope de (1510–65)
  Coloquio de Tymbria [Magic flower causes sleep]
  Comedia llamada Armelina [Medea motif. Necromancy]
  Comedia llamada Medora (c.1538)
  La tierra de Jauja (1547)
Ruibal, José (1925–)
  La máquina de pedir (1969) [Devils]
Ruiz de Alarcón, Juan (c.1580–1639)
  *Algunas hazañas de las muchas de don García Hurtado de Mendoza,
    Marqués de Cañete* (1622) [In collaboration with Antonio Mira
    de Amescua, Luis Vélez de Guevara, Guillén de Castro, and
    others. Araucanians]

El anticristo (1623) [Astrology. Devil]

La cueva de Salamanca (1617–20) [Marqués de Villena. Devil]

La manganilla de Melilla (1602–8) [Black magic]

La prueba de las promesas (1618 or 34?) [Based on a story in Don Juan Manuel's *El conde Lucanor:* "De lo que contesció a un Deán de Sanctiago con D. Illán, el gran maestro de Toledo". Don Juan de Espina. Necromancy]

Quien mal anda en mal acaba (1601–11) [First pact with the Devil in Spanish drama. Ramón Ramírez, a Moor arrested, tried and punished by the Inquisition as a magician]

Ruiz Iriarte, Víctor (1912–)

La señora, sus ángeles y el diablo (1947)

Rusiñol y Prats, Santiago (1861–1931)

El mistic (1904) [Life of Jacint Verdaguer]

El titella prodig (1911) [Puppets. Devil]

Saavedra, Angel de (Duque de Rivas, 1791–1865)

El desengaño de un sueño (1844)

Salas Barbadillo, Alonso Jerónimo de (1581–1635)

Celestina (1620) [Version of the novel. Celestina motif]

Salazar y Torres, Agustín de (1642–75)

El mérito es la corona y encanto de mar y amor

El encanto de la hermosura y el hechizo sin hechizo o La segunda Celestina (late 1600s) [Celestina motif]

También se ama en el abismo [Circe motif. Mythology]

Salvo y Vela, Juan (1700s)

El mágico de Salerno, Pedro Valladares (1715–20) [Five parts. Magic motif]

El mágico Lusitano (1743) [Magic motif]

Sánchez, Tomás Bernardo (1700s)

El mágico Muley (1736) [Magic motif]

El mágico Segismundo (1736) [Magic motif]

Sánchez de Badajoz, Diego (c.1479–c.1554)

Farsa de la hechicera (1552)

Sastre, Alfonso (1926–)

Las cintas magnéticas (1973) [In *El escenario diabólico*]

Frankenstein en Hortaleza (1973) [In *El escenario diabólico*]

La sangre y la ceniza (1965) [Miguel Servet]

El vampiro de Uppsala (1973) [In *El escenario diabólico*. Vampirism]

Sepúlveda, Lorenzo de (1500s)

Comedia Sepúlveda (1547)

Silva, Feliciano de (c.1492–c.1558)

Segunda comedia de Celestina (1534) [Celestina motif]
Solís y Rivadeneira, Antonio de (1610–86)
    El Pastor Fido (1678) [In collaboration with Pedro Calderón de la
        Barca and Antonio Coello. Devil:Luzbel]
Suárez de Deza y Avila, Vicente (1600s)
    El matemático (pub. 1663) [Sainete. Astrology]
Tamayo y Baus, Manuel (1829–98)
    Juana de Arco (1847) [Joan of Arc]
    Sancho García (1842) [Astrology]
Téllez, Gabriel. See Tirso de Molina
Timoneda, Juan de (c.1490–1583)
    Comedia llamada Aurelia (1564)
    Comedia llamada Cornelia (1559) [Reworking of Ariosto's *Il
        Negromante*. False necromancy]
    Farça llamada Floriana (1565)
    Farça llamada Paliana (1564) [Necromancy]
    Los Menecmos (1559) [Adapted from Plautus' *Menaechmi*]
    Tragedia llamada Filomena (1564)
Tirso de Molina (Gabriel Téllez, c.1584–1648)
    El burlador de Sevilla y convidado de piedra (1630) [Don Juan
        Tenorio. Specters]
    El castigo del pensequé (1627) [Allusions to enchantments]
    El colmenero divino [Auto. Devil]
    El condenado por desconfiado (1635) [Devil]
    El duende (1635)
    El melancólico
    Tan largo me lo fiáis [Attributed to Tirso de Molina. Don Juan
        motif]
Torres, Diego de (1700s)
    Fin de fiesta de la galería mágica y fiesta del mesón (1748) [Magic
        motif]
    Fin de fiesta del juego de la sortija (1719) [Conjuring]
Torres Naharro, Bartolomé de (c.1480–c.1530)
    Comedia Aquilana
    Comedia Himenea (1517) [Celestina motif]
    Comedia Serafina (1508–9)
Unamuno, Miguel de (1864–1936)
    El hermano Juan o El mundo es teatro (1934) [Don Juan motif]
    Medea (1933) [Medea motif]
    El otro (1932) [The Other—Double]
Urrea, Pedro Manuel de. See Jiménez de Urrea, Pedro

Valdivielso, José de (1560–1638)
El hombre encantado (1622) [Auto. Enchantment]
Valladares de Sotomayor, Antonio (1700s)
El encantador [Sainete. Witchcraft. Astrology]
Esposa y trono a un tiempo y mágico de Serván [Magic motif]
El mágico de Mogol (1782) [Magic motif]
El mágico en Cataluña [Magic motif]
Los mágicos de Tetuán [Magic motif]
Valle-Inclán, Ramón del (1866–1936)
Aguila de blasón (1907) [Superstition]
Cara de Plata (1922) [Superstition]
Comedia de ensueño (1903) [Witch]
Divinas palabras (1920) [Devil]
El embrujado (1912) [Bewitchment. Lycanthropy]
Ligazón: Auto para siluetas (1926) [Witchcraft. Blood pact]
El Marqués de Bradomín (1907) [Discussion of Devil. Witchcraft]
Romance de lobos (1908) [Santa Compaña. Superstition]
Vega, Alonso de la (c.1510–c.1565)
Comedia de la duquesa de la rosa (1566) [After Bandello]
Comedia llamada Tholomea (1566) [Necromancy. Medea motif]
Tragedia llamada Seraphina (1566) [Necromancy. Dream.
    Mythology]
Vega, Ventura de la (1807–65)
La segunda dama duende (1838)
Vega Carpio, Félix Lope de. *See* Lope de Vega
Vélez de Guevara, Luis (1579–1644)
*Algunas hazañas de las muchas de don García Hurtado de Mendoza,
    Marqués de Cañete* (1622) [In collaboration with Antonio Mira
    de Amescua, Juan Ruiz de Alarcón, Guillén de Castro, and
    others. Araucanians]
La corte del demonio [Devil]
La devoción de la Misa [Devil]
El Diablo está en Cantillana [False ghost. Devil]
El pleito que tuvo el diablo con el cura de Madrilejos (1632) [In col-
    laboration with Francisco de Rojas Zorrilla and Antonio Mira de
    Amescua. Devil]
Vicente, Gil (c.1453–1537)
Auto da barca do inferno (1517) [Hell. Celestina motif]
Auto de la sibila Casandra (c.1513) [The Sybil Cassandra]
Auto dos Reis Magos (1503) [Magi]
Comedia de Rubena (1521) [Magic. Spells]

Triunfo de Inferno
Villalón, Cristóbal de (1510?–1562?)
  El crotalón [Adaptation of the prose work. Transmigration]
Villegas Selvago, Alonso de (1534–1615)
  Comedia llamada Selvagia (1554) [Celestina motif]
Zabala (or Zavala) y Zamora, Gaspar de (1700s, 1800s)
  El soldado exorcista (1818) [Sainete. Adaptation of Calderón's *El
    dragoncillo*. Sham conjuration. Cave of Salamanca motif]
Zabaleta, Juan de (c.1610–c.1670)
  El hechizo imaginado
  La Margarita preciosa [In collaboration with Pedro Calderón de la
    Barca and Jerónimo de Cáncer. Devil:Egeo–El Mayor Dios]
Zamora, Antonio de (1664–1728)
  Aspides hay basiliscos (pub. 1721) [Zarzuela]
  La doncella de Orleans [Joan of Arc]
  Duendes son alcahuetes y el espíritu Foleto (1709) [Magic motif]
  El hechizado por fuerza (1697) [False enchantment. Goya did a
    painting on this subject, originally titled "La lámpara
    descomunal" but now known as "La lámpara del Diablo,"
    National Gallery, London]
  *No hay plazo que no se cumpla ni deuda que no se pague, y el
    convidado de piedra* (1722) [Based on Tirso de Molina's *El
    burlador de Sevilla*. Don Juan Tenorio]
Zorrilla, José (1817–93)
  Don Juan Tenorio (1844) [Don Juan. Specters]

LATIN AMERICA

Andrade Rivera, Gustavo (1921–72)
  Remington 22 (1961) [Puppets. Angels]
Arlt, Roberto (1900–1942)
  El fabricante de fantasmas (1936)
Arriví, Francisco (1915–)
  Caso del muerto en vida (1951)
  El diablo se humaniza (1941)
  Medusas en la bahia (1956)
  Vegigantes (1958) [Afro–Puerto Rican folklore. Masks]
Basurto, Luis G. (1920–)
  El anticristo (1942)
  Faustina (1942) [Faust motif]
Belaval, Emilio S. (1903–)
  Circe o el amor (1962) [Circe motif]

Bloch, Pedro (1914–)
  As maos de Eurídice (1951) [Surrealistic monologue]
Brene, José Ramón (1927–)
  Los demonios de Remedios (1964) [Santería rites. Possession]
  La fiebre negra (1964) [The Orisha Changó]
  Santa Camila de la Habana Vieja (1963) [Santería]
Buenaventura, Enrique (1925–)
  La adoración de los reyes magos (1956)
  A la mano derecha de Dios Padre (*En la diestra de Dios Padre*, 1960)
    [Devil. Christ. St. Peter. Death]
Carballido, Emilio (1925–)
  Medusa
  Yo también hablo de la rosa (1966) [Medium]
  La zona intermedia. Auto sacramental (1950) [Devil. Nahual]
Carril, Pepe
  Shango de Ima (1969) [The Orishas, Yoruba deities]
Cuadra, Pablo Antonio (1912–)
  Satanás entra en la escena (1938)
Cuadra Pinto, Fernando (1926–)
  El diablo está en Machalí (1958)
  Las Medeas [Medea motif]
Dias Gomes, Alfredo (1926–)
  O pagador de promessas (1960) [Candomblé]
Felipe, Carlos (1911–75)
  La bruja en el obenque (1952–56) [Witch]
  Requiem por Yarini (1954;1960) [Spiritism. Santería. Changó.
    Elegguá]
  Tambores (1943) [Changó]
Ferretti, Aurelio (1907–63)
  Las bodas del diablo (1947)
Heiremans, Luis Alberto (1928–64)
  Versos de ciego (*Sigue la estrella*, 1961) [Magi motif]
Huidobro, Vicente (1893–1948)
  Gilles de Raiz (1932) [Devil:Lucifer. Witch. Magician. Joan of Arc.
    Don Juan]
Imbert, Julio (1918–)
  El diablo despide luz (1954)
  Primer actor: el Diablo (*La baba del diablo*, 1954)
Lira, Manuel N. (1905–)
  El diablo volvió al infierno (1943)
  Vuelta a la tierra (1938) [Mexican folklore. Devil]

Milián, José
Camino para llegar a viejo (1964) [Santería]
Mamico Omi Omo (1964) [Afro-Cuban folklore. Santería]
Monterde, Francisco (1894–)
Proteo (1931) [Greek mythology. Masks. Transformations]
La que volvió a la vida (1923)
Montes Huidobro, Matías (1931–)
Las cuatro brujas (1950) [Witchcraft]
Morton, Carlos
El Jardín [Garden of Eden allegory: God, Serpent, Death]
Johnny Tenorio [Don Juan motif]
Pancho Diablo [Devil. Hell]
Nalé Roxlo, Conrado (1898–1971)
El pacto de Cristina (1945) [Demonic Pact. Devil:Maese Jaime]
Nascimento, Abdias do (1914–)
Sortilegio. Misterio Negro (1961) [Candomblé. Orixás]
Pontes, Paulo
Doutor Fausto da Silva (1972) [Faust motif]
Rein, Mercedes and Jorge Curi
El herrero y la muerte (1981) [Folklore. Devil. Hell]
Reyes, Alfonso (1889–1959)
Ifigenia cruel (1923) [Greek mythology]
Rojas, Ricardo (1882–1957)
Ollantay (1932) [Adaptation of Inca legend. Sun and snake
    worship]
Santana Salas, Rodolfo (1944–)
Moloch (1973)
Nuestro padre Drácula (1968)
Segura, Manuel Ascencio (1805–1871)
Ña Catita (1846) [Celestina motif in colonial Peru]
Seljan, Zora (also Seljam)
A festa do Bonfim (1978) [Version of *Historia de Oxalá*]
A Orelha de Obá (1958) [Orixás]
Historia de Oxalá (1958) [Oxalá, head of the Yoruba deities]
Iansan, Mulher de Xangô (1958) [Orixás]
Negrinha de Iemanjá (In *Os Negrinhos*) [Yoruba Orixá Iemanjá]
Negrinhos das Folhas [Light-hearted treatment of Orixás]
Oxum Abaló (1958) [Orixás]
Solorzano, Carlos (1922–)
El hechicero (1954)
Las manos de Dios (1956) [Devil:El Forastero]

Steiner, Rolando (1936–)
Antigona en el infierno (1958)
Suassuna, Ariano (1927–)
A pena e a lei (1959) [Puppets. Last Judgment]
O auto da compadecida (1955) [Christ. The Virgin Mary. Devil]
O auto de Joao da Cruz (1958) [Faust motif]
Triana, José (1932–)
Medea en el espejo (1959) [Medea motif]
La muerte del Ñeque (1964) [Afro-Cuban ritual chants]
La visita del ángel (1963)
Valdez, Luis
Bernabé [Pre-Hispanic deities]
Zapata Olivella, Manuel (1922–)
La bruja de Pontezuela (1971)

RECURRING MOTIFS IN THE PLAYS

CASSANDRA
Alivios de Casandra by Alonso de Castillo Solórzano
Auto da la sibila Casandra by Gil Vicente
La profetiza Casandra by Pablo Polop y Baldés
CAVE OF SALAMANCA
El arca, anonymous
El astrólogo tunante, anonymous
La cueva de Salamanca by Juan Ruiz de Alarcón
El dragoncillo by Pedro Calderón de la Barca
El enredo más bizarro y historia verdadera by Manuel Coello Rebello
Entremés de la cueva de Salamanca by Miguel de Cervantes
Entremés de un viejo ques casado con una mujer moza, anonymous
El fariseo, anonymous
Fortunilla, anonymous
El gigante by Jerónimo de Cáncer y Velasco
Los gigantes by Pedro Rosete Niño
El sacristán hechicero, anonymous
El soldado exorcista by Gaspar de Zabala y Zamora
CELESTINA
Auto da barca do inferno by Gil Vicente
Auto de Clarindo by Antonio Diez
Baile de Celestina, anonymous
El caballero de Olmedo by Félix Lope de Vega

Celestina, lost work by Pedro Calderón de la Barca
Celestina by Alonso Jerónimo de Salas Barbadillo
Comedia Clariana, anonymous
Comedia del infamador by Juan de la Cueva
Comedia Himenea by Bartolomé de Torres Naharro
Comedia intitulada dolería del sueño del mundo by Pedro Hurtado
   de la Vera
Comedia llamada Florinea by Juan Rodríguez Florián
Comedia llamada Selvagia by Alonso de Villegas Selvago
Comedia pródiga by Luis de Miranda
Comedia Radiana by Agustín Ortíz
Comedia salvage by Joaquín Romero de Cepeda
Comedia Tesorina by Jaime de Huete
Comedia Tidea by Francisco de las Natas
Comedia Vidriana by Jaime de Huete
Las conversiones by José Martín Recuerda
Egloga de Fileno y Zambardo by Juan del Encina
Egloga de la tragicomedia de Calixto y Melibea by Pedro Manuel de
   Urrea
Egloga de Plácida y Vitoriano by Juan del Encina
*El encanto de la hermosura y el hechizo sin hechizo o La segunda
   Celestina* by Agustín de Salazar y Torres
Entremés de la ropavejera by Francisco de Quevedo
Entremés de los gigantones by Francisco de Castro
Entremés famoso de la Celestina by Juan Navarro de Espinosa
Farça a manera de tragedia, anonymous
Ña Catita by Manuel Ascencio Segura
Segunda comedia de Celestina by Feliciano de Silva
Tercera parte de la tragicomedia de Celestina by Gaspar Gómez de
   Toledo
Tragedia Policiana by Sebastían Fernández
Tragicomedia alegórica del parayso y del infierno, anonymous
Tragicomedia de Calixto y Melibea, attributed to Fernando de Rojas
*Tragicomedia de Lisandro y Roselia llamada Elicia y por otro nombre
   cuarta obra y tercera Celestina* by Sancho de Muñón
CIRCE
Circe by Félix Lope de Vega
La Circe angélica by Félix Lope de Vega
Circe o el amor by Emilio S. Belaval
Los encantos de la culpa by Pedro Calderón de la Barca
Fieras de zelos y amor by Francisco Antonio de Bances Candamo

El mayor encanto, amor by Pedro Calderón de la Barca
Polifemo y Circe by Antonio Mira de Amescua, Juan Pérez de
Montalbán, and Pedro Calderón de la Barca

DON JUAN DE ESPINA

Casos prodigiosos y cueva encantada by Juan de Piña
Colegio de los Gorrones by Pedro Francisco de Lanini y Sagredo
Don Juan de Espina en Milán by Jose de Cañizares
Don Juan de Espina en su patria by José de Cañizares
Entremés de la Tataratera by Pedro Francisco de Lanini y Sagredo
La prueba de las promesas by Juan Ruiz de Alarcón

DON JUAN TENORIO

El burlador de Sevilla y convidado de piedra by Tirso de Molina
El burlador que no se burla by Jacinto Grau
Don Juan by Dionisio Ridruejo
Don Juan, buena persona by Serafín and Joaquín Alvarez Quintero
Don Juan de Carrillana by Jacinto Grau
Don Juan de España by Gregorio Martínez Sierra
Don Juan de Mañara by Antonio and Manuel Machado
Don Juan Tenorio by José Zorrilla
El hermano Juan o El mundo es teatro by Miguel de Unamuno
El hijo de Don Juan by José Echegaray
Johnny Tenorio by Carlos Morton
*No hay plazo que no se cumpla ni deuda que no se pague, y el
convidado de piedra* by Antonio de Zamora [Based on Tirso de
Molina's *El burlador de Sevilla*]
Tan largo me lo fiáis, attributed to Tirso de Molina
El nuevo don Juan by Adelardo López de Ayala

FAUST

El despertar de Fausto by Augusto Martínez Olmedilla
Doutor Fausto da Silva by Paulo Pontes
Faustina by Luis G. Basurto
Faustino by Emilio Lopez Medina
O auto de Joao da Cruz by Ariano Suassuna

MARQUÉS DE VILLENA

La cueva de Salamanca by Juan Ruiz de Alarcón
Los encantos de Amenón, anonymous
Los encantos del Marqués de Villena by Pedro Calderón de la Barca
Macías by Mariano José de Larra
Porfiar hasta morir by Félix Lope de Vega
Lo que quería ver el Marqués de Villena by Francisco de Rojas
Zorrilla

La redoma encantada by Juan Eugenio Hartzenbusch

MARTHE BROSSIER

El asombro de la Francia, Marta la Romarantina by José de
Cañizares

Marta abandonada y carnaval de París by Ramón de la Cruz.

Marta aparente by Francisco Antonio Ripoll

*Marta imaginaria, segundo asombro de Francia . . . y mágico
gaditano* by José de Concha

MEDEA

Comedia llamada Armelina by Lope de Rueda

Comedia llamada Tholomea by Alonso de la Vega

Los encantos de Medea by Francisco de Rojas Zorrilla

Jasón o la conquista del Vellocino, anonymous

Medea by Miguel de Unamuno

Medea en el espejo by José Triana

Las Medeas by Fernando Cuadra Pinto

Los tres mayores prodigios by Pedro Calderón de la Barca

El Vellocino de Oro by Félix Lope de Vega

MERLIN

Comedia famosa de la casa de los celos y selvas de Ardenia by Miguel
de Cervantes

Los encantos de Merlín by Andrés Rey de Artieda

Los encantos de Merlín by Manuel Fernández y González

ZOROASTER

El anillo de Giges, y Mágico rey de Lidia by José de Cañizares

Comedia de la constancia de Arcelina by Juan de la Cueva

Notes

I. Supernaturalism in Medieval Spanish Drama

Epigraph: Peter L. Berger, *A Rumor of Angels* (New York: Anchor Books/Double-day, 1990), p. 2.

1. Alfonso X, *Las Siete Partidas*, 1431. The following quotes from *Las Siete Partidas* are from the same translation, p. 1432. Law 12 of *Partida 1* addresses the kinds of plays that were deemed acceptable, such as religious works, and those that were forbidden under threat of punishment—among them, the vulgar, secular farces known generically as *juegos de escarnio*.

2. See chapter 3 of this study.

3. See Rodrígues, "*Iconografía angélica*," 53–80. See also Keller, "Drama, Ritual and Incipient Opera," 72–89.

4. The translation is mine. See original in del Rio, and del Río, eds., *Antologia general de la literatura española*, 1:18.

5. *Webster's New International Dictionary*, 2d ed., s.v. "Occultism."

6. Numerologists may find significance in the conjuration occurring in act 3, for the number three was of great import in the symbology of occultism, as a reading of Cirlot and Biedermann will verify. This and subsequent passages of *La Celestina* are in my translation.

II. Esoterica in the Golden Age Drama of Spain

Epigraph, Kurt Seligmann, *Magic, Supernaturalism and Magic* (New York: Pantheon, 1974), 131.

1. This and subsequent passages of *El caballero de Olmedo* are my translations.

2. Among his plays of this type are the *comedias El mágico de Mogol, Los mágicos de Tetuán, El Mágico en Cataluña*, and the *sainete* (farce) *El encantador*.

3. Respectively, they are: *El asombro de la Francia, Marta la Romarantina; Marta aparente; Marta imaginaria, segundo asombro de Francia; Marta abandonada y carnaval de Paris*.

4. This and subsequent passages of *El esclavo del demonio* are my translations.

5. The first and second acts (*jornadas*) were respectively written by Juan de Zabaleta and Jerónimo de Cáncer.

III. The Demonic Pact and the Quest for Esoteric Knowledge

1. See Justin Martyr, "Dialogue CV," 251, in which he states that the Witch of Endor was in league with demons and that it was one of these who spoke to Saul, not Samuel's shadow.

2. Among the rituals thought by medieval magicians to be most effective were those

found in the *Clavicle of Solomon*, sometimes referred to as *The Key of Solomon*, published in France as a pamphlet at an unknown time as *Les véritables clavicules de Salomon, trésor de sciences occultes suivies [de] grand nombre de secrets, et notamment de la grande Cabale dite du papillon vert.*

3. Magic is not based on worship, unlike Witchcraft and Satanism, but on the search for personal power, that is, knowledge, through control of cosmic forces.

4. In the Cabbalistic tradition of Judaism, the name of God was anagrammatized to enhance its efficacy, thus the form YHWH or IHWH as a "magical formula."

5. This is a remnant of or accommodation to dualism; later on, the Manicheans and Cathars would attempt to restore this concept.

6. Christianity developed its concept of Satan out of a misreading of such biblical texts as Isaiah and Job, as well as such pseudepigraphal writings as *The Book of Enoch*. For an exposition of this, see chapter 2.

7. The "nether world" becomes "Hell" in the King James Version, which is wholly inappropriate since the term comes from Nordic mythology and is not found in the Old Testament.

8. The pre-Christian world had its own variants on pacts, as Lucan points out in the *Pharsalia*.

9. *De doctrina christiana*, 2. Further views on his demonology are to be found in *De civitate Dei* (Books 8–10, 18, 21) and in *De divinatione daemonum*.

10. The legend of Theophilus, originally in Greek, was translated into Latin by Paul the Deacon in the ninth century. This version became the basis for all subsequent works on Theophilus, including those works by Adgar and Gautier de Coincy (both in verse) and Rutebeuf's *Le miracle de Théophile*, a play.

11. The head functioned somewhat like a familiar, an evil spirit in animal form associated with the Devil's disciples in later periods, who made communication with and action through Satan possible. The eleventh-century Cardinal Benno, a German, was the first to refer to Gerbert as a disciple of Satan. In Map's version of the story, the "talking head" was replaced by the she-demon Meridiana, who seduced Gerbert into a pact; Satan does not figure in that version.

12. Bacon's legend is the subject of Greene's play *Honorable History of Friar Bacon*.

13. The first was *Jeu de Saint Nicolas*, written by Bodel in the twelfth century.

14. In *Medieval French Plays*, 177–78.

15. For a thorough assessment of witchcraft see Murray's *Witch Cult in Western Europe* and *God of the Witches*.

16. *Errores Gazariorum* (ca. 1450) recounts how in the ritual of initiation a witch swore allegiance to the Devil, who then wrote a document with blood extracted from the neophyte and kept it as evidence of their special relationship. The *Malleus maleficarum* (1486) also promoted the idea of an eternal commitment by the witch through a pact.

17. Saint Albertus Magnus (ca. 1193–1280) was a Bavarian Scholastic philosopher who came to be called the Universal Doctor.

18. Written in reverse (a mirror image), this document purportedly stated the duty of the demonic signatories toward the human being. Such an element made the pact bilateral. A separate pact, signed by Satanas, Beelzebub, Lucifer, Elimi, and Astaroth was produced as evidence against Père Urbain Grandier at his trial in 1634; the document, written backward and from right to left, was held to be the ultimate proof against the priest, who had been accused of seducing the nuns at a nearby convent. John Whiting's play *The Devils* is based on this series of events.

19. The exact date is polemical. The drama is generally dated 1588, but this creates a problem in the supposed relationship of Marlowe's tragedy to the *Volksbuch* or *Faustbuch* (*Historia von D. Johann Fausten*), published in Germany in 1587 and not translated into English until 1592 as *The Damnable Life and Deserved Death of Doctor John Faustus*. Some date Marlowe's work to 1592.

20. There are many candidates for "the real Faust." A Faust is mentioned by Johannes Trithemius in 1507, by Mudt, by Johann Gast, and by Johann Wier (cf. Spence, *Encyclopedia of Occultism*, 158). The "biography" of Faust given by Passage in the introduction to his translation of Goethe's *Faust* mentions a figure known in the age of Luther as George, Georg, or Jörg, later rechristened as John, Johann, or Johannes, and Goethe's strange renaming of his character as Henry or Heinrich, all usually having Faustus as the surname. In *The Gnostic Religion*, Jonas posits that the surname derives from the Latin *faustus*, meaning "the favored one," and puts the Faust of Marlowe and Goethe in relationship to Simon Magus, to whom *Faustus* was attached and who also had a Helena in his life.

21. The original version of this devil's name was Mephostophiles in the *Volksbuch*. Other variants of the name are Mephisto, Mephistophilis, Mephistophiles, Mephistophilus, and Mephistophiel (see Butler, *Ritual Magic*, 164).

22. There is no evidence that Marlowe knew Rutebeuf's miracle play, however.

23. In the *Faustbuch*, Mephistopheles indeed tries to get Faust *not* to make the pact.

24. Similarly, in the Catholic tradition Tirso de Molina's Don Juan, in *El burlador de Sevilla* (1630), must be damned for his transgressions.

25. Among other English plays on the demonic pact are *The Divil's Charter* (1607) by Barnabe Barnes, which concerns Roderigo Borgia, who was to become Pope Alexander VI, and *The Witch of Edmonton* (c. 1623) by Thomas Dekker, William Rowley, and John Ford, which concerns Elizabeth (Mother) Sawyer. See the Bibliography for additional plays.

26. Its roots, too, were in medieval texts, among them, the prose pieces "De lo que contesçió a un omne que se fizo amigo et vasallo del Diablo" (Don Juan Manuel, *Conde Lucanor y Patronio*, ejemplo 45) and a second version of the same tale, which appears in Ruiz, *El libro de buen amor* as "Enxiemplo del ladrón que fizo carta al Diablo de su anima" (Coplas, 1454–75). Poetic works such as Berceo's *Los milagros de Nuestra Señora* and Alfonso el Sabio's *Cantigas de Santa María* contain numerable references to satanic pacts, most notably that of Theophilus of Adana.

27. Appears in a collection of *comedias* by Lope de Vega and others published in Barcelona. There is internal evidence that the play may have been written as early as 1605. Other important Spanish plays of the seventeenth century that contain demonic pacts are Rojas Zorrilla's *Marqués de Villena* and Ruiz de Alarcón's *La cueva de Salamanca* and *Quien mal anda en mal acaba*.

28. The motif of the seduction of a woman who is about to become a nun is a frequent one in Spanish literature; its best-known manifestation is in those works dealing with Don Juan Tenorio, among them Tirso de Molina's *El burlador de Sevilla* and Zorrilla's *Don Juan Tenorio*.

29. Act 2 (scene 4). This and subsequent passages from the play are my translations.

30. Act 1 (scene 1). This and subsequent passages from the play are my translations.

31. This is one of many instances in Calderón's religious dramas in which pagan deities are supplanted by the Christian Devil. Astaroth, sometimes Ashtoreth, was a "prince" or "duke" in the Christian hierarchy of Hell.

32. See chapter 6 of this volume.

IV. Ancient Ways

Epigraph cited in Lima, *Valle-Inclán, Theatre of His Life*, 93. The translation is mine.

1. On ophiolatry (the worship of serpents) which was first brought to the Iberian Peninsula by the Phoenicians, see Rodríguez López, *Supersticiones*, 52. The Celts named their sacred sites *Nemeton*; their settlements of clustered round and rectangular houses are today called *Castros* and are found throughout Galicia.

2. With the separation of Portugal (Lusitania) from Spain, Galician was transformed into Portuguese, becoming the language of that new political entity. In Galicia the language (Gallego) developed under the influence of Castilian. Today, the orthography and pronunciation of Gallego and Portuguese have many differences.

3. For biographical data, see Lima, *Valle-Inclán*.

4. Castroviejo, *Galicia*, 11. Variations of these lines of verse appear throughout the literature of Galicia, including the works of the poet Rosalía de Castro. In my translation, the version in the text reads: "I am fearful of a something / that I feel but cannot see."

5. In *El ocultismo en Valle-Inclán* Speratti-Piñero provides detailed assessments of these throughout all the genres in Valle-Inclán's writings.

6. John Henry Fuseli's *Nightmare* depicts an incubus atop a sleeping woman's chest. The male Devil sitting on Pedro Gailo represents an unusual variant that can perhaps be explained in that he has replaced the female succubus with the male Devil because of his drunken stupor. A Freudian analysis might interpret the substitution in terms of latent homosexuality.

7. This and all subsequent passages from Valle-Inclán's works are my translations. References are to page number.

8. The evil spell of the Moon is highlighted as well in two instances in *Cara de Plata* (conversation between Sabelita and the protagonist; description of Fuso Negro) and in *Divinas palabras* (description of the hydrocephalic dwarf).

9. This legend is related to the more encompassing one of the Mariños de Lobeira (seafarers of Lobeira) narrated by Molina in his *Descripción del Reyno de Galicia*: "Some say that the Mariños were born of a woman of the sea whose face was beautiful; and that a hidalgo of this Kingdom had her in his power and, once her fish scales were removed, had offspring from her. . . . They are called Mariños because they came by sea. There were blue waves on their heraldic shields" (my translation). See Castroviejo, *Galicia*, 152.

10. In ancient Greece, Lamia was the name given a goddess worshipped as a serpent and associated with other such goddess (e.g., Medusa).

11. Variants of this tale appear in prose works by Valle-Inclán from years previous to the play, among them, "Cartas galicianas" (1891), reproduced in Fichter, *Publicaciones periodísticas*, and the novel *Flor de santidad*, in which an old man relates the legend to other shepherds, one of whom utters the same phrase as Florisel and receives the same reply from the old narrator as that given by Doña Malvina.

12. See Cirlot, *Dictionary of Symbols*, 345–47.

13. See Cirlot, *Dictionary of Symbols*, 44, and Biedermann, *Dictionary of Symbolism*, 66–67, who states: "Chimeras appear occasionally in medieval mosaics (and in the capitals of pillars and columns) as embodiments of Satanic forces."

14. This Celtic belief survives in Ireland, Brittany, and other parts of Europe where the Celtic influence is strong. On the Isle of Man it is called the Company, in Ireland, the Gentry Army; elsewhere it is known as the Fairy Procession.

15. All over Europe there are bridges, aqueducts, towers, and stelae whose span, height, or difficulty of construction has given them an association with Satan, hence

such names as the Devil's Bridge, Devil's Gorge, Devil's Finger, etc. The bridge constructed by Valle-Inclán's witches is solely for the use of the dead, not even to be seen by the living, except in the case of Don Juan Manuel Montenegro, who is slated to die soon thereafter.

16. For a full discussion of the intricacies of color symbolism, see Cirlot, *Dictionary of Symbols*, 50–57. See Speratti-Piñero, *El ocultismo en Valle-Inclán*, 54 n.45, for a comparison of the color sequence of the cocks with other related tales.

17. For a discussion of the number symbolism behind Valle-Inclán's aesthetics, see Lima, "Triads of Valle-Inclán."

18. There are other occult motifs in *Romance de lobos:* the audience sees the materialization of Doña María as a shadow; Sabelita sees the candles in the chapel where she prays as two women consumed in flames; the voice of the penitent Montenegro is said to be that of Satan fighting to exit his body; and folkloric beliefs appear throughout.

19. Caamaño Bournacell, *Las rutas turísticas de Valle-Inclán,* 22 states that the models for the sons of Don Juan Manuel Montenegro were, to some degree, the playwright's own ancestors, the Valle-Inclán brothers of the eighteenth century.

20. According to Castroviejo, Moraña, in the Valley of Salnés near Pontevedra, is well known for its September pilgrimage during which miracles are said to be plentiful (*Galicia,* 201). La Lanzada is a beach famous since pagan times for its powers to cure female sterility and the effects of bewitchment, both of which are eliminated by "the nocturnal bath of nine waves" (169). Valle-Inclán does not need to mention the number of waves because nine is the accepted number in Galician folklore.

21. The first English translation appeared as *Blood Pact* by Robert Lima, in *Modern International Drama* 24 (Spring 1991); *Blood Pact* is included also in *Savage Acts: Four Plays* (1993).

22. "Mari," a contraction of María and Gaila, is typical of the Spanish feminization of the husband's name. "Lucero," in astronomy, means "bright star"; in its figurative sense, it means brilliance or radiance. Valle-Inclán uses it rather than the equivalent "Lucifer," meaning "shining star," the name erroneously associated with the leader of the fallen angels in biblical lore through a serious misreading of Isaiah's reference to the fall of Nebuchadnezzar, king of Babylonia. "Trasgo" is an imp, goblin, sprite, or demon; "Cabrío" means "goatish" or "goatlike." The figure here is Pan, half-man, half-goat, one of the pagan deities whose physical aspect was usurped and assigned to the Christian Devil.

23. See Rodríguez López, *Supersticiones,* 150–53.

24. See Rutebeuf's *Le miracle de Théophile,* the first pact signed in blood in dramatic literature, and Marlowe's *The Tragedy of Doctor Faustus* (also as *The Tragical History of the Life and Death of Doctor Faustus*). The tradition of a priest signing a pact with the Devil, as in Rutebeuf's play, was depicted by Goya as the cleric signing the Devil's book, held by a witch. In *Supersticiones,* Rodríguez López, speaking of the kingdom of Galicia, states: "In the sixteenth century, the greater number of those considered witches were priests. Canon 59 of the Second Council of Braga forbids clerics from casting spells or making pacts" (69, my translation).

V. Toward the Dionysiac

1. For a study of *Yerma* from this perspective, see Lima, *Theater of García Lorca,* 217–40. All passages from *Yerma* are my translations; page numbers appear in parentheses after each quote.

2. In *The Birth of Tragedy* (1872), Nietzsche distinguishes two modes of human behavior, the Apollonian and the Dionysiac. For the purposes of this essay, these dual approaches that create the tension of living symbolize the struggle between Christian principles and pagan tradition.

3. Yerma's father has chosen Juan, a farmer, over Victor, a shepherd, as husband for his daughter. The choice demonstrates an ancient prejudice among settled peoples in favor of the homesteader. The reason may be that in being tied to his land the farmer is more reliable than the wandering shepherd, at least in the eyes of the community. In quite a different context, however, it is the shepherd who wins favor. The story of Cain and Abel is, on one level, a tale of the contention between the homesteader and the shepherd. When Cain kills Abel, the given reason for the homicide is that the farmer resents the rejection of his offering and the acceptance of the shepherd's by God. The God of the Old Testament had a marked preference for blood sacrifices and an ironic enjoyment in having his "chosen people" live as nomads. It was, at best, a mixed blessing being a shepherd. Perhaps the rejection of Victor as a suitable mate for Yerma stems from a subconscious racial memory of such origins.

4. In Euripides' *Bacchae*, the conflict is between those who deny Dionysus his rightful place in the pantheon of the gods and those who acknowledge his divinity through worship. Dire consequences accrue to those who deny Dionysus his proper place in the scheme of things. Just as the Dionysia or Bacchanalia gave rise to tragedy in ancient Greece (most notably in Attica), so too the tragic manifests itself in *Yerma*'s modern Dionysian revels, the "Romería" scene at the play's end. The parallels will be discussed in this context.

5. See Campbell, *The Masks of God*, 458. See also Lindsay, *The Origins of Astrology*, 20–21.

6. See Herodotus, *The Histories*, 226. See also Tacitus, *Complete Works*, 728. For the association of earth with masculinity, see note 13 below.

7. See Guenon, *Man and His Becoming*, passim.

8. See Wilkins, *The Rose-Garden Game*, 102, 113–14, 124. See also Song of Solomon 5:2.

9. Although not normally used in Spain to refer to the sexual act in a vulgar manner, *coger* is widely employed in that way throughout Latin America, particularly in Argentina, Uruguay, and Cuba. García Lorca visited these countries and thus may have come across the taboo usage.

10. In Agrippa, *The Philosophy of Natural Magic*, 43, 49.

11. The collective title of those esoteric writings centered on Hermes Trismegistus, the syncretic Mediterranean deity who ruled the four elements.

12. Adamic Man is the protagonist of the familiar creation story in Genesis 2:7 ("Then the Lord God formed man out of the dust of the ground and breathed into his nostrils the breath of life, and man became a living being") and in Genesis 2:21–22 ("The Lord God cast the man into a deep sleep and, while he slept, took one of his ribs and closed up its place with flesh. And the rib which the Lord God took from the man, He made into a woman, and brought her to him." However, there is a *previous* creation, that of Primal Man, recounted in Genesis 1:26–28: "God said, 'Let us make mankind in our image and likeness,'. . . God created man in His image. In the image of God he created him. Male and female He created them. Then God blessed them and said to them, 'Be fruitful and multiply.'" (Quotations from the edition of the Bible published by the Catholic Book Publishing Co. (New York, 1962). This *first* creature, so-called Primal Man, was not made of the earth but in the "image and likeness" of God

and was a simultaneous creation of "male and female," possibly an androgynous creature representative of God's duality. The story of Primal Man ends abruptly, replaced by that of Adamic Man, a creature made of the earth.

13. Nietzsche, *The Birth of Tragedy.*

14. The God of the Hebrews manifested himself as fire on various occasions, most notably on Mount Sinai when he gave Moses the tablets of the law and again in the burning bush episode. He could not be seen because he emitted a searing light.

15. Horns are among the oldest symbols of male sexuality and are attributes of numerous gods in antiquity; among them are the Semitic El, the Greek Actaeon, Pan, and Zeus, the Egyptian Amen, and the Persian Mithras. These and other deities bore the horns of goats, rams, bulls, or stags, animals whose energy and sexual prowess made them fitting symbols for fertility gods. In Tantric yoga, the yoga of sexual energy, horns are the emanations of male vitality, which originates from sexual ejaculation, rises through the spine to the head in the form of mystic energy, and accumulates as "outgrowths."

16. Misidentification of the Horned God as Satan is typical of Christianity, which saw all pagan traditions of fertility as inspired by that personification of evil that the religion called the Devil. The concept of the Devil's wife stated here may stem from the Jewish folkloric personage named Lilith, said to have been Adam's first mate until she rebelled against God's authority and became an evil creature: the idea may also be based on those Mediterranean goddesses associated with fertility, likewise condemned by the Church. See Kelly, *The Devil, Demonology and Witchcraft*, Murray, *Witch Cult in Western Europe* and *God of the Witches.*

17. See Cavendish, ed., "Numerology," in *Encyclopedia of the Unexplained*, 158–67. See also Cirlot, "Numbers," in *Dictionary of Symbols*, 220–27.

18. The rose as a symbol of the female has a complex history. See Wilkins, *The Rose-Garden Game.*

VI. The Devil in the Blood

Epigraph: Saint Augustine, *De divinatione daemonum (Corpus scriptorum ecclesiasticorum latinorum)*, 41:608.

1. Casona, "Don Juan y el Diablo," 4. Reprinted in *Cuadernos del Congreso*, 69.

2. "Casona" means "large house." His real name was Alejandro Rodríguez Alvarez (1903–65).

3. Sáinz de Robles, Introduction to *La barca sin pescador*, 5–6.

4. Published as "El Diablo: Su valor literario, principalmente en España" in *Obras completas*, 2:1265–1368.

5. Sáinz de Robles, Introduction to *La barca sin pescador*, 6.

VII. Illuminati, Witches, and Apparitions

1. For a listing of Spanish plays of this type, see the Bibliography in this volume.

2. The particular grotesques by Goya are two series of etchings, *Los caprichos* (The Caprices) and *Los desastres de la guerra* (The Disasters of War), and several large paintings titled *El Aquelarre* (The Witches' Sabbat).

Valle-Inclán (1866–1936) was the precursor of what came to be called Theater of the Absurd through the creation of an aesthetic of the grotesque, which he called the *Esperpento*. The new norm is defined by Max Estrella, the protagonist of Valle-Inclán's first *Esperpento, Luces de bohemia* (1920): "Our tragedy is not tragedy. . . . [It is] the *Esperpento*. . . . Goya was the inventor of *Esperpentism*. Classical heroes have taken a stroll along Gato Alley. . . . Classical heroes reflected in those concave mirrors manifest the *Esperpento*. The tragic sense of Spanish life can only be rendered through an aesthetic that is systematically deformed. . . . In a concave mirror, the most beautiful images are absurd. . . . My present aesthetic is to transform classical norms through the mathematics of the concave mirror" (scene 12; my translation). For a listing of criticism on the *Esperpento*, see Lima, *Annotated Bibliography of Valle-Inclán*, 253–64, 278–83 and under entries for *Los cuernos de don Friolera* (286–88) and *La hija del capitán* (289). A wholly revised and updated two-volume edition of this bibliography will be published in 1995: *International Annotated Bibliography of Ramón del Valle-Inclán* (London: Grant and Cutler).

3. The term *Illuminati* was given to or taken by those said to be in possession of a higher wisdom than that of normal human beings, a knowledge acquired either through serious study (as in the case of Cabbalists) or through personal revelation (as in Gnosticism). More traditionally, those who followed the rigorous path of mysticism were also so called. In the context of the play, the term applies to the followers of a heterodox movement centered in Seville.

4. The names of the Prioress have symbolic resonance. In the context of a Spanish nun who is the prioress of a convent, the name Teresa undoubtedly makes reference to Santa Teresa de Jesús, Mother Superior of the Carmelite convent in Avila and a renowed mystic who was canonized in 1622. "Cerda" is the feminine form for pig, hog or swine; thus, it means "sow," an appellation sometimes given to women believed to be used by the Devil, either sexually or to achieve other ends. The association of sow with evil may stem from pre-Christian beliefs in the Goddess, among whose European manifestations were the Celtic Cerridwen and the Teutonic Freya, each of whom was the Sow Goddess, eater of corpses, when she represented the death aspect of her divinity. The Prioress, whose full last name means "valley of the sow," rules over a convent many of whose nuns have "died" to God by following the dictates of the devils said to possess them; in this negative mode, she is their symbolic Sow Goddess. Taken together, the names present the opposition of goodness (Teresa) and evil (Valle de la Cerda). This is the true state of the Prioress—a woman whose body and soul are the battlegrounds of the forces of good and evil.

The earlier accusation of the Conde Duque's sorcery is noted in chapter 15 of Marañón, *El conde duque de Olivares*: "Las hechicerías de Olivares."

5. Many churches in Spain feature a realistic image of the suffering Christ, either on the cross, in the arms of Mary, or lying-in-state. In such works, every puncture of the crown of thorns and every wound on hands, feet, and side are vividly depicted, the blood seeming still to ooze from the tortured body. Velázquez's figure does not conform to the traditional iconographic mode, as the Conde Duque de Olivares, who donated the piece to the convent, tells his companion Villanueva: "Come here and look, look at those two feet set and firm, those legs healthy and straight, and that body tranquil and at peace. Tell me that it hasn't been painted to console and quiet the spirit of those who look upon it rather than to instill sorrow and anguish. Notice that there is so little blood that it is as if there were none" (I, p. 30).

6. See *Razones por qué no se publicó el decreto de que los frailes no hablen con monjas* in Deleito Piñuela, *La vida religiosa*, 131.

7. Possession of more than one individual in a tightly knit group, such as a convent of nuns, is now seen as the result of mass hysteria rather than as caused by the interven-

tion of a supernatural force. Nonetheless, the Roman Catholic Church, and other denominations, still employ the ritual of exorcism in highly investigated cases in which no human agency can be determined to have affected the state termed possession.

8. In Defourneaux, *Daily Life,* 118.

9. The historical facts regarding the relationship between Doña Teresa de Silva and her spiritual mentor, Fray Francisco García Calderón, as well as the complex series of events that transpired during the years of their relationship in the convent, leading to the arrest and trials by the Inquisition, are recounted in Lea, *Religious History of Spain* 309–18, who adds in note 1: "It is scarce necessary to call attention to the similarity of the cases of Calderón and of Urbain Grandier, which were so nearly synchronous (Histoire des Diable de Loudun, Amsterdam, 1752)." The French priest was the subject of *The Devils of Loudun* by Aldous Huxley, and of the play based on that work, *The Devils,* by John Whiting.

10. The feast days of San Pascual and San Gil de Santarem fall on May 14, thus the title may imply that the entire action occurs during that day, but in fact it does not. However, there are three other Giles in the Church calendar, one with a feast on January 14 (fifteenth-century Neapolitan), another on April 23 (thirteenth-century Giles of Assisi), and the third on September 1 (ca. eighth-century Aegidus). If a period of time is intended by Miras in using the title, the time could be from May 14 (feast day of Saint Pascal) to September 1 (feast day of Saint Giles). The titular reference may not have a time function, however. San Gil was a famous church in Madrid. In 1627 a celebration of Franciscan martyrs was held in which a procession of about a thousand led from the church of Saint Francis to that of San Gil. In the play, the references to Saint Giles pertain to the encampment where the troops that rebelled against Isabel II were billeted. For a dramatic treatment of the Queen's court, see Valle-Inclán's *La reina castiza*.

11. Lea, *Religious History of Spain,* reports on the outcome of an official examination of her wounds: "Three physicians . . . examined the wounds. . . . On the backs of the hands were ulcers, produced by a mild caustic, and on the palms were scratches; there was no sign of bleeding, but they were covered with a dark red substance, insoluble in water, which was removed with difficulty. On the left side was a nearly healed sore, apparently produced by friction. . . . On the top of the feet were cicatrices nearly well, while the soles bore no mark of any kind. Around the forehead were three series of spots, each about fifteen in number, produced by a cutting instrument. . . . If interference could be prevented the physicians promised that all could be cured in from fifteen to fifty days" (417–18). Lea reports further that later Sor Patrocinio confessed under oath that a Capuchin, Padre Fermín de Alcaráz, "had given her what he called a relic and commanded her on her salvation to apply it to hands, feet, side and head, telling her that the sufferings it would cause would be salutary penance; she had done so, and in further obedience had never revealed it to anyone, even to her confessor" (418).

12. When Isabel's despotic father, Fernando VII, was close to death and had no male heir, he formulated the "Pragmática Sanción," abrogating the traditional Ley Sálica, which decreed that no female could ascend the throne when a male heir, even if in a parallel line, was available. Don Carlos, brother of Fernando, was the legitimate heir apparent, but upon the king's death in 1833, the child Isabel was declared queen under the regency of her mother, María Cristina. Don Carlos rebelled and so began the first Carlist War, which lasted until 1839. Thereafter, there were periodic rebellions by his followers and heirs. There is still a Carlist presence in contemporary Spain.

13. Lea reports in *Religious History of Spain:* "[A] story was circulated that on one occasion the demon had carried her through the air to Aranjuez where she witnessed

convincing proof of the immorality of the Queen-regent María Cristina and of the illegitimacy of her daughter Isabel" (416–17). When a public investigation of Sor Patrocinio's claims was made, "it was testified that about half-past ten one morning she had disappeared and between twelve and one was found lying insensible on the roof of one of the convent buildings, with her dress covered with dust and fragments of vegetation, as though she had been dragged through the fields. It appeared however that the roof was nearly flat, with a large window opening upon it from a room in the second story of the main building" (417).

14. In Defourneaux, *Daily Life*, 118–19.

15. The Little Formless Fears have a similar function in O'Neill's play *The Emperor Jones*.

16. *Primer Acto*, 74. Miras does not consider Arthur Miller's *The Crucible* as such a statement.

17. Witchcraft had been erroneously considered the worship of the Devil since medieval times when the gods of pagan religions were absorbed into Christianity either as saints (in the case of those who were benevolent) or as devils (in the case of those who represented ideas inimical to Church dogma or tradition). The god of those termed "witches" (usually a deity with horns) was transmogrified into the Satan of Christian belief, who then acquired the horns, hairy body, tail, and feet of the goatlike Pan.

18. I cite from the playwright's typescript.

19. Quiteria refers to the feast day of the fourth-century Pope Sylvester I, December 31.

20. Francisco de Goya y Lucientes (1746–1828) created many images of witches as popularly conceived from the Middle Ages to his time. In the series of etchings titled *Los Caprichos* (The Caprices), he drew a young witch holding on to the hair of the old hag as they ride through the night on a broomstick, the image that influenced Miras's description of the flight to the Sabbat.

21. This interpretation of the Devil stems from borrowings from Pan, half-man, half-goat, the great Satyr of Greek antiquity, and one of the supposed Horned Gods of Witchcraft (see Murray, *God of the Witches*).

22. The concept of night belonging to Satan is a remnant of ancient dualism, in which the positive deity was symbolized by light (the Sun) and his antithesis by darkness (the Moon). One such influential system of belief was Persian Zoroastrianism, whose opposing deities were Ahura-Mazda and Ahriman.

23. See Murray, *God of the Witches* and *Witch Cult in Western Europe*. She and those who follow her thinking believe in a worldwide worship of such deities throughout human prehistory (verifiable in cave art and artifacts) and into more recent times.

24. Seasonal changes were celebrated in four major Sabbats, starting with the end of the old year and the birth of the new—Samhain (October 31–November 1)—followed by Embolc (February 1–February 2), Beltane (April 30–May 1), and Lugnasa (July 31–August 1), as well as many lesser feasts, called Esbats. Many of these pagan festivals were Christianized when they could not be eradicated, as for example the superimposition of the Eve of All Hallows (Halloween) and All Saints Day on Samhain.

25. Cervantes, *Don Quijote*, part 2, chap. 41.

26. The flying scene is reminiscent of the flight of Don Quijote and Sancho aboard the wooden horse Clavileño (see note 25).

27. I cite from the playwright's typescript.

28. See note 1 of this chapter.

VIII. The Orishas of Ifé

Epigraph: Alejo Carpentier, "Prólogo," *El reino de este mundo* (México, D.F.: Compañía General de Ediciones, 1971), 15–16.

1. The Yoruba Empire was in the West African region known as Oyó, the ancient realm of Ulkamy, which is the possible antecedent or root of the Cuban *Lucumí*, the name given to all the Yoruba slaves regardless of tribe (see Ortíz, *Nuevo catauro de cubanismos,* 316, and Law, *The Oyó Empire,* 16, concerning such variants as Ulcumi, Ulcuim, Ulkami, Licomin, etc.). Just as their lineage was ancient, so too was their religion; in fact, the Yoruba consider theirs to be the oldest extant religion in the world. Their cosmogony is centered on Ifé, the sacred place in the East said by some to be in the western Sudan; it was there that the world, the Yoruba people, and their religion began (see Davidson, *History of West Africa,* 97–98). Thus, Ifé was the "Navel of the World" to the Yoruba. In the pantheon of the Yoruba religion were hundreds of Orishas who personified cosmic and other archetypal images; these entities often vied with each other for power and influence on both the supernatural and natural levels, as in the systems of ancient Egypt, Babylonia, and Greece. As in the beliefs of those ancient nations, fate is an important concept in the religion and divination of the Yoruba; indeed, it is an integral aspect thereof. Divination is done periodically through various means, the most significant of which is the Table of Ifá, a verbal system in which the *babalao* or *babalawo* (the priest; literally, the father of the secrets or the knowledge of the religion) recites the prognostication after casting seeds (in Cuba, *caracoles* [cowrie shells]; in Brazil, palm nuts and sticks are sometimes used) upon the "table"; his words convey the Orisha's revelation to his people.

2. In Haiti the African gods are called *Loas,* and the religion is known as Voudoun or Vaudun, what is called Voodoo outside the nation. Unlike its island neighbor, the Dominican Republic, where the Hispanic Santería is practiced, Haiti has a French cultural background and much of its syncretism refers to French Catholic influence. The present chapter deals exclusively with Cuba and Brazil, thus Voudoun, Obeah, Ju-Ju, and other African-root religions of the Americas are not discussed.

3. The *Odú* is a body of learning that consists of 256 chapters, each with its own character and distinct contents. The name *Babalawo* or *Babalao* means "Father of the Tradition" because it is his responsibility to know the *Odú* by memory. Like the *Odú,* the *Patakín* is a complex system. According to Martínez Furé, *Diálogos imaginarios,* there are "hundreds of myths and fables, lists of refrains, Yoruba-Spanish vocabularies, ritual formulas, recipes for enchantments and sacred meals, the relationships of the Orishas, and particulars on their avatars, chants, systems of divination, and their secrets, the names of herbs of the deities, their utilization in rituals and in popular pharmacopeia, etc. In short, the entire knowledge of the ancient Yoruba and their culture, which refuses to die out" (211–12).

4. For a discussion of such cults in Cuba, see Cuervo Hewitt, *Aché, presencia africana,* an excellent synthesis of Yoruba culture and its integration into Cuban life and narrative literature.

5. There are other prominent systems of belief in Brazil that have some African roots. *Macumba* is the general name given any ceremony that courts the spirits or deities through ritual and voluntary possession. *Umbanda* is the practice of "white" (i.e., positive) magic, which was started in 1920 by Zélio de Moraes. It is a mixture of African animism and Catholicism. Its name may come from the Sanskrit *Aum-Bandha* ("Limit of the Unlimited") or, more likely, from an African root word meaning "the art

of healing." *Quimbanda*, whose name is derived from the Bantu *Ki-mbanda*, is the practice of "black" (i.e., negative) magic centered on the worship of Exú, both trickster and tempter, and his demonic cohorts, male and female; among the latter is Pomba-Gira, whose origin is in indigenous Indian lore. In Africa, Exú's counterpart is the messenger and intermediary of the gods; his name may be Legbara, Leba, or Elegara. *Batuque* is a religion of mixed African and Catholic elements that stresses spirit possession and is practiced in the northern Brazilian city of Belém and its environs. *Spiritism*, the least African in orientation, is the practice of seeking contact with the spirit world through trance possession and mediumship. It is a European import based on *The Book of Spirits* (1897) by Allen Kardec, pseudonym of the Frenchman Hippolyte Leon Denizard Ravail.

6. In many cases, the syncretism is threefold: Yoruba-Bantu (Congo)-Christian, which designates the fusion of the major African and European strains, or African-Indian-Christian, which includes the sometimes important incorporation of indigenous beliefs (Carib and Taino in Cuba and other islands of the Greater Antilles; Tupi in Brazil, etc.).

7. First performed in Havana in 1969 at the Teatro Guiñol; its U.S. premiere in Susan Sherman's adaptation took place at La Mama Dance Drama Workshop in New York City in 1970.

8. Variants of the tale appear in Cabrera, *El Monte*, as in other texts. See also Cuervo Hewitt, *Aché, presencia africana*, on the broad spectrum of African motifs in Cuban literature.

9. The most powerful Orishas grouped together are called the African Powers. Although most often seven in number, here they include Babalú Aye (Saint Lazarus), Elegguá (Holy Child of Atocha), the twins Los Iberi Taebo y Kainde (Saints Cosmos and Damian), Obatalá (Immaculate Conception, Our Lady of Mercy), Ochosí (Saint Norbert), Ochún (Our Lady of Charity of Cobre), Oggún (Saint Peter), Oko (Saint Isidore the Worker), Orunla (Saint Francis of Assisi), Osaín (Saint Joseph), Oyá (Our Lady of Candlemas), and Yemayá (Our Lady of Regla).

10. The syncretism of Santería in the Caribbean is, curiously, transferred back to the character Africa in her identification with the seven daggers that pierce her heart, which are symbolic of the seven sorrows of the Virgin Mary, also shown as daggers in paintings and statues of her under the name Our Lady of Sorrows, one of the titles in her litany. The translations that follow are mine.

11. See review by Lima, "In Celebration of Life."

12. Curiously, the playwright's works have appeared both under Seljan and Seljam. The former will be used here to avoid confusion.

13. Langguth, *Macumba*, gives quite a different story of the relationship between Oxalá and Changó, here called Obatalá and Sàngo in the original Yoruba version: "His grandfather, who was Obatalá, had heard reports of Sàngo's hard heart. Taking the disguise of an impoverished old man, he went to investigate. Upon entering the land of Oyo, the first thing Obatalá saw was a starving horse, and he gathered up grasses and fed the poor beast.

"He had barely finished when Sàngo's guards appeared. Using the pretext that the horse had been stolen, they beat Obatalá for his kind deed and dragged him before the king for sentencing.

"Sàngo laughed at the old man's plight. Indolently he ordered that Obatalá be thrown into prison. It was a sentence the king had seven years to regret. For during that time, the harvests failed throughout Oyo. Lakes went dry, dead fish stank in the riverbeds. Sàngo himself became impotent and his wives infertile. At last, his soothsayers told him about the man who had been unjustly imprisoned. Although he still did not recognize him, Sàngo ordered his grandfather released. Whereupon the kingdom bloomed once more" (280–81).

14. See Jonas, *The Gnostic Religion.*

15. Oxum is also the goddess of fresh water, thus her assumption of the river form later in the play. According to Langguth, *Macumba,* there exists a confusion of names that has given Oxum aspects of two similarly named Orixás: Oshun, "[g]oddess of the river Oshun, daughter of Iemanjá . . . the beloved second wife of Xangô" and Oxun, "goddess of fresh water . . . Was she once Oshun, Xangô's scheming wife? . . . Sometimes her name is written Oxum, which might imply—incorrectly—a connection with Oxumaré" (279).

16. Seljan, *Historia de Oxalá,* explains the association of these indigenous spirits and the African Orixá: "These *caboclos,* although they do not belong to the rituals of the *gegê-nagô,* were added to the play expressly to give it a Brazilian quality. In the '*caboclo candomblés,*' in the '*macumba*' of Rio de Janeiro, and in the diverse '*terreiros*' of the other states, the African 'orixá' of the hunt became syncretized with similar Amerindian entities, becoming something of a 'king-of-the-vegetation' whom the spirits of the indigenous ancestors obey" (35–36).

17. Bombonjira is a variant name of Pomba-Gira, the indigenous Indian spirit who in Quimbanda is the consort of Exú.

18. Nascimento's *Sortilégio: Mistério Negro,* written in 1951, may have been influenced by Eugene O'Neill's *The Emperor Jones,* produced in 1920, or by the film scenario written by DuBose Heyward and starring Paul Robeson. Nascimento's play, like O'Neill's, has overtones of Shakespeare's *Macbeth,* most obviously in the opening sequence with the incantations and prognostications of the three Filhas de Santo, but also in the acceptance of guilt and its consequences in the mind of the protagonist.

Works Cited

Agrippa, Henry Cornelius. *The Philosophy of Natural Magic*. Secaucus, N.J.: University Books, 1974.

Alfonso X [el Sabio]. *Las Cantigas de Santa María*. Madrid: Edilan, 1979. [Facsimile edition in two volumes.]

——. *Las Siete Partidas*. Translated and annotated by Samuel Parsons Scott. New York: Commerce Clearing House, 1931.

Aquinas, Saint Thomas. *Summa theologica*. Translated by Fathers of the English Dominican Province. Westminster, Md.: Christian Classics, 1981.

Augustine, Saint [Aurelius Augustinus]. *De civitate Dei* (The City of God). New York: Hafner, 1948.

——. *De divinatione daemonum* (On the divination of demons). In *Corpus Scriptorum Ecclesiasticorum Latinorum*. 41:608. Vienna, n.d.

——. *De doctrina christiana* (On Christian instruction). In *Patristic Studies* 23. Washington, D.C.: Catholic Univ. of America, n.d.

Auto de los Reyes Magos. In Angel del Río and Amelia A. de del Río, *Antología general de la literatura española*. Vol. 1. New York: Holt, Rinehart and Winston, 1960.

Bastide, Roger. *The African Religions of Brazil*. Baltimore: Johns Hopkins Univ. Press, 1960.

Berceo, Gonzalo de. *Los milagros de Nuestra Señora*. Granada: Univ. de Granada, 1986.

Berger, Peter L. *A Rumor of Angels*. New York: Anchor Books, Doubleday, 1990.

Biedermann, Hans. *Dictionary of Symbolism: Cultural Icons and the Meanings behind Them*. New York: Facts on File, 1992.

Bodel, Jean. *Jeu de Saint Nicolas*. Oxford: Blackwell, 1963.

Brene, José R. *La fiebre negra*. In *Teatro*. La Habana, Cuba: Ediciones Unión Contemporáneos, 1965.

Burns, Robert I., S.J., ed. *Emperor of Culture: Alfonso X, the Learned of Castile and His Thirteenth-Century Renaissance*. Philadelphia: Univ. of Pennsylvania Press, 1990.

Butler, E.M. *Ritual Magic*. Cambridge: Cambridge Univ. Press, 1949.

Caamaño Bournacell, José. *Por las rutas turísticas de Valle-Inclán*. Madrid: Gráficas Valencia, 1971.

Cabrera, Lydia. *El monte: Igbo-finda*. Miami: Ediciones Universal, 1975. First published in LaHabana: Ediciones C.R., 1954 (Col. de Chcherekú).

Calderón de la Barca, Pedro. *Las cadenas del demonio*. In *Obras completas*. Vol. 1. Madrid: Aguilar, 1959.

————. *La dama duende.* In *Obras completas.* Vol. 2. Madrid: Aguilar, 1960.

————. *El José de las mujeres.* In *Obras completas.* Vol. 1. Madrid: Aguilar, 1959.

————. *El mágico prodigioso.* In *Obras completas.* Vol. 1. Madrid: Aguilar, 1959.

————. *La Margarita preciosa.* Comedia de Juan de Zabaleta, Jerónimo de Cáncer y Velasco, Pedro Calderón de la Barca. In *Parte veinte y una de comedias nuevas escogidas de los mejores ingenios de España,* 405–45. Madrid: Ioseph Fernández de Buendia [para] Agustín Verges, 1663.

Campbell, Joseph. *The Masks of God: Primitive Mythology.* New York: Viking, 1959.

Cáncer y Velasco, Jerónimo de. *La Margarita preciosa.* Comedia de Juan de Zabaleta, Jerónimo de Cáncer y Velasco, Pedro Calderón de la Barca. In *Parte veinte y una de comedias nuevas escogidas de los mejores ingenios de España,* 405–45. Madrid: Ioseph Fernández de Buendia [para] Agustín Verges, 1663.

Carpentier, Alejo. "Prólogo" to *El reino de este mundo.* México, D.F.: Compañía General de Ediciones, 1971.

Carril, Pepe. *Shango de Ima: A Yoruba Mystery Play.* English adaptation by Susan Sherman. Garden City, N.Y.: Doubleday, 1970.

Casona, Alejandro. *La barca sin pescador.* Estudio y Edición de Federico Carlos Sáinz de Robles. Madrid: Ediciones Alcalá, 1966.

————. "Don Juan y el Diablo (Las dos negaciones del amor)." *El Universal* (Caracas), October 19, 1955. Reprinted in *Cuadernos del Congreso por la Libertad de la Cultura* (Paris) 16, January–February 1956.

————. *Obras completas.* 2 vols. Edición de Federico Carlos Sáinz de Robles. Madrid: Aguilar, 1967.

————. *Otra vez el Diablo.* Madrid: Escelicer-Alfil, 1968.

Castroviejo, José María. *Galicia. Guía espiritual de una tierra.* Madrid: Espasa-Calpe, 1960.

Cavendish, Richard, ed. *Encyclopedia of the Unexplained.* New York: McGraw-Hill, 1974.

Cervantes Saavedra, Miguel de. *Don Quijote de la Mancha.* 2 vols. Madrid: Alhambra, 1979.

————. *El rufián dichoso.* In *Teatro completo.* Barcelona: Editorial Planeta, 1987.

Cesarius of Heisterbach. *Dialogus miraculorum.* Cologne, 1851.

Cirlot, J.E. *A Dictionary of Symbols.* New York: Philosophical Library, 1962.

Cuervo Hewitt, Julia. *Aché, presencia africana. Tradiciones Yoruba-Lucumí en la narrativa cubana.* New York: Peter Lang, 1988.

Davidson, Basil. *History of West Africa.* New York: Doubleday, 1966.

Defourneaux, Marcelin. *Daily Life in Spain in the Golden Age.* New York: Praeger, 1971.

Deleito Piñuela, José. *La vida religiosa bajo el cuarto Felipe: Santos y pecadores.* Madrid: Espasa-Calpe, 1952.

Don Juan Manuel. *Libro del Conde Lucanor y Patronio*. Madrid: Alhambra, 1982.

Eliot, T.S. "Four Quartets. Burnt Norton (I)." In *The Complete Poems and Plays, 1909–1950*. New York: Harcourt, Brace and World, 1962.

Felipe, Carlos. *Requiem Por Yarini*. In *Teatro*. Edited by José A. Escarpanter and José A. Madrigal. Boulder, Colo.: Society of Spanish and Spanish-American Studies, 1988.

Fichter, William L. *Publicaciones periodísticas de don Ramón del Valle-Inclán anteriores a 1895*. Mexico, D.F.: El Colegio de México, 1952.

García Lorca, Federico. *Yerma*. Buenos Aires: Editorial Losada–Biblioteca Clásica Contemporánea, 1967.

Goethe, Johann Wolfgang von. *Faust*. Translated by Charles E. Passage. New York: Bobbs-Merrill, 1965.

Gratian [Gratianus]. *Decretum*. In *Corpus Juris Canonici*. Vol. 1. Leipzig: B. Tauchnitz, 1879.

Greene, Robert. *The Honorable History of Friar Bacon and Friar Bungay*. In *Typical Elizabethan Plays*, edited by F.E. Schelling and M.W. Black, 163–96. New York, 1949.

Guazzo, Fra Francesco Maria. *Compendium maleficarum*. Translated by E.A. Ashwin. Edited by Montague Summers. London: J. Rodker, 1929.

Guenon, René. *Man and His Becoming According to the Vedanta*. London: Luzac, 1945.

Herodotus. *The Histories*. Translated by Henry Cary. New York: Appleton, 1899.

Jonas, Hans. *The Gnostic Religion*. Boston: Beacon, 1963.

Jung, Carl. *Symbols of Transformation*. Vol. 5 of *Collected Works*. London: Routledge and Kegan Paul, 1956.

Justin Martyr. "Dialogue CV." In *The Ante-Nicene Fathers*, edited by Alexander Roberts and James Donaldson. Grand Rapids, Mich.: William Eerdmans, 1953.

Kardec, Allan. *Les Livres des esprit*. Paris, 1897.

Katz, Israel J., and John E. Keller, eds. *Studies on the "Cantigas de Santa María": Art, Music, and Poetry. Proceedings of the International Symposium on the "Cantigas de Santa María of Alfonso X, el Sabio (1221–1284) in Commemoration of its 700th Anniversary Year—1981*. Madison: Hispanic Seminary of Medieval Studies, 1987.

Keller, John E. "Drama, Ritual and Incipient Opera in Alfonso's *Cantigas*." In *Emperor of Culture*, 72–89. edited by Robert I. Burns, S. J.

Kelly, Henry Ansgar. *The Devil, Demonology and Witchcraft*. Garden City, N.Y.: Doubleday, 1968.

Kramer, Heinrich, and James Sprenger. *Malleus maleficarum*. Translated by Montague Summers. New York: Dover, 1971.

Lachatañaré, Rómulo. *¡¡Oh, mío Yemayá!!*. Manzanillo, Cuba: Editorial "El Arte," 1938.

Langguth, A.J. *Macumba: White and Black Magic in Brazil.* New York: Harper and Row, 1975.

Law, Robin. *The Oyó Empire.* Oxford: Clarendon, 1977.

Lea, Henry Charles. *Chapters from the Religious History of Spain Connected with the Inquisition.* Philadelphia: Lea Brothers, 1890.

Leacock, Seth, and Ruth Leacock. *Spirits of the Deep.* Garden City, N.Y.: Doubleday, 1972.

Lima, Robert. *An Annotated Bibliography of Ramón del Valle-Inclán.* University Park: Pennsylvania State University Libraries, 1972.

———."In Celebration of a Special Kind of Life." Review of *The Tent of Miracles,* by Jorge Amado. *Philadelphia Bulletin,* August 22, 1971.

———. "The Orisha Changó and Other African Deities in Cuban Drama." *Latin American Theatre Review* 23, no. 2 (Spring 1990): 33–42.

———. "Xangô and Other Yoruba Deities in the Plays of Zora Seljan." *Afro-Hispanic Review* 11, no. 1–3 (1992): 26–33.

———. "Spanish Drama of the Occult through the Eighteenth Century: An Annotated Bibliography of Primary Sources." *Crítica Hispánica* 15 (Spring 1993): 117–38.

———. *The Theatre of García Lorca.* New York: Las Américas, 1963.

———. "The Triads of Valle-Inclán: *La lámpara maravillosa.*" *Letras Peninsulares* 3 (Fall–Winter 1990): 309–19.

———. *Valle-Inclán. The Theatre of His Life.* Columbia: Univ. of Missouri Press, 1988.

Lindsay, Jack. *The Origins of Astrology.* New York: Barnes and Noble, 1971.

Lope de Vega Carpio, Félix. *El caballero de Olmedo. Obras completas,* 1: 793–824. Madrid, Aguilar, 1969.

Lucan [Marcus Annaeus Lucanus]. *Pharsalia.* London: J. Tonson, 1718.

Map, Walter. *De Nugis Curialium.* Edited by M. Rhodes James. Oxford: Clarendon, 1914.

Marañón, Gregorio. *El conde duque de Olivares o la pasión de mandar.* Madrid: Espasa-Calpe, 1936.

Marlowe, Christopher. *The Tragedy of Doctor Faustus.* New York: Washington Square, 1965.

Martín Recuerda, José. *Las conversiones.* Madrid: PREYSON, 1985.

Martínez Furé, Rogelio. *Diálogos imaginarios.* La Habana, Cuba: Editorial Arte y Literatura, 1979.

Medieval French Plays. Translated by Richard Axton and John Stevens. Oxford: Blackwell, 1971.

Meredith, Peter, and John E. Tailby, eds. *The Staging of Religious Drama in Europe in the Later Middle Ages: Texts and Documents in English Translation.* Kalamazoo, Mich.: Medieval Institute Publications–Western Michigan Univ., 1983.

Mira de Amescua, Antonio. *El esclavo del demonio.* In *Diez comedias del Siglo de Oro,* edited by José Martel and Hymen Alpert. New York: Harper and Row, 1968.

Miras, Domingo. "El Doctor Torralba." Manuscript.

———. *Las alumbradas de la Encarnación Benita*. Madrid: Colección la Avispa, 1985.

———. *Las brujas de Barahona*. *Primer Acto* 185 (August–September 1980).

———. *De San Pascual a San Gil*. Madrid: Editorial Vox, 1980.

———. "Fragmentos de la memoria." *Primer Acto* 185 (August–September 1980): 72–77.

Misteri d'Elx. In *La Festa o Misteri d'Elx*. Elche: Patronato Nacional del Misterio de Elche, 1989.

Molina, Licenciado. *Descriptión del Reyno de Galicia*. Mondoñedo: Imprenta de Agustín de Paz, 1550.

Molina, Tirso de [Fray Gabriel Tellez]. *El burlador de Sevilla y convidado de piedra*. New York: Doubleday, 1961.

Murray, Margaret. *The God of the Witches*. New York: Doubleday-Anchor, 1960.

———. *The Witch Cult in Western Europe*. Oxford: Oxford Univ. Press, 1967.

Nalé Roxlo, Conrado. *El pacto de Cristina*. In *Antología total*. Buenos Aires: Editorial Huemul, 1968.

Nascimento, Abdias do. *Sortilégio: Mistério Negro*. In *Dramas para Negros e Prólogo para Brancos: Antologia de Teatro Negro Brasileiro*. Rio de Janeiro: Ediçao do Teatro Experimental do Negro, 1961.

Nietzsche, Friedrich. *Die Geburt der Tragödie au dem Geiste von Musik (The Birth of Tragedy from the Spirit of Music)*. Leipzig: Verlag von E.W. Fritzsch, 1872.

Origen. *De principiis*. Torino: Unione Tipografico–Editrice Torinese, 1968.

Ortíz, Fernando. *Nuevo catauro de cubanismos*. La Habana, Cuba: Editorial de Ciencias Sociales, 1974.

Otto, Rudolf. *The Idea of the Holy*. London: Oxford Univ. Press, 1969.

Rivas, Duque de. See Saavedra, Angel de.

Rodrígues, Ana Domínguez. "*Iconografía angélica* en las *Cantigas de Santa María*." In *Studies on the "Cantigas de Santa María,"* edited by Israel J. Katz and John E. Keller, 53–80.

Rodríguez López, Jesús. *Supersticiones de Galicia y preocupaciones vulgares*. Lugo: Ediciones Celta, 1974.

Rojas, Fernando de. *La Celestina (Tragicomedia de Calixto y Melibea)*. Edited by Julio Cejador y Frauca. Madrid: Espasa-Calpe-Clásicos Castellanos, 1972.

Rojas Zorrilla, Francisco. *Lo que quería ver el Marqués de Villena*. In *Comedias escogidas,* edited by Ramón de Mesonero-Romanos. Madrid: M. Rivadeneyra, 1866.

Ruiz, Juan [Arcipreste de Hita]. *El libro de buen amor.* Zaragoza: Editorial Ebro, 1963.

Ruiz de Alarcón, Juan. *La cueva de Salamanca*. In *Primer (Segunda) parte de las obras completas,* Vol. 1. Valencia: Castalia-Hispanófila, 1966.

———. *Quien mal anda en mal acaba*. In *Biblioteca de Autores Españoles*. Vol. 20. Madrid: Imprenta de los Sucesores de Hernando, 1907.

Rutebeuf. *Le miracle de Théophile*. Paris: Librairie Ancienne Edouard Champion, 1925.

Saavedra, Angel de [Duque de Rivas]. *Don Alvaro, o la fuerza del sino*. In *Tres dramas románticos*. Garden City, N.Y.: Doubleday, 1962.

Seligman, Kurt. *Magic, Supernaturalism and Religion*. New York: Pantheon, 1974.

Seljan[m], Zora. *Historia de Oxalá: Festa do Bonfim*. Rio de Janeiro: Ediçoes de Ouro, 1965.

————. *The Story of Oxala: The Feast of Bonfim*. London: Rex Collings, 1978.

————. *3 Mulheres de Xangô*. Rio de Janeiro: Ediçoes GRD–Livraria Clássica Brasileira, 1958. Contains: *Oxum Abalô, Iansan, Mulher de Xangô, A Orelha de Obá*.

————. *3 Mulheres de Xangô e outras peças afro-brasileiras*. São Paulo: IBRASA, 1978. Contains: *Oxum Abalô, Iansan, Mulher de Xangô, A Orelha de Obá, Os Negrinhos, A festa do Bonfim* (a version of *Historia de Oxalá*).

Spence, Lewis. *An Encyclopedia of Occultism*. New Hyde Park, N.Y.: University Books, 1960.

Speratti-Piñero, Emma Susana. *El ocultismo en Valle-Inclán*. London: Tamesis, 1974.

Spies, Johann. *Faustbuch*. Frankfurt am Main, 1587. [Also known as *Volksbuch*.]

Tacitus. *Complete Works*. New York: Modern Library, 1942.

Thompson, Stith. *Motif-Index of Folk Literature*. Revised and enlarged edition. 6 vols. Bloomington: Indiana Univ. Press, 1955–58.

Valle-Inclán, Ramón del. *Aguila de blasón. Comedia bárbara*. Madrid: Espasa-Calpe, 1964.

————. *Cara de Plata. Comedia bárbara*. Buenos Aires: Espasa-Calpe, 1946.

————. *Divinas palabras: Tragicomedia de aldea*. Madrid: Espasa-Calpe, 1970.

————. *El embrujado: Tragedia de tierras de Salnés*. In *Retablo de la avaricia, la lujuria y la muerte*. Madrid: Espasa-Calpe, 1968.

————. *Ligazón: Auto para siluetas*. In *Retablo de la avaricia, la lujuria y la muerte*. Madrid: Espasa-Calpe, 1968. Translated by Robert Lima as *Blood Pact: A Play for Silhouettes*, in *Savage Acts: Four Plays* (University Park, Pa.: Estreno Contemporary Spanish Plays, 1993).

————. *Luces de Bohemia*. Madrid: Espasa-Calpe, 1971.

————. *El Marqués de Bradomín: Coloquios románticos*. Madrid: Espasa-Calpe, 1961.

————. *La reina castiza*. In *Tablado de marionetas para educacíon de príncipes*. Madrid: Espasa-Calpe, 1990.

————. *Romance de lobos: Comedia bárbara*. Madrid: Espasa-Calpe, 1961.

Wilkins, Eithne. *The Rose-Garden Game*. London: Victor Gallancz, 1969.

Zabaleta, Juan de. *La Margarita preciosa*. Comedia de Juan de Zabaleta, Jerónimo de Cáncer y Velasco, Pedro Calderón de la Barca. In *Parte veinte y una de comedias nuevas escogidas de los mejores ingenios de España*, 405–45. Madrid: Ioseph Fernández de Buendia [para] Agustín Verges, 1663.

Zorrilla, José. *Don Juan Tenorio*. In *Nineteenth Century Spanish Plays*, edited by Lewis E. Brett. Englewood Cliffs, N.J.: Prentice-Hall, 1935.

Index

Since the authors and their respective plays in Part Three: Bibliography are listed alphabetically therein, they and their works are excluded from this index, except where discussed in the text proper.